Advance Praise for *Riding Behind the Padre*

"A history lesson of the borderland life. Our group, Los Caminos de Kino, is not formed by Mexicans or Americans, it is formed by families who share land, ecosystem, economy, and dreams. While we do have differences between both sides of the border, all people have the same dream: that their families develop in a peaceful environment. Reading *Riding Behind the Padre: Horseback Views from Both Sides of the Border* could help governments from both countries make laws that could contribute with keeping the border's peace and harmony."

José Luis Salgado B.
Coauthor of *Por Los Caminos de Kino*
Hermosillo, Sonora

"For all the [mostly negative] attention the borderlands gets these days, we have few seasoned, balanced voices speaking to us who know the terrain like the back of their hands. Forget *God's Middle Finger* and *No Country for Old Men*, the borderland dystopias that distort realities more than seeking them out. *Riding Behind the Padre* has writing in it as eloquent as Cormac McCarthy and Graham Greene, but it is not a drive-by shooting of border cultures, it is an immersion in the richly nuanced and often contradictory lives embedded in this region."

Gary Paul Nabhan
Author of *Cultures of Habitat*
The Southwest Center, University of Arizona, Tucson

"I found *Riding Behind the Padre: Horseback Views from Both Sides of the Border* to be a significant work, weaving the history of Anglo involvement in the Pimería Alta through the legacy of Father Kino, with contemporary accounts of border life, both exhilarating and tragic. The book is culturally and environmentally astute, blending the author's own remarkable knowledge of landscapes and ranching with sensitive observations on humans, nature, and of course, horses."

George B. Ruyle
Marley Endowed Chair for Sustainable Rangeland Stewardship
University of Arizona, Tucson

Riding Behind the Padre

*Horseback Views
from Both Sides of the Border*

Richard Collins

Riding Behind the Padre: Horseback Views from Both Sides of the Border

Published by Wheatmark®
1760 East River Road, Suite 145
Tucson, Arizona 85718 U.S.A.
www.wheatmark.com

ISBN: 978-1-62787-133-4 (paperback)
ISBN: 978-1-62787-134-1 (ebook)
LCCN: 2014905811

rev201401

At the Caborca Corrals

For Oscar and Lea Ward,
borderland vecinos and friends

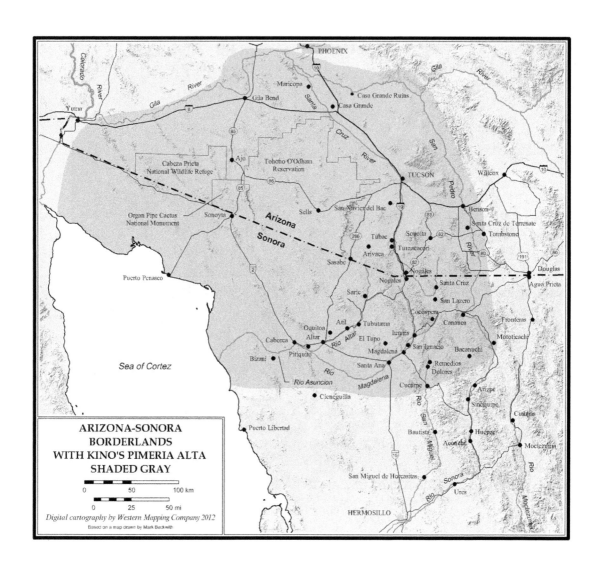

ARIZONA-SONORA
BORDERLANDS
WITH KINO'S PIMERIA ALTA
SHADED GRAY

0   50   100 km

0   25   50 mi

Digital cartography by Western Mapping Company 2012

Based on a map drawn by Mark Beckwith

Contents

"It was not a border between civilization and wilderness, or civilization and savagery, because those terms were nothing more than value judgments of the conquerors. Instead it was contested ground, a place where no single group—tribe, nation-state, or empire—held uncontested sway."

—Thomas E. Sheridan

Prologue

JUST BEFORE DAWN, I saddle and leave the Britten corrals on the western margin of the Sierrita Mountains, fifty miles southwest of Tucson, Arizona. For the first hour we ride south across the gently sloping *bajada*, a stony alluvium scattered with creosote bush, burro weed, and prickly pear, crossing over sand washes that meander down to the bottom of the Altar Valley. Approaching the San Juan windmill, a dozen black, humpy cows trot away from the water trough and vanish into the mesquite thickets. An abandoned mining road climbs into the hills, and we follow it into an interior basin treed with mesquite and juniper and framed by three high ridges. Two whitetail deer stare at my horse, more out of curiosity than fear, and then bound over the north ridge, waving their white flags good-bye. We climb steadily on for another hour, weaving through thickets of ocotillo and wait-a-bit thorn. A herd of javelina is feeding on shindagger agave, a rooting more suggestive of the pig than the aberrant dog-like relative that they really are. They catch our scent as the wind shifts, and bound away down the hillside, leaving a rank, musty stink floating in the air. The day brightens and fills with birdsong: cactus wrens, Gambel's quail, and a splendid cardinal in full breeding plumage.

On the mountaintop, the air is clear—so clear, the beyond becomes visible. I can see south, deep into the neighboring state of Sonora, Mexico. To the west, Baboquivari Peak, revered by the O'odham people as the home of I'itoi, their "Elder Brother," stands radiant and shining above a fringe of dark clouds. The air is rich with the native smells of damp creosote and horse sweat, the kinds of scents that lodge in memory like a childhood dream.

In the distance, a rugged, wide-open landscape rises and falls and rises again toward the southern frontier. This is the Sonoran Desert basin and range—a harsh, thirsty land of rare beauty, few people, and a rich history that stretches back past antiquity. A little of it I know from riding over the ranches on the Arizona side. But across the border in Sonora is a wider sky, pulsing with the exotic—a new language and culture as well as other things only half imagined and illusory.

I WAS IN my twenties then, and I could not have guessed that four decades later in the midst of all the turmoil over immigration and drug trafficking that I would be riding over the borderlands with a happy-go-lucky group of riders from Sonora. But even less could I have imagined that a Doubting Thomas like myself would be following the trails of Eusebio Francisco Kino, the Jesuit priest who explored this same land over three hundred years before.

So why did I go along when I had plenty to do on my own ranch? Out of curiosity and a sense of adventure—at least in the beginning. I wanted to experience the borderlands and its people with the full dimensions of sight, sound, smell, and texture in the same way the earliest explorers had—from the back of a horse. Also, I wanted to find out what my peers in Sonora thought about the borderland immigration and drug wars, since they live and work in the middle of the action and their voices are seldom heard in the United States.

But over the years, these rides the Mexicans called *cabalgatas* became more than just the fulfillment of curiosity. The book you hold in your hands is a story of personal exploration into the history and present-day state of affairs of my native land. And one goes exploring not only to discover new landscapes and cultures but to gain new perspectives—or to paraphrase a famous explorer, to gain new eyes with which to see.

Along the way, our trails would cross the modern-day escape routes for Mexico's poverty-stricken immigrants, trudging hopefully toward a paying job. During their exodus, they often fall prey to their own countrymen, like migrating wildebeests to hyenas—the Mexican guides who lead them to the border and across; the criminal cartels who use them as drug mules to deliver their contraband into America's heartland. The southern end of my ranch is located a scant twenty-five miles north of the line, and I regularly bump into not only the immigrants and *burrero* drug mules heading toward Interstate 10 but also the wreckage and refuse they leave behind.

But despite the damage, I understood the immigrants' plight, having lived and worked in the rural villages of Central America and southern Mexico during the civil war decades of the 1970s and 1980s, places where extreme poverty often amounted to extreme violence. In those days, landless people lived in cornstalk and cardboard huts, men and women who cut sugarcane and picked coffee and cotton for one dollar a day, when they could find work. These were societies where any plea the workers made for a better deal was ruthlessly suppressed. On my last trip to the region in 2006, little had changed except that about one-quarter of the able-bodied men had fled to *El Norte* (United States), either as migrant or immigrant workers.

A word on labels: an immigrant is one who moves to another country with the intention of taking up residence. Documented immigrants have legal permission to be in the United States. Illegal immigrants do not, and most of the immigrants I bumped into were probably illegal. For them, the difference is real, but they cross over anyway because they have no opportunity in their homelands. A migrant is one who travels in search of work and intends to return home after the job ends. Many of the people I have met in Mexico, Central America, and on my ranch are migrants who will eventually return home by choice. In the book, it seemed bootless to make the distinction (even if I knew) every time immigrant or migrant is mentioned, but neither one is an "alien," as if from outer space. They are real people. Also, I use the border slang term "narco" for a drug smuggler or drug runner, rather than for a narcotics law enforcement officer. The label in Spanish is *narcotraficante*. People who carry drugs across the border are *burreros*, or drug mules. *Coyotes* are Mexicans who put together groups of people to cross the border and often work for the drug cartels who now control illegal immigration. The bad guys are the narcotraficante managers for multinational criminal organizations labeled as Mexican drug cartels. Today, they operate in the United States as well as Mexico, feeding on America's addictions.[1]

Richard Collins
September 30, 2013
Sonoita, Arizona

Part 1

The Western Desert: 2008

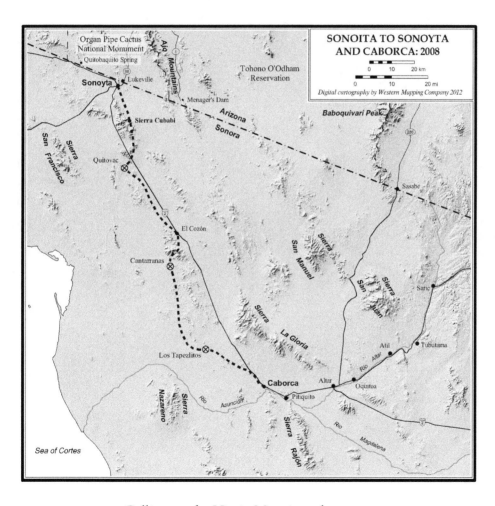

Calling on the Virgin Mary is useless.
Instead, one must know the language of the land.

—Ofelia Zepeda, Tohono O'odham poet

THE CABALGATAS WERE dedicated to retracing the steps of the pioneering Jesuit priest Father Eusebio Francisco Kino, who, from 1687 until his death in 1711, rode thousands of miles over this thirsty land he labeled the Pimería Alta (see map). This designation came from the Spanish recognition of a native people living in the upper (Alta) Sonoran Desert who spoke a common dialect of the Uto-Aztecan language family that stretched all the way from Central Mexico to the Gila River. (The Spanish term *Pima* comes from the first indigenous peoples' response—"*Pi ma:c*"—to the Spaniards' incomprehensible queries. Their response translates to "I don't know what you are talking about.") Kino's overarching goal was to "civilize" the natives by converting them to the Catholic faith, but he was a vigorous man with other more worldly interests.

Born in 1645 in the Tyrolean Alps of northern Italy, Kino as a young man worked on his family's farm. Although he was unaware of it as a boy, growing crops and caring for livestock was good preparation for missionary work among the tribes of the Sonoran Desert region. Also, the youthful Kino was an able student. When his father died, the family sold the farm to finance Kino's education in private Jesuit and Austrian schools. Struck down by a mysterious illness, he vowed to commit to the priesthood if God would restore his health. Inside the cloistered halls of the university, he excelled in mathematics, astronomy, geography, and cartography, in addition to religious studies. After completing formal training, Kino taught school, another experience that served him well as a missionary. The fifteenth and sixteenth centuries saw Spain's conquest of vast new continents, and the Jesuit order was pledged to impose the Catholic worldview on people who had evolved a simpler communion with their earthly surroundings.

Ordained at the age of thirty-two, Kino volunteered for overseas missionary service several times before he embarked for New Spain at the age of thirty-six.

A physical sketch of Kino, the man, has emerged from descriptions in Jesuit and Spanish documents, anatomical studies of his remains, and studies of his relatives in Italy. Eusebio Francisco Kino, was about five and one-half feet tall and bowlegged from a lifetime spent on horseback. Artists' paintings show him as lean-faced with a prominent nose, deep tan, high cheekbones, black hair, and always wearing a long black robe. How he managed the robe for thousands of miles on horseback remains a mystery even today.

The cabalgatas were the inspiration of Jesús Enrique Salgado Bojórquez, the eldest brother of the large Salgado family living in Hermosillo. Bilingual and gregarious, Enrique had a gift for capturing the essence of a situation with succinct, to-the-point statements. His first trip in 1984 had been a family outing with brothers José Luis and Arturo Oriol, riding the 150 miles from Hermosillo to Caborca, where the family patriarch, Enrique Salgado Martínez, lived. "We had grown apart," Enrique recalled, "so we made that first ride to become brothers again." The next year, the three brothers rode from Kino's home mission of Delores to Cerro el Nazareno near Caborca, starting the cabalgatas—*Por Los Caminos de Kino*. A devout Catholic and aficionado of Sonora's colonial history, Enrique then came up with the ingenious idea of annual cabalgatas to highlight the remarkable accomplishments of Father Kino, promoting the cause of his sainthood. Each year, starting in 1987, they have retraced a section of the Jesuit's trails that meandered over the Pimería Alta.

Kino, according to his biographer Herbert Eugene Bolton, was unlike some colonial Jesuits in that he became like family to his converts, and the Salgados followed that example. Each in his or her own time, the Salgado spouses and children joined the rides when and wherever possible. With each succeeding year, the cabalgata attracted new riders, and out of the adventure, hardships, and camaraderie, they too became like family. In 2008, my first year, twenty-five cabalgantes (the individual riders) rode from Sonoyta, Sonora, southeast to the town of Caborca, an ancient settlement that figured prominently in Pimería Alta's history, dating from Kino's era and continuing on to the immigration and drug wars of today.

MY NEIGHBOR, BIOLOGIST Oscar Ward, had invited me to ride the cabalgata several times, but I had been unable (or unwilling) to go. One reason was that our ranch required constant attention. Diane and I had a herd of cows spread out over a few thousand acres of the Canelo Hills and a band of broodmares to take care of. But other reasons stood in the way, as well, including the fact that I would be going without her. Although we worked the ranch together on horseback, Diane didn't fall for my vacation scheme of riding daylight to dark over the hinterlands of Sonora.

Lots of times on the ranch, I go prowling alone, just to see what I can see. Diane jokingly accuses me of preferring inarticulate company, but the horse is inarticulate only if you don't know what to look for: the position of its ears, the direction of its gaze, how it holds its mouth; or the tension coming up through its legs that can signal a panicky runaway, a threat to start pitching, or readiness to work a cow.

The second reason I hesitated was that as an Arizona native with an amateur's interest in its history and literature, I didn't like what I had read about the Spanish conquest of Mexico and the Southwest. The conquistadors arrived, cuirassed and mounted on horses, heavily armed with crossbows, muskets, lances, swords, and attack dogs. Entering a native settlement, they read the natives the *Requierimiento*, an edict written in 1513 requiring the natives to pledge allegiance and everything they owned to the "two Majesties," the Catholic pope and the Spanish crown. If they did not, then "with the help of God . . . we shall take you and your wives and children, and your lands, and make slaves of them."

Afterward came the Jesuits, captains of a faith too sure of its own righteousness. Their courage was excessive—so addled by faith that they did not fear death by the hands of the heathen nor from the heat and thirst of the desert. While the conquistadors scoured the land for gold and silver, the priests tallied their wealth in the number of converts to the faith. For those who rejected Catholic paternalism, forced labor in Spanish-owned mines and haciendas often awaited. But Oscar and Lea claimed that Kino was also an explorer, horseman, rancher, and farmer, as well as an apostle to the native people. The first four pursuits resonated with me, but I was indifferent to the proselytizing part, believing that each person and culture has an inalienable right to their own views of spirituality. Nevertheless, one had to be impressed by anyone who rode thirty and forty miles a day in unpaid service to others. In fact, Caballero Kino rode so hard and long that sometimes his followers had to tie themselves in the saddle to keep from falling from exhaustion.

In an emergency, Kino did not hesitate to ride alone. On May 3, 1700, Kino was engaged in saying Mass at Tumacacori, a mission on the Santa Cruz River in what is now southern Arizona, when he got word that the Spanish were going to execute an innocent Indian in the town of San Ignacio, Sonora, seventy-five miles to the south.

Kino struck out on his mule, arriving in San Ignacio at dawn the next morning in time to stay the execution, demonstrating not only his endurance riding skills, but also a commitment to justice. (In December, 2013, the cabalgata retraced Kino's heroic ride, but it took us three days what with navigating the border crossing maze at Ambos Nogales).

Illegal immigration and narcotics-related violence was my third reason for staying home. Over the past four decades or so, Sonora's border towns and the nearby mountains have become the staging grounds for immigrants and narcotics destined for the United States. Even so, Lea and Oscar still traveled to Sonora, avoiding the conflicted areas. Lea had continued to lead the Father Kino tours for Arizona's Southwestern Mission Research Center that she had started in 1974. Over the decades, Lea has taken busloads of Tucsonans and others to visit Kino's churches in the Pimería Alta. Raised in Magdalena, Sonora, the gregarious Lea wanted to make Arizonans aware of their historical connections neighboring Sonora, introducing thousands of history buffs to the legacies and realities of the borderlands. "Father Kino's missions in Sonora are just as beautiful as those Spanish missions in California," she has exclaimed, infecting everyone with her spontaneous enthusiasm.

Finally, I was not excited about riding borrowed horses from people I didn't know. Aging is a matter of selectively eliminating enthusiasms while holding on dearly to the ones you will never quit. As I've gotten older, I have become less interested in horses bred and trained for competition. These days, the kind of horse I ride depends a lot on the country and the work to be done. What I chiefly need is a sure-footed mount with a smooth gait, especially at a trot. There is little pleasure in riding all day on a stumble-footed horse or one that jars your teeth with each step.

But Les Shannon, a neighboring rancher, enlightened me on just how good Mexican ranch horses could be, especially in rough country. Small-bodied and barrel-chested, hard-footed and tractable, they are descendants of the Spanish Barb, the horse the Moors left behind in Spain during the twelfth and thirteenth centuries. Crossing this rock-footed transplant from Africa's rugged Barbary Coast with native Iberian stock produced a durable and courageous mount with an exceedingly smooth way of going. After all, Cortés and his army had conquered Mexico sitting on their loins.

Oscar and I shared several things in addition to an affection for horses. We both enjoyed the writings of Konrad Lorenz and E. O. Wilson, fellow biologists who wrote about small creatures in ways that explained some hard-wired human behaviors, such as aggression and deep attachment to particular places. We also loved Temple Grandin, who used her autism to see the world as our horses saw it, thus helping us to become more humane. Over the years, I had grown to value Oscar's opinion and enjoyed his company. He had a manner and lifestyle that made him content and pleased everyone around him—a willing attitude and an open smile that beamed from underneath his narrow-brimmed Stetson. In fact, when we worked the Sonoita Quarter Horse Show together, Oscar always got started while the others wrangled over who had to do what. True, he hadn't much opportunity to perfect his riding seat while occupying his tenured professorship at the University of Arizona, but he rode a horse well enough to help me on the ranch now and then. What's more, Oscar knew the Sonoran Desert, and I looked forward to learning from him as we rode together.

And so I went, in late January 2008, as soon as the racehorses had been retired and our son, Richard West, returned home to take over the ranch. To a horseman, Sonora had the authentic pull of western American antiquity, even though writer Wallace Stegner and others claimed the American West started at the one hundredth meridian during the 1800s. Though Stegner was a westerner, he had unwittingly adopted an eastern perspective: "Eastward I go only by force," said Henry David Thoreau, the Massachusetts sage of Walden Pond, "but westward I go free."

But Stegner and Thoreau both got it wrong. The American West did not begin at Plymouth Rock or on Walden Pond, or with Lewis and Clark at the one hundredth meridian. It started in 1519, when Hernán Cortés and his troops unloaded their horses near Veracruz, starting Spain's conquest of northern New Spain that much later became Mexico. The Aztec emperor Moctezuma received word back from his terrified warriors that the newcomers were swift beasts with two heads and six legs, carrying sticks that spit fire and made horrible noises. Rumors quickly spread that their horses fed on human flesh. Cortés landed with 350 foot soldiers [some say 650] and sixteen horses in fighting fit, according to Bernal Díaz del Castillo in his 1568 eye witness history of the conquest. Díaz del Castillo listed each horse by the name of its owner, its color and sex, along with its assets and liabilities; for examples:

> *Capitán Cortés*: a vicious chestnut horse...
> *Francisco de Morla*: a bright-colored chestnut horse that was speedy and handled well.
> *Pedro de Alvarado* and *Hernán López de Ávila*: a sorrel mare, excellent at both fighting and racing.

Gonzalo Domínguez, who was a fine horseman: a dark chestnut horse, very good and a fine runner.

Juan de Escalante: a light-colored chestnut horse with white feet that wasn't any good.

Pedro de Alvarado and *Hernán López de Ávila*: a sorrel mare, excellent at both fighting and racing.

These horses and others that arrived later were crucial to Cortés's astonishingly rapid conquest of the Aztec empire. "Next to God they protected us the most." By "they," Díaz del Castillo meant the Spanish cavalry. To survive and triumph in the chaos of battle, war horse and rider had to trust each other completely and without hesitation. What horsemen today call "unity" between horse and rider was for the conquistador and his horse a matter of life or death.

A few decades later, in 1540, the conquistador Francisco Vázquez de Coronado trotted around the south flank of the Huachuca Mountains with hundreds of horses, crossing into what is now Arizona, less than fifty miles from my home. Coronado was looking for houses roofed with gold and streams shimmering with silver, a fruitless search that took him all the way to Kansas. Sixty years later, Juan de Oñate colonized Santa Fe, establishing large breeding herds that quickly drew the attention of Native American tribes whose economies were already based on raiding: Apache, Navajo, Zuni, and, decades later, the Comanche, who migrated into the region from Wyoming. For the next three hundred years, these horse-mounted marauders ruled the southern plains and southwestern deserts.

Perhaps no other foreign frontiersmen of the New World exceeded the Spanish soldier in physical courage, resilience, and brutality. Conquistadors were more soldiers of fortune for the Spanish throne and the Catholic Church than they were an organized military. Díaz del Castillo defended his compatriots unapologetically: "We were there to serve God, and to get rich." As the conquistadors made their way north from the Valle de México, pillaging, ravaging, and enslaving indigenous Americans, they left behind an implacable hatred for the Spanish settlers and soldiers who followed.

Yet another soldier, Alvar Núñez Cabeza de Vaca had a different experience, proving that stereotypes don't always hold true. Shipwrecked in a hurricane in 1528 with six hundred other soldiers, only Cabeza de Vaca and three other men survived, including an African slave, after they finally washed up on the shores of Galveston Island. They too had come seeking riches but got lost instead. Few have ever been so utterly lost: naked, starving, and sick, without even words for the new landforms, plants, animals, and people they found themselves among. The only direction they knew was where the sun set, and in that direction they might find their countrymen. At first enslaved by a voluptuous tribe of coastal aborigines (probably the Karankawas, who reputedly enjoyed a "manbake" as much as a clambake), the Spaniards became godlike creatures by withstanding diseases they themselves had brought. For almost nine years, Cabeza de Vaca and his compatriots wandered westward, living as faith healers and attracting large crowds of acolytes, while they wandered over the Gulf Coast of Texas and northern Mexico. Estevanico, the polyglot Moorish slave, got them through.

When at last they encountered a Spanish slaving party in Sinaloa, Cabeza de Vaca's native disciples refused to believe that he and his three companions were of the same race as the conquistadors. In his 1542 memoir, Cabeza de Vaca recorded their reaction, one of the few direct accounts of what indigenous Americans thought of the Spanish when their cultures first collided:

> We came from the sunrise, they came from the sunset; we healed the sick, they killed the sound; we came naked and barefoot, they came clothed, horsed, and lanced; we coveted nothing but gave whatever we were given, while they robbed whomever they found and bestowed nothing on anyone.

Cabeza de Vaca's conversion reads like an Old Testament parable—wandering in the wilderness, stripped naked of everything but hope and direction, losing all pretensions in order to become truly human.

The Spanish and multicultural Jesuits also left behind a wealth of reports, maps, and journals. These histories, of course, contained only the perceptions of conquerors and priests; only they had a written language. Even so, as I continued to read, my interest surged. To know as completely as possible where I might be going and why seemed instinctual; the history of place, people, and region made them what they are today. Kino had worked in the heart of the Sonoran Desert, a near-mythical land of great beauty and complexity. For the newcomer, the unprepared, or the foolhardy, this was hostile country—its plants and animals armed by spine, venom, or fang as if to repel an invasion; elevations ranging from sea level to ten thousand feet above; a thirsty land, prone to extremes of temperature, violent thunderstorms, and prolonged droughts. But to many indigenous Americans, it was home, and for a few biologists, artists, and ranchers, the most interesting landscape on earth. And the most authentic way to experience it all was from the back of a horse.

IN EARLY JANUARY, Lea told me that the Salgados had decided on the route—Sonoyta to Caborca; 125 miles; February 1–4—and that they would be glad for me to come along. Over the next few days as we prepared for the trip, e-mails zipped back and forth between José Luis Salgado, Enrique's younger brother and general manager of the Salgado family business, and the other riders spread out over Sonora, Arizona, and California. The horses would leave Hermosillo by trailer on January 31 at seven in the morning, and the riders should be at the stockyards in Sonoyta no later than the same afternoon.

"Are you and Oscar going?" I asked Lea over the phone toward the end of January. Oscar's hip had been giving him trouble recently, and he had not been able to ride much. Also, the last time I saw him, a slight tremor in his left hand suggested other problems, but Oscar didn't say anything, and it didn't seem to affect his usual optimism.

"Of course," she replied. But I had the feeling that if we were going to ride a cabalgata together, it would have to be this year.

In one e-mail, José Luis sent a map showing our route. The staging place was the border town of Sonoyta on the edges of the Organ Pipe Cactus National Monument and the Tohono O'odham Indian Reservation. Sonoyta was on the crossroads of the highway going south to Rocky Point and Mexico's Route 2, which cut across the waist of Kino's Pimería Alta and linked Tijuana on the Pacific Ocean with Ciudad Juárez across from El Paso, Texas.

Although Kino was one of the first Europeans to see it, the O'odham and other indigenous Americans had traveled the same landscape for a thousand years, trading medicinal plants, shells, basketry, feathers, and other goods from as far south as Valle de México and west to the Pacific Ocean. Nowadays, these highways carry other kinds of commerce: hundreds of thousands of destitute immigrants and billions of dollars of illegal narcotics, both destined for America's heartland. Sonoyta sat right in the middle of it all.

Father Kino made many trips through Sonoyta, establishing San Marcelo de Sonoyta early on as a supply base for his explorations into California's geography. Following O'odham guides west, Kino cut trails over the western desert to the Gila and Colorado Rivers, generally following what today is the US–Mexico border. On one trip in 1702, he and Father Rector Manuel Gonzales reached the confluence of the Gila and Colorado Rivers, descending to northern flood tides of the Sea of Cortés. The trip home was so arduous that Kino's companion expired on the way.

Their route later became a deadly shortcut during the California gold rush of 1849. The bones of hundreds of Argonauts (and their livestock) littered the highway, nameless pilgrims who dreamed of riches but died of sunstroke and thirst instead. To the south, the giant sand dunes and lava fields of the Gran Desierto de Pinacate were even more forbidding. Once, the optimistic Kino tried a shortcut back to Sonoyta by going directly east from the Colorado River Delta: "After eighteen leagues [46 miles] over the most difficult sand dunes and continuous wind, we found not a drop of water nor the least bit of pasturage." Though adventurous, the Jesuit was not foolhardy. He reversed course and followed the Gila River home instead. Prudence was another of his many virtues.

On May 19, 2001, twenty-five Mexicans looked at this landscape, having been assured by the coyotes that it would be a boulevard to a better life. Luis Alberto Urrea painstakingly reconstructed their round-trip journey, from when they left their villages in the state of Veracruz until they returned there in coffins. The *alambristas* stepped over the barbed-wire border fence near Quitobaquito Spring, following a Mexican guide called Méndez into the scorched landscape. The second day out, Méndez got lost. Then the "asshole" took their money and went looking for water. Five days later, fourteen were dead. The survivors included Méndez. The incident caused a great outcry because of the numbers, eclipsing the previous record of thirteen Salvadorans who died here in July 1980, unable to quench their thirst with their own urine. They had paid $2,500 each for the guided tour.

KINO'S PROSELYTIZING THE O'odham did not interest me as much as their adaptations to arid living in a region that often received less than six inches of annual rainfall. With the looming realities of global warming, their life ways could be useful guides for modern Arizonans, including ranchers struggling to conserve water and land resources in the face of climate change. On the first night out, we would pitch camp at the Hia C-ed O'odham (Sand Papago) village of Quitovac, a sacred place because of its perennial springs. Along the way, we would ride cross-country over Mexican ranches with stands of giant columnar cactus found nowhere else on earth. Cowboy Kino's bestiary included criollo cattle that originated from North Africa's barren Atlas Mountains. By today's standards, their descendants were mostly horns, hide, and testicles, but they thrived in an environment where the Hereford and Angus breeds would starve or die of thirst.

Lea planned to pick me up at eight, so I packed a duffel and bedroll the night before and got up at daylight to get my saddle and tack together. At nine, I got itchy and called her house. "We are on our way," she sang out over the phone. At ten thirty, the pickup finally rolled into the driveway of our ranch headquarters, with Lea driving. Oscar stepped slowly out of the truck like a man feeling his way in the dark. I hadn't seen him in over a month and was startled by how much he had slipped. He still wore that winning smile, but his red vest hung off his shoulders like a feed sack.

"Whee, we made it," Lea said, hopping down. She gave Diane a hug and hurried around to the breezeway where I had piled my saddle and bedroll. "Sonoyta is only about four hours, so we have plenty of time." After all the years, now that I was finally able to go, Oscar couldn't ride. Despite that, he was not giving up. He and Lea would follow the supply truck and stay in the homes of their Sonoran friends or in motels along the way.

I offered to drive, but Lea said we'd better get going and jumped up into the driver's seat. Diane and I hugged each other, and she closed the ranch gate behind us, waving good-bye. Looking back, I noticed that Oscar had already dozed off in the backseat of the double-cab pickup. We dropped off the Sonoita Plains north to Interstate 10 and headed west through Tucson toward the Tohono O'odham Reservation on Highway 86.

On the western outskirts of Tucson, Lea whizzed past Robles Junction, where State Route 286 branched off to the south. Highway 286 dead-ended at Sasabe, a flea-bitten border town notorious for being the busiest crossing point for illegal immigrants in the Border Patrol's Tucson sector. Here, Homeland Security had wasted $1 billion on Boeing Corporation's wide-optical, digitized radar—the so-called "virtual fence"— that couldn't penetrate through the deep arroyos or dust storms or tell the difference between a human or a horse. Instead, seven miles of steel fence, fifteen feet high, shielded the town, forcing the immigrants to cross deeper in the boondocks.

"Hey, Lea," I said as we crossed over the Brawley Wash bridge. "See that blue flag above the mesquite thicket? It's a water station for immigrants. I leased the Buckalew Ranch for grazing last winter and the Humane Borders people had water barrels out all over the place."

Lea lifted herself up to see over the steering wheel, swerving into the opposite lane. "*Yes!* So that's what my church gives money for!" she cried out happily, swerving back just in time to miss a head-on collision with an oncoming car. Oscar's big truck didn't fit the diminutive Lea, and she had trouble reaching the pedals.

Alarmed by the soaring death rate—five hundred border crossers died in 2005—Reverend Robin Hoover, a veteran of the sanctuary movement of the 1980s, organized the Humane Borders to put out water stations on the footpaths that streamed down the Altar Valley toward Interstate 10. But dry statistics seldom create much sympathy, especially if the dead are anonymous Mexicans. To mobilize public support, Hoover illustrated the awful truth with a death map on the Humane Borders website.

Picture a map with Sasabe on the border at the center. Then draw concentric half circles around the town at one, two, and three days' walking distances toward Robles Junction, located forty-five miles north on Highway 86. Finally, plot a red dot on the map at each location where a dead migrant was found. Hundreds of dots fanned out away from the border, clustering along the well-used trails paralleling the Brawley Wash in the valley's bottom. A little way south of Highway 86, the dots bled into a solid red mass, vividly exposing the limits of human endurance. Upon leaving Sasabe, most immigrants carry enough water for two or three days, if they ration it wisely. Exhausted and stunned by the heat, the unlucky ones run out of water and die just hours from sanctuary, like snow-blind skiers freezing within sight of the cabin. These days, many are native to the humid climes of southern Mexico, Guatemala, and El Salvador, verdant lands teeming with shade and streams of water in every arroyo—landscapes that are a far cry from the Sonoran Desert, where water jugs run dry and people die. They have no understanding of how quickly heatstroke, dehydratiown, and the merciless desert sun can kill.

The Humane Borders program has encountered resistance, and not just among the right-wing vigilantes who say they would just as soon see the immigrants die if they refuse to stay in Mexico. Longtime residents of the borderlands, including ranchers, the O'odham tribe, and conservationists, worried that water stations would encourage illegal border crossers, increasing the damage to the fragile landscape and property and endangering American lives. The program also could increase immigrant deaths, because it fools people, especially women and children, into thinking that the journey is less hazardous than it really is. But Hoover saw the situation as a humanitarian crisis that demanded immediate action. While unquestionably true, water barrels have not changed—and will not change—the poverty in Mexico that drives illegal immigration. Nor will they satisfy the United States' appetite for cheap labor and illegal drugs. A supervised guest-worker program could go a long way in meeting the needs of both countries and reduce the human and environmental carnage.

HIGHWAY 286 CLIMBED the creosote-covered bajada and we rounded the north flank of the Coyote Mountains, passing the turnoff to Kitt Peak Observatory.

"Did you find any bodies on the Buckalew Ranch?" Oscar perked up in the backseat.

"No. It was a wet winter," I answered, "and I had the cattle out of there before it got hot. I did lose a cow to a drug overdose, though. She ate a marijuana brick. When I opened her up, her rumen was crammed with the black plastic and the yellow clothesline rope they bundle the stuff with."

"Did you talk to any of the walkers?" Lea asked.

"I usually stayed back, because if I rode up, they'd scatter like quail. One might get separated from their group."

"Did you call the Border Patrol?" Oscar asked.

"When they needed help, I did. To tell the truth, I felt sorry for them. I used to live down there, so I know what their life was like. The farms where I worked were like the pre–Civil War South, except the slaves were brown."

We crossed the Tohono O'odham reservation and turned south at Why, entering the Organ Pipe National Monument. The setting sun fired the Ajo Mountains crimson, and giant saguaro and organ pipe cactus cast long, thin shadows over the asphalt. The desert floor was carpeted by a dwarf forest of spiny things: clusters of prickly pear, ocotillo thickets, brittle brush in yellow bloom, treed by foothill paloverde, mesquite, and ironwood. Soon, we entered Lukeville at the border, a bleak settlement with one store, a small cluster of government buildings, and an empty RV park.

We crossed the border from Lukeville to Sonoyta and drove to a motel on the main road, appropriately labeled Hombres Blancos (White Men's) Street, where Lea and Oscar would spend the night. While they checked in and rested up, I walked out into the hectic energy of the border town. Hombres Blancos led to the highway going south to Rocky Point's fabulous beaches and points further down the seacoast. Early arrivals from Tucson and Phoenix were already in the stores, stocking up for the coming weekend.

The American traffic kept to their street—sleek 4x4 trucks, pulling trailers loaded with dune buggies, Sea-Doos, and cool boxes; fat-tired jeeps with surfboards strapped on top; lumbering RVs, one with a hairless Chihuahua that yipped at me through the windshield as I walked by. They had crossed the border to spend money, lots of it, in their separate enclaves of gringo affluence in Sonora's version of Cancun.

Going in the opposite direction, a Mexican bus rattled past, coughing up great clouds of diesel smoke, its destination San Luis Río Colorado, across from Yuma, Arizona. A sign in the driver's window proclaimed "*Dios Es Mi Guía*," which translated to the very Mexican sentiment that "God Is My Guide." Off the main road, smells of ripe fruit and hot grease from sidewalk vendors floated out of the alleys, where immigrants were buying provisions for their trek into America. A heavy-set woman with empty plastic water jugs hanging from both ends of a pole draped over her broad shoulders stalked the back streets. "Fifty pesos each," she cried out. Trudging behind her, the ice cream vendor pushed his bicycle cart, the tinkling bells adding a cheerful aspect to the fading day.

Two contrasting cultures streamed past each other without making contact, each one intent on separate destinations—one poor, the other rich; one dark-skinned, the other pale; one spicy, the other mild; one hungry and the other well fed; one focused on work, the other on play. Most Americans, with some notable exceptions, didn't give a rat's ass about the immigrants' plight. The immigrants, in turn, dreamed about paying jobs at the opposite end of the rainbow—useful, needed work like harvesting America's crops or tidying up hotels and hospice centers—fulfilling their hopes by sending their wages back home.

When I got back to the motel, Oscar and Lea were in the pickup, talking to Enrique Salgado on the cell phone, getting directions to the stockyards. The day died beautifully in a violent sunset of red and purple as we drove into the corrals of the Asociación Ganadera de Sonora.

"Yippee! We made it," Lea chirped, hopping down from the truck. The campsite had been set up on freshly plowed ground behind the corrals, where a dozen or more tents rose up from the damp earth. The cabalgantes stood or squatted around a bonfire behind the cook trailer. The Salgados greeted Oscar and Lea with back-slapping hugs without saying anything about Oscar's obvious condition. Dinner was over, but Gaspar, the cook, had saved us some tortillas and grilled strips of meat (*carne asada*). Around the campfire, talk flared like struck matches, then died out, and then flared again, often punctuated by laughter. I listened quietly, trying to put names with the faces and personalities of the people with whom I would be riding for the next four days.

José Luis Salgado Bojórquez, leader of the cabalgata, stood across the fire from where we sat. The youngest Salgado brother was a tall man, forty years old, with an easy smile, likable manners, and a fin of a nose hanging above a bushy mustache. He wore a potato-chip straw hat and a tan saddle coat with the blue insignia of Caminos de Kino stitched on the left front pocket. Standing beside him, his willowy teenage daughter, María José, had big brown eyes and a sparkling, toothy smile. She wore a quilted vest, jeans, boots, and straw hat, the riding attire of an expert horsewoman. Jesús Enrique, the elder statesman of the Salgado clan, gazed through black-framed glasses with the studious appearance of a college dean, complete with a narrow-brim felt hat and leather vest. When Enrique spoke, it was about some historical fact related to Kino's journals, and everyone paid attention.

The middle Salgado brother, Arturo Oriol, was a short, burly man whose conversations often ended in outbursts of laughter. His physique, full round face, bushy black eyebrows, and beard suggested Basque ancestry from the Pyrenees Mountains of northern Spain and southern France, a lineage well established in the Spanish-Mexican frontier. In fact, Adjutant Nicolas Bohórques accompanied Father Kino on the 1701 expedition to the upper reaches of the Sea of Cortés. A century and a half later, Juan Bohórquez was on the roster of the last Mexican soldiers to leave Tucson after the 1854 Gadsden Purchase was completed.

Pichi, as everyone called Arturo, was a small animal veterinarian who practiced in Hermosillo with his veterinarian wife, Susy. Their son Pichito had followed their lead, except that he specialized in equine medicine and attended to our horses on the ride. Pichito is the diminutive for Pichi, but Pichito outweighed his father by a hundred pounds and was built like a lineman for the Norte Dame football team, his puckery face split by a happy grin and punctuated with twinkly dark eyes.

Ricardo Ramonet, a farmer, sat next to me. A short, trim man in his mid-forties, Ricardo was eager to practice English, and I, Spanish, so we chatted in both languages. Years had passed since I had been completely immersed in the Spanish language, and its rhythms felt like old friends returning after a long absence. Ricardo had studied agronomy at the University of California at Davis and grew oranges, garbanzos, and watermelons on irrigated land west of Hermosillo. He was a veteran of the rides, beginning with the third one that also started here at Sonoyta-Lukeville, but went west in the opposite direction, ending at the Colorado River at Yuma. His oldest son, David, a teenager with red hair and blue eyes, would be starting on his first ride tomorrow.

Perhaps because we were at the same starting point, Ricardo and the three Salgado brothers retold the story of the ride to Yuma over *El Camino del Diablo* (the Devil's Highway). On December 11, 1989, eight riders, plus a horse wrangler named Jerry, started out on a pilgrimage worthy of the intrepid Kino, crossing the desert from Lukeville to the confluence of the Gila and Colorado Rivers, a distance of 160 miles in five days.

Since Kino's time, the Devil's Highway had become fettered by rules and regulations. To avoid air force bombs on Barry Goldwater's bombing range, the cabalgantes squeezed their ride into one specific week when the planes were grounded. Unable to bring their own horses because of the border quarantine, they had to find mounts in Arizona. Dr. Mike Weber, a historian and cabalgante from Arizona Historical Society, rented a string from a dude ranch in Tucson.

But the Park Service prohibited keeping horses overnight on the monument. That presented several difficulties: first, they needed a place to stable the horses the first night; second, the cabalgantes would have to ride forty miles the first day in order to make camp off the monument and thirty miles every day thereafter; third, their supply trucks were forced to make daily runs to Yuma for water and hay because water and pasturage on the refuge were reserved for wildlife; and fourth, the Park Service office in Lukeville that issued the required permits was closed on Sunday, the day the riders had to leave. Another call from Mike Weber persuaded the Park Service to make an exception and issue the permits early. José Luis solved the problem of stabling horses that first Sunday by renting parking spaces in Lukeville's empty RV park.

For the cabalgantes, overcoming the obstacles had become points of pride, in the same way that story becomes legend fondly remembered with the passage of time and the retelling. Ricardo said he had ridden a horse only now and then in the years before El Camino del Diablo. Once they got past noon on the first day, he recalled, the only option was to continue, in spite of the pain. Mike Weber had been on a horse only once before in his life!

Enrique and José Luis had driven the route earlier that year and knew the campsites and distances. Fourteen miles out, they passed by the lovely Quitobaquito Spring. Unable to water their horses there and in a hurry, they missed seeing the most beautiful scenery on the entire trip. They reached the first camp long after sundown, but their supply trucks were nowhere to be seen. The horses needed water, and everyone was hungry. After Jerry the wrangler got panicky, José Luis settled everyone down by stating the obvious: all they could do was wait. The two trucks finally rolled in after midnight. For safety, they wisely drove in tandem but still got stuck in the deep sand because neither truck had four-wheel drive.

Father Kino had similar problems on his February 1699 ride. Exhausted and out of water, his caravan finally came to a halt after dark beside a giant shard of granite rising up from the sand. The Jesuit, instead of collapsing like everyone else, scrambled to the top, where the moonlight revealed a deep pool of precious water that he named Moon Springs (*Aguaje de la Luna*). For the cabalgantes, this act of faith and curiosity captured the essence of Father Kino's indomitable spirit, and they were resolved to celebrate it. When they finally arrived at Aguaje de la Luna in the afternoon, they made camp early to wait for the full moon and the arrival of Father Gabriel Gómez Padilla with the supply trucks, in order to celebrate a moonlit Mass on the mountaintop.

During the scouting trip, Enrique met John Annerino, photographer and writer, accompanying four *campesino* (small farmers) immigrants from Sinaloa. They had left the border in the fierce heat of May, each one carrying six-gallon jugs of water and a sack of food that would hopefully last until they reached Interstate 8. To Enrique, these Mexicans represented the great potential of his country being squandered by a political system that denied them the opportunity to work and share in Mexico's wealth. Mexicans fleeing to the United States was the escape valve that allowed the entrenched bureaucracy to maintain itself in power. Correcting this should be the job of all Mexicans, he wrote.

At Aguaje de la Luna that night after Mass, Enrique had a dream that he shared. The Mexican president took action by crossing the desert hand in hand with the campesinos. On television each night, all Mexicans saw the image of their president, tired and sweaty, sharing the suffering of those who could not find decent work at home. His example so inspired the whole country that industry began to produce more, politicians began working for the people instead of for themselves, farmers returned to the land, teachers really became teachers again, and students learned better. Mexico pulled itself up by the bootstraps and was transformed within a few years, with Father Kino's compassion, intelligence, and energy as the example.[1]

THE SIERRA CUBABI is a low, broken range of mountains lying east-southeast of Sonoyta. Today, we were to ride into those hills, José Luis said, to visit a ranch owned by a local family, where Father Claudio Murrieta would dedicate a new chapel. From Rancho Cubabi, the route would take us across Mexico's Highway 2 to the O'odham oasis village of Quitovac.

At dawn, Ricardo Ramonet and I went to the corrals to feed his horses, including the mare I had been assigned, a pretty palomino called Alejandra, who was a twenty-year-old veteran. I slipped the nosebag of grain over her head, looking down at her legs and black hooves. Her knees seemed big, but she was, for now, completely unconcerned about the journey we would impose on her. Returning to the campfire, I was delighted that Oscar and Lea had come to see us off. Gaspar called out for breakfast, a delicious concoction of scrambled eggs, a spicy dried meat called machaca, green chile, and onions, with refried beans and flour tortillas as thin as snakeskin, warmed on a sheet of tin over the fire.

The Mexicans loved ceremony. As we prepared to leave, the mayor of Sonoyta made a speech wishing us well. Next, Father Claudio Murrieta, a cabalgante from Pitiquito mission, recited a brief prayer invoking the spirit of Padre Kino. A police car from the town preceded us down the dusty road, lights flashing and siren screaming, until the land opened up, and we turned off into the unbroken desert. Looking back, I saw Oscar and Lea standing by the Los Caminos de Kino banner, which was waving brightly in the morning breeze. Oscar was smiling, but I had an uncomfortable feeling about riding without him. I would miss the companionship and his encyclopedic knowledge of the desert. And in spite of Lea's competence, I was worried about them traveling alone in this conflicted region. Oscar was meticulous about pulling maintenance on his big truck, but still, things could go wrong, and Lea couldn't lift the spare tire.

It was a lovely, high-ceiling day, the sky platter blue and the air brisk and clear. José Luis and our cowboy (vaquero) guide took the lead, and the riders strung out in no particular order. As we quit the road and entered unmarked landscape, we all felt the exhilaration that comes with the start of a journey, with senses heightened and mind receptive to what might lie ahead. Enrique rode beside me on a smooth-striding, sturdy, buckskin-colored gelding with black mane, dorsal strip, and zebra-striped legs—

the color prized by the conquistadors. Alejandra started out with an easy walk, but as the hour passed, she began to strain for the lead and broke into a trot. Once in front, she slowed and fell behind and then trotted again to catch up. *Okay*, I thought, *we will do it your way, and maybe you'll get tired.*

We had entered the land of organ pipes, the columnar cactus the Mexicans called *pitaya*. To me, they looked more like gigantic candelabra than the pipes of an organ, or Jewish menorahs with multiple branches rising up out of a thick base. To the tribes of the Sonoran Desert, pitaya fruit was a staple food and, along with the fruit of the saguaro, was fermented to make the wine drunk at summer festivals held to bring rain. The Ópata and Mayo tribes also claimed that pitaya wine, in addition to being mildly alcoholic, had aphrodisiac effects. Narratives of Coronado's expedition referred to these natives as "sodomites," saying they became stupefied by the concoction. Scandalized by the natives' joyous reproductive behavior, the glum Jesuits denounced cactus wine as ungodly. The Mayo people also claimed the fleshy meat of the stem relieved the pain of hemorrhoids when applied directly to the anus (provided the spines were removed first).

Clusters of gigantic granite boulders loomed up from the desert floor and foothills, like dry-land archipelagoes, the house-sized stones often stacked precariously on top of each other. Beneath the clusters, badgers, foxes, and coyotes had excavated small caves. The vaquero and José Luis turned into a wide canyon that split the mountain, arriving at Rancho Cubabi, a small village nestled on three sides by the natural rock walls. Children ran out on the road to greet us as if we were a l iberating army as we rode into the corrals and dismounted. Even though it was only midmorning, the ranch had laid out an open-air feast of carne asada and various sweets made of pitaya fruit. The strips of meat from the loin had been grilled over an open fire and were served rolled up in warm flour tortillas, with strips of green chile and a dollop of guacamole. An early visitor from the eastern United States once described Sonora as the place where civilization ended and carne asada began.

Rancho Cubabi recently had completed a chapel to serve the isolated small ranches in the area, and Father Murrieta had been asked to dedicate it to Saint Francis. Dressed in a denim jacket and straw hat, he appeared quite unpriestly, with a heavy beard and bushy eyebrows that looked like black, furry caterpillars. Going inside, he stood alone, bareheaded and bald for a moment, and then turned and came outside to address the people who crowded around. He told the story of John the Baptist—how he had preached on the River Jordan, calling men to penance. As the crowd returned to the fiesta, I entered the chapel and gazed at the clean, whitewashed walls, a crucifix mounted over the altar, and the Virgin of Guadalupe overlooking the pews. Outside, a pair of unadorned bell towers framed the peaked roof, each one topped with a simple, elongated cross. Behind them loomed the Sierra Cubabi, lending the little building an importance out of proportion to its size.

The ranchers had dish-faced, tail-twisted Arab show horses, the kind seen in Lawrence of Arabia movies. They saddled and rode to show us pictographs of antlered deer, hunters, and geometric figures etched into the rock of a shallow cave, a place that spoke silently of the ancient presence of humankind, long before Kino arrived. Looking at these figures, I wondered about the artists. What color and size were they? What sounds did they utter? Did they go about dressed in skins or were they naked? What did they hope for the future? This cave had surely been a chapel to the O'odham pantheon long before Kino's arrival. Leaving the questions unasked because there were no answers, I followed the others to Highway 2, where the ranchers turned back while we crossed over and rode in the bright midday sun toward Quitovac.

Alejandra stayed with her stiff-kneed trot, fighting to hold the lead. Trying to hold her back only made matters worse. Thinking priestly company might help, I pulled her up next to Father Claudio's horse, and she relaxed long enough that Father Claudio and I could have a conversation. Claudio's home mission was Pitiquito on the Río Altar, not far from our destination of Caborca. I was curious about which of Sonora's many missions had the most to offer for a visitor.

"Álamos is the most beautiful," he replied without hesitation. "That was where it all started."

Located in the southwestern corner of Sonora, the Jesuits began the mission there in 1630, and silver was discovered soon afterward. Álamos thrived as the mining and religious center for northern New Spain, funding many of the expeditions that established settlements and churches in the Pimería Alta, including Kino's maiden voyage in 1687. Silver also paid for Álamos's massive La Parroquia de la Purísima Concepción church, completed by the Franciscan order in 1826.

In 2001, the cabalgata extended from El Fuerte in the state of Sinaloa, through Álamos, on the way to Quiriega, Sonora. According to Lea and Oscar, it had been a journey plagued by very bad luck. While loading the horses for transport to El Fuerte, Oscar suffered several broken ribs when he was smashed by a horse inside the truck. In El Fuerte, Mike Weber's blood sugar dropped precipitously and he had to be rushed to the hospital. On the final day of the ride, Domingo Pesquiera's horse kicked Ricardo

Ramonet, breaking his ribs. It seemed as if this cabalgata needed the touch of Teresa Urrea, the Saint of Cabora, the legendary faith healer who lived on the nearby Cabora Ranch in the late 1800s. She became the most celebrated and sought-after healer in the history of the borderlands. Some say she helped precipitate the Mexican Revolution.

The Mexican Joan of Arc, Saint of Cabora, Queen of the Yaquis, or simply Teresita, Teresa Urrea was born in October 1873, the illegitimate daughter of a wealthy ranch owner, Tomas Urrea. Her mother, Cayetana Chavez, was an indigenous girl who worked on the Urrea ranch. Chavez abandoned her daughter to the care of the ranch's native herbalist and midwife shortly after Teresita's baptism. In colonial Mexico, the wealthy upper class often had liaisons with the kitchen help, and Don Tomas was no exception. He had two "official" wives, with whom he had nearly a dozen offspring, but he also had several children with his peon lady friends. Usually, those children went unrecognized and were cast out, but Teresita proved an exception. By age sixteen, she had learned the names and uses of nearly two hundred medicinal herbs and several tribal rituals. The local tribes—Yaqui, Tomochic, and Mayo—though nominally Catholic, had retained their traditional beliefs. Teresita became renowned as a midwife; her touch on a woman in labor was said to cause the pain of birth to immediately fade away.

As Teresita's fame grew, Tomas grew aware of her and adopted her into his home, along with several of her half siblings. At one point, a jealous worker tried to rape her. The attempt left her in a coma, and she was later pronounced dead. As the women of the ranch prayed over her coffined body, Teresita suddenly stirred from her narcolepsy, declaring, "I will not sleep here!"

Teresita claimed to have met God while asleep and said that he had shown her many things, including the power to heal his earthly children with a touch and a prayer. As word of her miracles spread, thousands of pilgrims surrounded her house, day and night, including warriors from the militant tribes. Fearful of her influence, the cowardly dictator Porfirio Díaz deported Teresita to the Arizona Territory and massacred the Indians who venerated her. Teresita died in Clifton, Arizona, in 1906. Among the impoverished communities of the borderlands, Teresita has become an ascendant saint, not of the Catholic Church but with a growing role in revolutionary thought and indigenous awareness.

Father Murrieta shrugged his shoulders when I mentioned Teresita's name, saying only that she was an errant Catholic, which was true. The next mission to see should be Arizpe on the Río Sonora, he said, and then Tubutama and Pitiquito.

"Let me know when you are coming," Claudio offered, handing me his card with e-mail address and cell phone number. I felt a twinge of incongruity, passing e-mail addresses while on horseback in the heart of the Sonoran Desert, talking about a journey launched 321 years ago and a heroine of the people from the previous century, who, like Kino, still lived brightly in the culture of the borderlands.

Some say that beautiful music has the power to abolish pain. Fernando, a rider from California, had an Apple iPod with speakers strapped to his saddle. A small, cheerful man, he wore the traditional outfit of a Spanish caballero: wide hat with flat brim and crown, a horsehair stampede string that trailed down his back, black singlet that covered his neck like a turtleneck sweater, and tight toreador pants festooned with silver conchos. His horse was a small, energetic gelding with a short stride that did not need the encouragement of the rawhide quirt Fernando insisted on carrying. The pony had to trot anyway to keep up, bouncing Fernando up and down like a lid on a boiling pot.

Fernando had omnivorous musical tastes, from opera to Mexican folk ballads. Perhaps in honor of Kino's birthplace of Signo, Italy, he brought a fine selection of Luciano Pavarotti, singing operas by Italian composers. Pavarotti's magnificent tenor voice ringing off the Sierra Cubabi, coupled with the energy of Vivaldi's violin concertos, nearly abolished the ache building in my groin from Alejandra's stiff-kneed trot.

Our stopover that night at Quitovac, the Hia C-ed O'odham (Sand Papago) village, was short and disappointing. We were met by Eugenio Velazco, a village elder with a wry smile and a mustache flecked with gray. He led us afoot down the dusty road to the vacant schoolhouse, where Brenda Lee, an O'odham teacher, kindly let us camp because the children were gone for the long weekend. Velazco was tall and lean for a Papago, and his broad forehead and narrow chin made his chestnut-brown face appear wedge shaped. I wondered if these Papago had managed to escape the epidemic of obesity affecting the O'odham on the main reservation.

While we set up camp, Velazco and Lee disappeared for good. Later, I noted that the Salgado's journal entry for this leg of our trip was brief:

> We rode into the village in the late afternoon and were met by the natives Eugenio Velazco and Brenda Lee. They allowed us to stay beside the schoolhouse because the children were gone on Friday. Several of the riders slept inside San Francisco's chapel, but on the following morning, Saint Francis left at dawn, disturbed by the snoring of the Kino-ites.

My strongest impression of the village was a big well with a rusty motor and the exit pipe hovering over a crumbling cement ditch. Extending out at right angles from the ditch were abandoned fields with long borders, as if they had been intended for alfalfa or grass. Irrigation on this scale seemed strangely out of place in a Hia C-ed O'odham oasis. Looking for the subsistence gardens I had read about, I led the mare at dusk in the opposite direction to a small set of pens surrounded by tangled hedgerows on three sides, stopping by a ditch for a well-deserved drink. A pig scampered away through the mud but the mare kept drinking, her ears flicking backward each time she swallowed. The gardens were barren except for a few dried-up pumpkin shells.

The day died beautifully with palm trees casting shadows over the oasis and doves calling in the twilight. The town seemed empty of people as I walked among the houses; perhaps we had frightened them away. Or maybe the O'odham were just being polite, knowing we had ridden far that day and were tired. After a quick supper, I pitched my bedroll on the ground away from the others and instantly fell asleep, grateful for level ground and mattress pad.

February 2

Cock-a-doodle-do! A rooster crowed proudly in the predawn light and then sounded off again to make sure that I'd heard. I walked to the horse pens, where a few goats were nibbling on the leftover hay. Gnatcatchers flitted in the hedgerow bushes, like smudgy mice with wings. Beyond the pens was a broad, shallow pond, covered by green scum. A great blue heron stalked around the far edge, carefully lifting one leg and then the other, intent on spearing what might be wriggling in the greenish water. As I looked around the village, there was no one in sight except other riders, tending to their horses.

I went back to the fire, where Gaspar had coffee ready and was working on breakfast. The Salgados seemed to have mastered a crucial aspect of a happy journey: eating well and on time. I recalled from his journals that Kino seldom traveled far without servants to handle such chores.

"How did you sleep?" Pichi Salgado asked.

"Good," I said. "I didn't hear a thing until the O'odham alarm clock went off."

"*Así es*," Pichi guffawed.

By now, the others were coming to the fire.

José Luis spread his hands over the flames, palms down. "We need to be saddled and riding by eight o'clock," he said. "The maps say fifty-eight kilometers to Cantarranas."

"How many did we do yesterday?" I grunted.

"Fifty-one, according to my GPS," Heriberto Robles said. Heriberto was a PhD toxicologist from Los Angeles and calculated our daily itineraries in hours and minutes, as well as feet, miles, meters, and kilometers. His brother, Arturo, and nephew, Arturo Jr., also came for the ride, driving the several hundred miles from their ranch in the state of Chihuahua.

"Is Eugenio Velazco coming for breakfast?" I asked. "Maybe he'd give us a tour of the village."

"I told him last night that we had to leave early," José Luis said.

"How did Kino get by without a GPS?" Arturo López queried. Three López brothers—Arturo, José, and Angel—ran cattle and farmed on the Río Sonora near Huepac in addition to operating a trucking company in Hermosillo.

"They had the Indians to guide them," Enrique answered.

"Where are the Papagos this morning?" I wondered again.

"Who knows? The Papago wander around a lot," Pichi said. "Sometimes they visit relatives on the reservation or go to Caborca."

"The farm looked abandoned," I said. "I was surprised to see the big well and cement ditches. Somebody spent a lot of money here."

"It was a government project to help the Papago," Enrique said. "But they ran out of money when the peso was devalued, and the Papago didn't care anyway."

"They do not farm that way," Ricardo interjected. "The Papago are happy to grow their small plots of squash and beans and to graze a few cows."

"The Gila River O'odham in Arizona have thousands of acres under cultivation," I added, "but they have lots of river water."

"Here is a different kind of Papago," Ricardo replied, "and a lot less water, not enough for commercial farming."

"Breakfast!" Gaspar yelped. Everyone dove for their dishes and stood in line. Each rider was required to bring his or her own utensils and to wash them. No disposables were allowed, and the cabalgantes were scrupulous about cleaning up their campsites. The first thing out of the supply truck was a special shovel, and we buried our stools like cats. Other sensible rules included no firearms (they are illegal in Mexico anyway); no narcotics; each rider must care for his or her horse; and those who snore too loud are banished from sleeping near the campfire.

Kino had camped at Quitovac more than once on his explorations of the western desert, as well as at Quitobaquito Oasis located forty miles north of where we were. But his brief journal entries about them suggested that he had little interest in either place as centers of O'odham culture or for their adaptations to arid living.

Kino's soldier sidekick, Lieutenant Juan Mateo Manje, gave a brief description of Quitovac on his first visit in 1694, calling it "San Luis de Bacapa y Moicapa, a place close to a high hill at whose feet were some springs of water and some lakes."[2] Manje described the natives as "naked and so poor" that he gave them all his supplies and so had to return to Caborca prematurely. Yet the Bacapa village at the Quitovac oasis must have been a sizable settlement at certain times of the year, as Kino was greeted four years later by 160 natives and given great quantities of pitaya.

Even small springs like Quitovac were precious in such a dry country, giving rise to feelings of the sacred and divine. This took expression in O'odham mythology in the form of the water serpent, a large, boa constrictor–like snake that guarded each spring.

The O'odham believed that killing the water serpent would cause the spring to dry up. The *mestizo* (mixed-blood) people of Sonora adopted a version of this myth, calling the snake a *Coría*.

Ethnologists claim this myth helped preserve the vital and often fragile connection between the O'odham and the few perennial water sources by making them aware of the need to be thrifty. In fact, early in the Spanish/Jesuit intrusion, they gave voice to concern over water. When Kino first entered the Pimería Alta in 1687, the natives of Remedios, a village on the upper Río San Miguel, told him that "they did not wish to be Christians or to have a missionary father,"[3] because they pastured so many cattle and horses that their watering places were drying up.

Clearly, this complaint didn't register, because Kino's strategic vision for the Pimería Alta included vast herds of livestock for missionary expansion throughout the region and into Baja California. With little competition from native herbivores like bison, Kino's cattle multiplied like the biblical loaves and fishes on the Pimería Alta's nutritious grasses. Before long, Kino became the first large-scale rancher of the Southwest. By 1701, the industrious Jesuit had established five missions with a collective herd of 4,200 head.[4] To manage an enterprise of such size and scope required molding herdsmen and vaqueros from foot-bound natives who had never before seen horses or cattle. The semi-agricultural tribes like the Ópata and Pima took to the new tasks relatively well, although the missionaries and Spanish settlers recorded many frustrations with their casual work habits. The more nomadic hunter–gatherers of the region adapted to the sedentary life of farmer and stockman with greater difficulty. Some, like the restless Seri and Apache, never did.

Another constant source of friction between Jesuits and natives was the required work on church farms and herds—three days per week was the norm—which did not leave them enough time to tend their own gardens and other business, such as hunting, gathering agave, and visiting relatives and neighbors in outlying settlements. The Jesuits viewed the entire mission complex, including its farms and livestock, as beneficial to the new church community and compelled the natives to see things their way.

Before the Jesuits came and even afterward, O'odham life ways inherently required cooperation, sharing of the scant resources, and the equitable division of labor between men and women. When the priests arrived, the O'odham already had a complex society; a precise, eloquent, and colorful language; and a belief system that embodied the way they lived each day. To be sure, food was at times in short supply, and the O'odham readily accepted most of the Old World crops, livestock, and tools offered by the missionaries. Kino and the others established their missions and chapels along rivers to take advantage of the fertile land, pasture, and water for irrigation. In one sense, the Hia C-ed and Tohono O'odham were fortunate because much of their homeland was deemed undesirable. They were able to take advantage of the benefits brought by the missionaries, while retaining their native culture and avoiding the intense mission environment enforced by the persistent and sometimes pestiferous padres.

A century and a half later, the United States acquired the land south of the Gila River from Mexico via the 1854 Gadsden Purchase. When the border between the two nations was finally surveyed, Quitovac village remained inside Mexico, while Quitobaquito fell inside the United States by about one-quarter mile. Today, Quitovac still belongs to the O'odham, but in 1937, the Department of Interior seized O'odham land for the Organ Pipe Cactus National Monument. There was no request to the tribe, no congressional act, no payment proposed for the taking. The Papago living at Quitobaquito were allowed to continue farming and grazing until 1957, but the park rangers did not appreciate their presence. They posted a sign to warn tourists: "Watch Out for Cattle, Deer, and Indians." Under pressure from Park Service bureaucrats, who wanted to build up ecotourism, one of their last descendants "sold" their improvements and aboriginal rights to use the land. Yet the old people knew the land belonged to all O'odham, rather than to an individual and certainly not to a government they didn't recognize.

The Park Service then gouged out a pond for bird watching tourists and bulldozed the cluster of homes, gardens, and corrals, desecrating a holy place that had nurtured humans from time immemorial. They also took down the warning sign, now that two of the three creatures had been expelled from the diminished habitat. This same exclusionary ideology that warehoused the O'odham (and other tribes) onto reservations conspired to convert Quitobaquito into an exclusive playground, thus exposing the white middle-class elitism and contempt for local culture that has defined the environmental movement until recently. The irony intensified when ethno-biologists Gary Nabhan and Amadeo Rea compared the biodiversity of Quitobaquito with Quitovac thirty years later. The wetland habitat and farms clustered around the spring in Mexico had many more species of birds, plants, insects, and small mammals than the "protected" one in the monument. Because of its larger diversity of habitats, more creatures found Quitovac more to their liking. Forty miles south in that old Papago village, O'odham farmer Delones Lewis remarked, "The birds [here] are still our friends."[5]

TODAY, THE ORGANIZED crime syndicates trafficking illegal drugs and immigrants through the reservation is the greatest threat to O'odham life ways. This menace plays out from two directions: the first is the co-option and corruption of the younger O'odham generations in the smuggling itself; the second comes from the Border Patrol's attempts to block entry into the United States.

Unemployment on the reservation is high (40–50 percent in the last decade), while the average employed O'odham earns less than $10,000 per year. For the old people, this was more choice than hardship, because the O'odham have always been subsistence farmers and herders who also migrated seasonally to gather wild foods. But the younger O'odham, who daily bump into the twenty-first century, want something like the images they see on television, the Internet, and in Tucson and Phoenix: electronic gadgets, pickup trucks and fast cars, and the whole enticing, corrupting consumer culture, including bad food and booze. For merely driving a loaded pickup across the border and dropping it off, they can earn $5,000.

In August 2008, authorities found one such vehicle near the settlement of Gunsite that contained 2,800 pounds of marijuana, worth $1.6 million. In 2009, the Border Patrol seized 750,000 pounds of pot on "the rez," worth about $1 billion on the streets. Even so, the Border Patrol catches only about 20 percent of the total passing through. Ned Norris Jr., tribal chairman, said, "We are in a crisis…we have too many of our people brought into that system."[6] Thirty percent of all drug cases presented to the US Attorney from this region involved tribal members, including some who were relatives of tribal leaders.[7]

The temptations are rife—for the tribe, the Border Patrol, and Mexican law enforcement. To cite only one example of many, Sonoyta's ex-police chief, Ramon Robles-Cota, was sentenced on February 19, 2008, to seven years in prison for attempted bribery on behalf of a Sonoyta-based drug-trafficking ring. He offered a Border Patrol agent $80,000 as down payment and $25,000 for each pickup load of marijuana, if the agent would look the other way when it entered the reservation.

O'odham have helped immigrants for a long time, out of their traditions of sharing and kinship. All of the immigrants were poor, and many came from indigenous cultures in Mexico and Central America. More recently, some O'odham have elbowed their way into the human smuggling rings operated by Mexican cartels.

The motorized army of the Border Patrol, new restrictions on travel, and the proposed border fence collectively represent the second threat to O'odham culture. Today, about eighteen thousand O'odham live in the United States, mostly on the reservation, and two thousand in Mexico in isolated villages like Quitovac or Pozo Verde, on the Mexican side of San Miguel Gate and Menager's Dam or in the barrios of Caborca and Magdalena. The tribe in Sells has extended full membership to the Mexican O'odham (who prefer to be called Papago), including education and health benefits. Instructors from Sells are sent to the school at Quitovac to teach O'odham culture and language.

For a thousand years, the O'odham moved freely over the Pimería Alta—a landscape they considered home—visiting relatives and burial sites and attending religious ceremonies, including the summer Wi'igita dances at Quitovac, held to coax on the monsoon. The boundary established in 1854 by the Gadsden Purchase divided their homeland between the two empires, although the O'odham still thought of themselves as "the People," rather than as Mexican or American. Many still do. One tribal official restated the often-quoted sentiment: "The border crossed us; we didn't cross the border."[8]

Nowadays, an official identification card is required to cross, which is difficult for some because they were born at home and have no birth certificate. Eugenio Velazco, who greeted the cabalgata at Quitovac, said he didn't go to Arizona anymore because of the new restrictions, preferring to live out his life where he was born over seventy-five years ago. The new border fence proposed by the Department of Homeland Security would further suppress exchange between US and Mexican O'odham.

Ofelia Rivas, organizer of O'odham Voice against the Wall, put the issue squarely in terms of family and spirituality, saying:

> For all time, we just went to Mexico and visited families, and people would come here. The authorities don't seem to realize that we have spirits walking before us when we do these things…and we have to explain to them that our history is being eradicated.[9]

Other desert people have been fenced off from their holy places, and the results have been catastrophic. The burden of Jerusalem is division. The Wailing Wall has been fought over by Jew, Muslim, and Christian for centuries. It is, of course, unlikely that the US-Mexico fence will cause a religious war, but it could be the beginning of the end of O'odham culture and spirituality in Mexico. The borderland war against drugs has already been enjoined, and the once bi-national Hia C-ed O'odham may be one of its collateral casualties.

Leaving Quitovac, I looked back at the vacant village and wondered if it would still exist five years from now, given all the converging, corrosive pressures coming to bear on the O'odham life ways and their land. Then I recalled that the Hia C-ed O'odham had thrived for millennia in this bitter land that made even the intrepid Father Kino turn back. They are nothing if not resilient. As the renowned ethnologist Bernard L. Fontana noted, "They are perennial. It is the rest of us who are exotic and ephemeral."[10]

OUTSIDE OF THE border towns, I had pictured Sonora as a quiet land of stunning deserts, rugged mountains, and whitewashed villages, centered on peaceful plazas. I didn't know about Mexico's Highway 2. Leaving Quitovac, we followed it east-south-east toward Caborca, staying as far as possible from the pavement's edge. The highway carried the east-west traffic from Tijuana to Ciudad Juárez, the equivalent of Interstate 10, except that it had only two lanes, only sometimes separated by painted lines. Not long ago, railroads carried most of Mexico's long-distance commerce because paved roads were few and poorly maintained. These days, eighteen-wheelers are common, and the buses range from giant land yachts with sleepers and restrooms to local vans with iron seats. All of them drive fast, and none is shy with its horn. They toot for warnings, to say hello and good-bye, or just for the joy of it.

Scratch any *Sonorense*, and he or she will bleed equine blood. Somewhere not too far back in their family pedigree, horses were present and fondly remembered; their grandfather worked on a ranch, or an uncle was *muy caballero* (skilled horseman).

Many of the pickups zipping down the highway sported mud flaps with chrome horses, and stirrups hung from inside mirrors. The sight of twenty-five riders strung out alongside Highway 2 proved an irresistible temptation for Mexican drivers to express their *compañerismo* (good fellowship). Some of them applied a polite tattoo of toots, while big-rig drivers leaned on their air horns. Children in buses pushed their faces to the window and waved shyly. María José, riding the pretty sorrel mare, drove some truckers into a frenzy with their air brakes and horn blasts. Alejandra was unfazed by it all, including a jet-like swoosh from a mammoth intercontinental bus. Fernando switched his iPod to Los Tigres del Norte, but with the traffic rushing by, we heard only snatches of their falsetto lyrics, crying out the agonies of love and betrayal.

Starting out, Alejandra seemed tired, but as the morning wore on, she again strained for the lead. Alejandra and María José's mare both belonged to Ricardo Ramonet, so I pulled alongside and learned that María José had been training her horse to run barrels, an event in which Jackie, my daughter-in-law, also competes.

Barrel racing is a speed event. Each horse runs around a cloverleaf pattern of three barrels. The one with the fastest time wins. Unlike other rodeo events, it has no counterpart on the working ranch, but the ladies love it nonetheless. The horse has to run all out but under enough control to make tight turns around each barrel. In the same way that people are right- or left-handed, horses have different preferences for which front leg, or "lead," they start on. Daisy, María José's mare, preferred the right lead, taking the right barrel first and then switching to the left lead for the second and third barrels and the final sprint to the finish line.

Horses hate surprises, and their training for any event (including combat) requires patience, concentration, and the trainer's ability to hold on to small details for sustained periods of time. Three years would not be an excessive length of time to produce a finished barrel horse—or cow horse, for that matter. Once the horse consents to having the rider on its back, teaching is a matter of constant repetition until the desired move has been built into its muscle memory—each move becoming a foundation for the next lesson. Gradually, the horse's training becomes cemented in, growing like the slow accrual of a coral reef. The best trainers are quiet people, consistent in what they ask the horse to do and how they ask for it. Competition horses, like human athletes, need a change now and then to free up their minds, and the cabalgata was an excellent opportunity to relax from the rigors of race training. And riding straight ahead for four long days can definitely dumb-down both horse and rider.

For María José and Daniel Sotelo (who also was riding a young horse), the Sonoyta-to-Caborca sojourn was a schooling opportunity. In Daniel, I recognized someone who got along well with horses and probably children, too. He was soft-spoken and even-tempered, and he moved with deliberate speed, but when he corrected his horse, he did it firmly and then immediately released the pressure. Later, I learned that Daniel taught science and math in Hermosillo schools.

Riding the right-of-way on a major Mexican highway confirmed the throwaway cultures of both our countries. Just like on Arizona's I-10, the roadside glittered with broken glass and bottles, pop-top cans, old tires, cardboard cartons, plastic, and more plastic. A couple of hours out of Quitovac, we happily turned toward the mountains again, where we entered Rancho El Cozón. *Cozón* means packrat in Spanish, but the ranch headquarters was the opposite of a packrat's midden. The small adobe house

Retaque Fence

sat in a manicured mesquite grove, with corrals tucked in behind an expansive yard that had been raked clean. Beneath the shade, Oscar and Lea were waiting in their pickup.

Oscar was feeling better, and we walked around the corrals, admiring the workmanship. The whole place spoke of adaptation to local materials and pride of ownership, standing in stark contrast to the trash and buildings tagged with graffiti that we saw along the highway and in both border towns. The corrals were constructed in a style called *retaque*, used since colonial times. Pairs of heavy posts are sunk in the ground, separated by about eighteen inches, and each pair is spaced about four feet apart along the full length of the corral. Mesquite limbs are then stacked horizontally in between the paired posts, up to six feet tall, and the tops of the posts are lashed together with heavy wire. The result is a solid fence where cattle do not feel threatened or think they can escape because they cannot see through or over it. Local materials, free for the taking, are another big advantage. On some older ranches at home, retaque corrals are still in use, but the craftsmanship and work ethic needed to build them is fast disappearing. These days, most corrals are made of welded steel and see-through panels that cost a lot of money, a commodity always in short supply on a ranch.

We entered the corral through a gate where Oscar pointed to the hand-forged hinges and gate latch. A shallow water trough, just wide enough for the muzzle of a thirsty cow, lined one complete side of the corral. At home, water troughs are big, with large surface areas where water evaporates quickly in the dry desert air. In one corner of the corral, a windmill turned in the soft breeze, filling a covered cistern fashioned from rock and mortar. We filled our canteens from the standpipe, grateful that the Corúa of Rancho El Cozón was alive and content. Sitting down on the concrete trough, we ate our burrito lunch, glad to be in a place and time that honored frugality and caretaking, making the most of what the desert offered.

From El Cozón, we would climb the hills westward in the direction of the Sea of Cortés, José Luis said. The roads on the other side were little more than rude dirt tracks, and he advised that Oscar and Lea not to try to make Cantarranas camp tonight but stay in Caborca instead. In fact, this would be the last we would see of them until reaching the end of the ride at the Caborca stockyards.

Sand River at midday. We rode up it toward our next campsite at Cantarranas, following the wide, sandy arroyo carved between two rock-strewn hills. On the hillsides, a forest of saguaro cactus, each one thirty feet tall, grew together as evenly spaced as if they had been planted by the hands of men. Oscar claimed the odds were fifty million to one against a single seed surviving to a cactus of this size. Who could guess what exceptional set of events coincided here a hundred years ago that favored their collective survival and growth—a wet year or decade, some disease that killed off the wood rats that eat most of the seedlings, a particularly fertile soil? Thrusting up from the steep incline like old roots of life, the saguaro must be endowed with an uncanny sense of the vertical; otherwise, they would topple over, given their enormous weight and shallow root system. And why do they grow so tall anyway? One cactus ecologist theorized that height places their flowers where nectar-feeding bats might see them better—the better for pollination.[11] If the flowers were lower down, the bats would have to flit through a thorny gauntlet of cholla and prickly pear to find them.

The O'odham consider it sacrilegious to damage a saguaro, and these Sonoran giants were unmarked by bullet holes or carvings in their flesh like the ones around Tucson and Phoenix. A few years back, one saguaro made news by getting revenge. A "sportsman" tried blasting off a limb with a high-powered rifle, and the severed limb fell on him, killing him instantly, according to the Maricopa County Sheriff's Department.

I grew up in Saguaro County, and saguaros have always been a source of awe and fascination for me, even though where I live now is too high and cold for them to grow. The books I read as a boy called them solemn and stately, but to me, they bestowed a sense of comic relief to the otherwise sober landscape. Most of them raised their arms in greeting, while others dropped an arm as if to shake hands. A scattered few grew top hats, just to show off—an aberration botanists call crestate. Some had smiles chiseled in their flesh by woodpeckers, while others had eye sockets claimed by elf owls. Feisty cactus wrens darted between pleated columns of toothpick-sized thorns, their daring exceeded by other feathered folk nesting in cholla clones. Two woodpeckers inhabited the saguaro-pitaya forest, according to Oscar: the gilded flicker and the gila, which sports a scarlet cap. Their looping flight and chattering *churr-churr-churr* sounded like an appreciative audience's applause for the desert pantomime, and I thought I saw both kinds.

Two hours later, we reached a thin stream of water, with heart-shaped deer and javelina tracks pressed into its sandy margins. Pichi and José Luis unsnapped the lead shanks on the spare horses. Suddenly free, they exploded ahead to a wide spot in the wash and dropped to roll in the sand, wriggling on their backs with obvious pleasure. The hillsides closed in as we climbed into the canyon's interior. Halfway up the left-hand hillside, a motley herd of cows browsed the prickly pear pads, their jaws milling sideways as they read our disinterest in the relaxed attitude of the horses. No threat from these dudes, they knew.

At the crest, we gazed down the long, weathered slope of the bajada toward the

Sea of Cortés, where the lowering sun glared through a reef of clouds. A chill wind blew toward us, signaling a change in weather. I could tell Alejandra was hurting in the knees, but I didn't think she would quit me. Dismounting, I led her through a boulder field, but she got nervous as we fell behind, so I got back on. Finally, we rode into Cantarranas at dusk, a remote camp on the far side of the divide. The good Gaspar was waiting at the corrals, and we were all very glad to see him. I led Alejandra into the corral and let her drink while I unsaddled. Putting on the nosebag of grain, I rubbed her down with an empty sack. On the way out, I mentioned to Pichito that Alejandra seemed sore in the knees.

Gaspar had set up the kitchen under a saguaro-ribbed shelter that covered a wood-burning stove. To guard against ants, a closed shelf for salt and sugar was suspended on greased wires from the roof. Rough-sawn planks beneath the shade completed our banquet table. The camp showed recent use, probably by vaqueros from the El Cozón ranch, José Luis said, as we were still on their land. Daniel Sotelo thought it might have been a Papago camp, because the ramada roof was so low that no one except Pancho Almada and the twelve-year-old Alejandro Robles Jr. could stand up under it. I asked if it could have been immigrants from Mexico's interior.

"Not likely," Enrique replied. "They take the bus up Highway 2."

The others agreed. Highways and border towns contained most of Mexico's present danger, according to the cabalgantes.

We had come fifty-eight kilometers—thirty-five miles—in eleven hours, according to Heriberto's GPS, an accomplishment that José Luis counted as a good day. Tomorrow would be about the same, he announced with a mischievous grin.

Pancho Almada, the quiet man who owned an auto parts store in Hermosillo, sighed: "We have arrived happily without problems, so let's not talk of tomorrow, please."

"I'll drink to that," I said, raising my cup of Agave Azul mescal. We toasted to the excellent day and the best campsite of the trip. After two days, we had started to regain that precious gift of living for the present moment. We had seen beautiful country and arrived safely; our horses were fed and watered; and we shared food and drink. It was enough to be thankful for—but not quite, as Oscar, who was in a motel in Caborca, flashed to mind.

"A toast to Oscar's health" I said.

"Saludos!" thundered back the voice of the cabalgantes.

Pichito and David Ramonet dragged in a gigantic pitaya skeleton for the fire, a fitting finale to a perfect day. Kino and Manje had recorded how the O'odham carried tubes of flaming pitaya when traveling in very cold weather. Pichito pulled the stump over the campfire, and we watched as the fire danced inside the lattice-work tubes until tongues of flame shot out the ends. The night air was cold and damp, and we sat in a circle with feet toward the wind-tattered flames, drowsy and spellbound by nature's gift.

Sand River

THE NEXT MORNING, both veterinarians watched Alejandra hobble as I led her out of the corrals. "She needs an injection of Bute," Pichi said. Pichito drew the medicine into the syringe while I rubbed down Alejandra's neck with alcohol. Pichi pushed his thumb against her vein, the skin bulging up behind it. With his right hand, he slid the needle easy-like into the bulge and then pulled back on the plunger. Blood from the jugular vein swirled darkly into the glass, mixing with the clear fluid. Releasing his thumb, Pichi slowly pushed on the plunger, injecting the horse aspirin where it would immediately go to work on Alejandra's knees. The mare scarcely winced when he pulled the needle out, and he spoke to her softy in praise.

"Acts like she's had this before," I said, rubbing her neck. "She didn't help her knees any last night when she came into heat and teased Alejandro Robles's stallion. I had my bedroll close to the corral, and she like to drove him crazy, pissing down her legs."

"You better saddle the black gelding," Pichi said. "She is too sore to ride."

"How about a shot for me?" I queried.

"Bend over." He grinned, holding up the toothpick-sized needle.

"Years ago, the docs gave me the same medicine for my arthritis. It really worked," I said. "But I only took the pills."

"*Con razón.*" Pichi snorted.

"You take the sorrel," José Luis interrupted. "You will thank me for this later." And thank him I did. The sorrel horse had an easy way of going all day long and into the night.

Our new guide was a vaquero from Domingo Pesqueira's ranch. The original Pesqueira had been a caudillo strongman of Sonora during the 1800s. One of his descendants usually rode with the Cabalgata, but this time he had sent Pastor Palacios instead.

Our overland route zigzagged across the west-facing foothills. On the horizon, a storm was making up in a low, laminar band of dark clouds, and a stiff wind blew at us sideways from the Sea of Cortés. At midday, we rode up on an adobe hut, the walls of which were eroding away like a gigantic termite mound. Just outside the open door, a small, dark-skinned man wearing a palm-leaf hat stood in front of a fire pit, scorching the hair off a chunk of meat that still had its cloven hoof attached.

"Dogs cornered this javelina yesterday," he explained, offering up slices of the meat to Pastor and me.

"Gracias," Pastor said, taking a sliver off the man's knifepoint.

In the doorway, a thin boy pulled the tarp aside and stood looking at us. Then he looked at the meat. A girl half his size peeked out from behind his back.

I started to decline but then realized that would have been taken as an insult.

"Muchas gracias," I said.

The man nodded and asked where we might be going. "Al Rancho Tapeztitos," José Luis replied.

The man gave a low whistle, looking up at the angry sky. "That's a long way to go in the rain," he said.

We rode on, trailing behind Pastor Palacios like Father Kino must have followed his Papago guides. Our guide was a brawny man, crinkled by the sun and wind. He had the weathered hard look of the country and the life that had shaped him—the slender legs of a horseman but with a bullish chest and arms from a youth of flanking calves and building fence. I would have called him middle-aged, but his dark face showed only a few wrinkles tucked into the corners of his eyes, and his drooping mustache was coal black. The oldest-looking part was his leathery hands, gnarled and rope-scarred and folded over the brass horn of his saddle. Had this been 1915 instead of 2008, I would have expected crossed bandoliers over his chest. Only the baseball cap, which he wore at a crooked angle, was out of character. All his other gear had the well-used, well-cared-for look, including the sixty-foot-long braided leather rope (*reata*) tied tightly below the right-side saddle swells. Mexican saddles are shaped to hold the rider on, with front swells extending out over the thighs and a high cantle in back. They are great for staying on green, half-broke horses and for bracing for a quick loop, but they can be a death trap for the rider if the horse falls.

But as handy as Palacios looked, the bald-faced sorrel mare he rode was equally so. She was tall for a Mexican horse and a little high-headed, but her gaits were so smooth that Señor Palacios appeared to be standing on the moving sidewalk at Phoenix Sky Harbor Airport. Her large ears whisked back and forth as they floated over the rocks, forward in the direction of travel and backward to see if Palacios was in agreement. Her mane had been clipped off so as not to interfere with the reata when Palacios had to rope something. *Padre Kino would have blessed this horse and kept her for himself*, I thought. Oscar needed a smoother-gaited horse with his bad hip, so I asked the vaquero if he had another one like her for sale.

Señor Palacios chewed on this possibility for a full minute, and then asked if I would be interested in this one.

"How much?" I asked.

He glanced at me sideways and then quickly looked ahead. "How about I go to work for you?" he asked.

"Do you have a green card?" I asked.

"No, but you tell me where you live, and I'll be there in a week." He proceeded to rattle off the names of Arizona ranches where he had worked, some of them my neighbors.

"With the mare?" I asked.

"With the mare," he said.

"But the mare has to be in quarantine for a month," I replied.

"How much you pay for the horse?"

"How much are you asking?"

He looked at me again and then looked away. "One thousand five hundred," he whispered.

"Expensive," I murmured, thinking she would be worth it in Arizona.

"How much you pay me to work?" he asked, following up the negotiations.

"No can do without a green card, unfortunately," I replied.

"*Pinche* green card!" The vaquero spat out the words. "I cross the border anytime I want. I don't need no fucking green card!"

Señor Pastor Palacios, I mused to myself, *you are right where you should be, doing the work you were born to do, riding that splendid mare over the country of your own choosing. These days, such good fortune is not to be looked down upon.*

Dark clouds began to cover the sun, and a veil of rain drifted toward us up the bajada. José Luis had his GPS out, fiddling with the buttons. Then he called Gaspar on his BlackBerry and found out our cook was lost and had a flat tire. *Thank goodness, Oscar and Lea are in Caborca instead of following the food wagon*, I thought. That the high-tech gadgets worked here was a bit of a shock, but we had seen cell phone towers on Highway 2. And we, too, were lost, heading for the wrong ranch; whether it was due to Pastor Palacios's misunderstanding or José Luis's GPS malfunction was not determined. Mexicans do not dwell on finding fault. To a gringo, their language with the reflexive verb form implied a shared fate, as when they say, "*Se perdió la vereda*" A literal translation might be, "The trail lost itself." We stopped and put on slickers while José Luis and Pastor Palacios conferred on the route.

Palacios started off in a different direction, and we fell in behind. An hour later, we topped out on an ocotillo-covered ridge and gazed down into an immense mesquite-covered flat. The setting sun winked back like a lighthouse from a tall, distant building. José Luis asked him how far. Palacios held up his hand with thumb folded across the palm.

A horse can easily walk four kilometers in an hour but not in heavy brush without a trail. We lined our horses out single file, ducking mesquite limbs and pushing aside ocotillo stalks that scratched our hands and wrists. Finally, at sunset, we broke out into an open field planted with sorghum stubble. The dim outline of Sergio Lizarraga's two-story hunting lodge of Los Tapeztitos came into view, rising above the mesquite forest in the background.

A savage whirlwind swept over the corrals as we unsaddled and hurried to the lodge through the fading light and a vicious, slanting rain. The circular tower and windows afforded a 360-degree view of the ranch—open grain fields in one direction, mesquite forest in the other. Sergio's hunting clients could look over the country with binoculars for trophy mule deer in comfort. Downstairs in the carport, we looked at a huge antlered buck in the back of the manager's pickup that must have weighed three hundred pounds. A client from Mexico City had booked a hunt and then couldn't come, but the "sportsman" called with instructions to kill the animal and send him a picture, a photo for which he had paid $4,000. The big deer would feed the ranch hands, so at least the meat would not go to waste.

In the past, the lodge's clientele included many Americans, but the recent notoriety about drug violence had scared them away. Other hunts included desert bighorn sheep that cost up to $40,000 and which were tightly regulated by Mexican wildlife authorities. Hunters paid only for big rams with big horns, which incentivized good wildlife management—in theory at least.

When local people and landowners shared in the profits, they would take better care of the habitat and animals, according to many wildlife managers in the United States and Africa. But whether or not this was the same in Sonora, I couldn't say. The manager did mention that the older O'odham were the best game scouts for the bighorns.

The youngsters—María José, Alejandro Jr., and David Ramonet—slept in the tower, while the rest of us moved to the bunkhouse, where Gaspar whipped out an impromptu supper of refried beans, spicy meat stew called *birria*, and tortillas. I had reached critical mass for beans and settled for just the tortillas. We spread out the bedrolls on the floor and turned in, oblivious to each other's snores and broken winds.

FEBRUARY 4

AT DAWN, I walked alone at the edge of the mesquite bosque, hoping to glimpse deer, but the disturbance of our arrival last night had frightened them away. The mesquites were huge and heavily infested with mistletoe. Deer had stripped the mistletoe from the lower branches, leaving a browse line six feet above the ground. Heart-shaped tracks were pressed into the damp earth, some prints the size of a large calf.

Crested phainopeplas fluttered in the treetops—the slim-bodied males a glossy black color; the females a dark gray. They were gobbling up the mistletoe berries that were too high for the deer to reach. Seeing the birds now, I recalled a sunny winter morning when Oscar and I were riding past the mesquite thickets in my Red Rock pasture when he called them flycatchers.

"So why flycatchers when they are eating mistletoe?" I asked.

"Nature's example of 'Help thy neighbor; help thy self,'" he said enigmatically.

"So how does that work?"

"The berries have to pass through the bird's digestive tract so the outer covering is removed and the seeds can germinate. When the bird poops, it poops in the mesquite tree near its nest and a new mistletoe plant sprouts on the limb. The chicks can't digest the berries, so the adults catch and feed them flies until they are out of the nest. Having watched their parents eat mistletoe, they do the same thing, and the cycle is repeated, generation after generation—phainopeplas get berries, mistletoe gets mesquite to grow on, and the chicks get bugs."

"But I've heard that too much mistletoe can kill the mesquite, right?"

"Correct, but mesquite is like a weed. It will take over unless there is some sort of biological checkmate. But don't get the idea that all this is part of some grand, altruistic scheme. Evolution operates by chance."

Talking with the analytical Oscar, nature made sense if I kept asking questions. To his finely trained mind, science was the avenue to adventure, figuring out the intricate, innumerable, and often circular connections of life. Seeing the lovely flycatchers again, I wished that I had asked Oscar how he rationalized the fact of evolution with Catholic dogma. I suppose that like the O'odham, he may have integrated the parts that seemed to fit while ignoring the rest. Another scientist I know with Catholic persuasions said for him the matter was uncomplicated: "Everything evolved except the pope and Virgin Mary."

Being more orientated toward the sensory than the scientific, I had always looked at the *National Geographic* magazine's photographs before reading the text. But hanging around with Oscar had taught me to appreciate nature at a different, deeper level, and I was grateful for that gift.

High above the fields of Los Tapeztitos, a pair of red-tailed hawks soared on the morning thermals, swooping and diving in an aerial ballet. One let go a piercing scream that was immediately answered by the other. Back at the corrals, Alejandra, her knees freed from pain by the medicine, was still in heat and again had driven Alejandro Robles's stallion into fits of passion during the night.

From Tapeztitos to the town of Caborca, where the ride would end, was only a half-day ride, but most of it was through thick stands of teddy bear cholla clones, its menacing spines glistening in the morning light. Our savvy Mexican ranch horses gave them a wide berth, and all the cabalgantes wore leather leggings for protection. The early Spanish explorers also wore leather skirts around their horses' chests that wrapped back around to cover the riders' legs. Even the horseback bronzes of Father Kino that adorn the boulevards and churches in Arizona and Sonora have these *armas*, as the Spaniards called them.

Cholla spines have an array of tiny hooks that grab onto anything they touch, and the joints break off so easily that the cholla has rightly earned the name "jumping cactus." The automatic reaction is to brush the joint off, which often makes matters worse. Immigrants from cactus-less country have been found immobilized, with cholla joints in their elbow creases, anchoring bicep to forearm. Even the gentlest horse becomes a savage kicker when stabbed by cholla. Scraping off the joint with a knife blade or a stick sometimes works, but that can also drive the spines deeper. Leather chaps, tweezers, and caution are required when riding in Kino country.

We pushed on. At midmorning, we arrived at sacred ground for the Salgados. The family patriarch, Enrique Salgado Martínez, had a plan to grow crops at the confluence of several large arroyos. Señor Salgado Martínez had constructed a Sagrado Corazon de Jesús statue on the top of a nearby hill, hoping that his show of faith would be blessed with rain. The water didn't come in sufficient quantities to make a crop, but the statue was still standing, and every Salgado clamored up the hill to pay homage. The O'odham used ceremonies of dance and cactus wine to bring rains, which didn't always work either.

Their poet laureate, Ofelia Zepeda, wrote, "You need a new kind of prayer to negotiate with this land."[12]

We plodded along in the midday sun through a bitter land, made more desolate by abandoned farms. An exception was a huge vineyard of white grapes, processed for raisins, making Caborca the raisin capital of Mexico. A nearby *ejido* village—a pleasant, prosperous-looking place, judging by rural Mexican standards—provided farm labor.

Francisco replayed the Pavarotti operas as we rode along the highway for another hour before reaching the outskirts of Caborca and the corrals of the Asociación de Ganaderos de Sonora. Families of the riders rushed out to greet each rider with a jigger of celebratory tequila. I rode beside Pichi and was pleased to meet his veterinarian wife, Susy. Oscar and Lea were standing by the corrals, smiling as we rode through the gate. Lea clapped her hands and cried, "Hooray! You guys made it!"

But before tucking into the good-bye dinner, more ceremonies were in order. José Luis presented engraved Caminos de Kino breast collars to María José, Pichito, Pancho Almada, and Daniel Sotelo for their past participation, which they promptly strapped to their saddles. Then, in a more formal proceeding, Ricardo Ramonet presented the mare Daisy as a gift to María José, thus cementing the close relationship of the two families. To Mexicans, family is everything. And to these folks, horses ran a close second.

We lined up on horseback for photographs, with Oscar and Lea standing front and center. Oscar looked tired but very happy. As we walked to the banquet table, he said, "Well, we finally made this happen."

"Thanks to you and Lea," I said, putting my arm around his thin shoulders.

As we left Caborca, I offered to drive but Lea again said no. After four days on horseback and sleeping on the ground, I was too tired anyway. The intimate views of the lower Sonoran Desert had been stunning, and I loved the tangible connection with borderland history—our shared past with Sonora. I had been made to feel welcome. The cabalgantes were a happy-go-lucky, unpretentious, and well-organized troupe. My only complaint was that we hurried past some places I would have liked to have seen and known more about, like Quitovac and the hunting ranch.

At home, most trail rides catered to high-octane, turbo-charged businessmen, who blew off steam by riding an hour or two and then retired to an open bar, sumptuous meals, all-night poker games, and feather beds. An ambulance was kept on standby for broken limbs, heart attacks, and a ready supply of Alka-Seltzer and Bloody Marys. In contrast, our ride had been a family affair with purpose and direction.

Lea wanted to show me the route taken by the Kino mission tours, up the Altar River valley, through the towns of Altar, Oquitoa, Pitiquito, and Tubutama. At Oquitoa, we stopped at the church, which stood on a barren hilltop surrounded by the village cemetery. We entered the grounds through a handsome gate made of hand-hewn *sahuaso* logs, for which Lea had helped raise money. The church front had an arched, two-story façade, rising up in support of two open towers, each one containing a bell. Its smooth plaster walls were unadorned and painted white. I suppose by European standards it would be considered small and plain, but to the O'odham of the seventeenth century, living in brush huts, it must have seemed colossal and imposing. To me, the uncomplicated rectangular architecture was appealing, although the tombs surrounding the building reflected the Catholic Church's preoccupation with death and afterlife, rather than the here and now.

Walking back to the pickup, we noticed the ruins of a flour mill across the road near the river. Its water wheel protruded out of the crumbling adobe like the skeleton of some ancient reptile. Lea had hoped to raise funds to restore the mill, but the prospects were bleak, given that the Kino tours had been canceled this year.

"So much to be done," she sighed as we climbed in the truck and continued up the Altar River. We drove past Pitiquito, Father Murrieta's church, and went on to Tubutama. I wanted to stop at both, but Lea turned around. The sun was almost to the western horizon, and we needed to be on the main highway toward Nogales before dark. Father Murrieta had cautioned that the farms and haciendas along the river had been taken over by the cartels that used them as staging sites for loads of immigrants and drugs being moved to Sasabe on the border, forty miles north of Tubutama. The Altar River Road continued northeast over the mountains to Nogales, but we took the toll road back to Magdalena instead. Kino's mission highway was no longer safe after dark, and even the lionhearted Lea hesitated to take the risk.

JUNE 15: C6 RANCH

FOUR MONTHS HAD passed since the Cabalgata had ended, and hot, dry June was dragging on, as usual. By eleven in the morning, the thermometer in the barn reached ninety-five degrees, and the haze from grass fires lay like a quilt over the Canelo Hills. I rode out at daylight to check water lines, a daily chore until the monsoon started. At Cheese Tanks, I adjusted the float valve to fill a five-hundred gallon water trough. Wizened bees and yellow wasps sucked at the precious liquid, soon to be followed by cattle, thirsty immigrants, drug mules, and sundry wildlife.

The Border Patrol claimed that fewer immigrants were crossing the border these days, but I hadn't noticed the traffic slacking off. As temperatures rose, so did the vandalism. We had troughs about a mile apart on the pipelines, where they could get water, but from the number of holes we had to patch, every walker must have had a Swiss army knife. Under one big mesquite, the burreros tied the pipeline up and punched holes for a shower—a bar of soap was stuck conveniently in the crouch of the tree. Such vandalism struck me as a prime example of the general selfishness of the human race. If one group drains the line, the next one coming along could be in dire straits. I could perhaps see them not worrying about my cows or the wildlife, but these were blood brothers, in a manner of speaking. Like many borderland ranchers, our waters encouraged illegal foot traffic over the land.

Our solar-powered well pumped water into two ten-thousand-gallon tanks that we kept in reserve for emergencies. The tanks had become landmarks for immigrants and burreros who trudged up from the border; they called the tanks *tanques de queso*, because they looked like two giant rounds of yellow cheese. Once, a man came to the ranch, asking about his son who had disappeared months earlier on his way back to Phoenix for a construction job. The group he was traveling with said they left him at Cheese Tanks. We didn't have any information to help, and the man had already been up to the area and contacted the Mexican consulate. Even so, I rode all that country over the next few days, looking for a sign. All I found were fresh tracks that showed the route was still in use.

I rode toward home in the full heat of the midday sun, over the hot, rocky ground that followed the rim of Oak Grove Canyon, a deep arroyo floored with stands of ash and walnut. Halfway along, a new backpack lay open beside the trail, with bottles of orange Gatorade, tin cans, and some clothing scattered around. Such trash was not uncommon; these bottles, however, were all unopened—except for one.

Nobody, not even a first-time walker, leaves that much liquid behind unless...unless. I dismounted and walked a circle, finding another pack, several tins of tuna fish (all unopened except for one), more clothing, and an unopened bottle of Coca-Cola. I collected all the discarded objects (they had now acquired more status than just trash), stuffed them in the packs, and hung them from the saddle horn. The ground was rocky, but here and there, I could make out fresh footprints—a day or two old, judging from the still-sharp outlines.

The track was the herringbone pattern of canvas gym shoes, such as those sold in Walmart—cheap and the worst kind for navigating this country. A few weeks before, I'd found a man from San Luis Potosi, immobilized, with toenails filled with blood, and raw, weeping sores on the soles of his feet. Unable to walk, his group had ditched him. He begged me to call the Border Patrol, which I did.

Mounting up, I rode in widening circles, paying attention to my dogs. The low humidity would have made the scent difficult to pick up, even for cow dogs. Still, if we had gotten within a hundred feet of a person, they would have let me know. The afternoon sun was on the way down when I gave up. Tracks, fizzy soda, and grease in the bottom of the one open can said they had been here less than a couple of days ago.

At home, Diane and I took the packs out to the barn and spread the contents out over the floor of the breezeway, looking for identification. If we had names, maybe the Border Patrol knew something.

"Look here," Diane said, pulling out a plastic bag of tortillas. "These are store-bought, not the kind Mama made." The food included powdered Tang, Rockstar energy drink, and a can of hominy. Tucked away in a side pocket, we found a statue of the Virgin of Guadalupe, hands pressed together in her saintly pose. In the same pocket, we found a crumpled boarding pass for Joel Palma on Interjet, dated January 18, from Mexico City to Hermosillo, Sonora—a name, a date, a destination, and a saint for protection.

The next day, I called the Border Patrol. They looked over the items and said that burreros carried top packs like these on their marijuana bundles. When surprised, they'd drop the top packs and run for cover with the loot. Another possibility was that local gangs had robbed and kidnapped them. Every immigrant has a phone number of relatives back home or in the states that they can call for help. The kidnappers hold the immigrants for ransom in "safe houses" in Tucson or Phoenix, according to local law enforcement and the FBI. I showed the boarding pass to the patrol and said I had looked for Joel and the other one for the rest of the afternoon. That could have been risky, they said, and they asked what I'd planned on doing if I'd found them.

So I told them about the man who'd lost his son at Cheese Tanks and that if I'd lost my son like that, I would be grateful for any help. I told them also about another lost immigrant who had found me at a dry water tank on another sunny summer afternoon a few years prior. He jumped from behind a juniper and grabbed at my horse's bridle, but the horse reared up and bolted. When I stopped and turned around, the man was still coming at me, holding out an empty jug, crying "*Agua, agua*" through his swollen lips. I tossed him my canteen and rode to the top of the ridge, where I could call the Border Patrol.

The officers agreed that those were good reasons to keep searching and added that rescuing immigrants was half their job. They kept the boarding pass and left, saying that the intelligence unit would be interested that burreros were being recruited all the way from Mexico City. I kept the Virgin of Guadalupe and mounted her on a special shelf in the horse barn breezeway, where we saddled in the mornings before riding out. Perhaps she would bring me better luck than she had for Joel Palma.

Cheese Tanks

SEPTEMBER 13: A CELEBRATION FOR OSCAR

ST. MARK'S PRESBYTERIAN Church on East Third Street in Tucson had the feel of a Spanish mission, with its whitewashed adobe walls, red brick parapets, and solid wooden doors recessed into an arched entryway. The tall, white columns of the bell tower rose from a lovely patio on the east side of the sanctuary, shaded by big mesquite trees. Inside, the wooden altar held a gilt-edged Bible and two big candles, one on each side. Two wooden pulpits rose up from either corner of the altar floor, lending a towering presence to those who spoke there. Upon entering, my eyes were immediately drawn to the heavy wooden beams supporting the high ceiling. The beams were trimmed in pale blue, with a single ivy vine running the full length. The whole interior spoke of strength and a reverence for simplicity.

Diane and I took our seats next to the center aisle. The wooden pews forced one to sit up straight, making it impossible to slouch down and hide from the preacher as I had done as a child when I alternated between boredom and fear of damnation. The large church filled rapidly, all except one front pew, where Lea sat looking down at her hands. Oscar had passed away during surgery a few weeks after the ride. Lea had waited until today, September 13, to organize this gathering with daughter, Annie, and son, Oscar Jr., as a celebration of their lives together.

The audience segregated itself according to the many facets of Oscar and Lea's fifty-three years of marriage—colleagues from the University of Arizona, in casual professorial dress; organizers from the Kino mission tours and the Southwestern Mission Research Center; ranchers and neighbors from Sonoita and Patagonia, wearing jeans with their bare foreheads white as porcelain; the cabalgates from Hermosillo, Sonora, clustered alongside one wall; the League of Mexican American Women and fellow Presbyterians who had supported the sanctuary movement and the "Humane Borders" campaigns for immigrants; and a Marine Corps honor guard, standing at attention for one of their comrades in arms who served during the Korean War.

I don't remember the minister's speaking, though he may have. Oscar was a good man (as Lea said, reminiscing on a later trip with the Kino riders), and I, for one, did not think he needed an intermediary. Annie and Oscar Jr. went to the pulpit separately, each telling stories of favorite memories of their father—traveling in a VW camper van on vacations to national parks, where Oscar instilled in them a love of nature and the outdoors; his keen scientific mind and attention to detail; his affection for a gray gelding called Weston.

The honor guard escorted Lea down the aisle, and the rest of us filed out behind them. In the entryway, I noticed a poster commemorating the anniversary of the assassination of Archbishop Oscar Romero in El Salvador, an event leading to the church's sanctuary movement for Central Americans fleeing political persecution in the 1970s and '80s.

The poster stunned me for a moment. I had been in San Salvador on the day Romero was assassinated after he delivered a fiery sermon chastising the Salvadoran military for the persecution and murder of peasant farmers. The next week, our Public Health Service laboratory was ordered out of El Salvador when the American embassy eliminated all "nonessential" personnel and strengthened its support of the military regime. Next to the poster was the mission statement of St. Mark's Church, ending with "Strive for justice for the poor and marginalized." Some of the Salvadorans who had worked for me eventually fled to the United States. Ronald Reagan had called them Communists, but they were refugees, fleeing the death squads of the Salvadoran oligarchy backed up by American military might. Thus began the Central American exodus to the United States that today amounts to 40 percent of the illegal immigrants crossing the borderlands.

THE RECEPTION TOOK place in the patio beneath the thin shade of mesquites. Diane and I were visiting with José Luis, Enrique, and Ricardo, chatting about the San Pedro River for a future cabalgata, when Lea came up. Her wan smile and hugs eased the sense of awkwardness that we all felt.

"I would like to go with you, but I need to be with Oscar and Annie," she said.

"Of course," Enrique said. "We were thinking of getting a motel in Sierra Vista tonight and going to the river tomorrow."

"Why don't you stay in Sonoita? Cheryl and Tom Rogos have a very nice bed-and-breakfast. They are around here somewhere," Lea said.

The next morning, Diane and I joined the Sonoran contingent for breakfast at Cheryl and Tom's hacienda-style inn. As we started to leave for the river, José Luis asked for the bill.

"Lea already paid for everything yesterday," Tom replied. I was not surprised by Lea's generosity, nor by the fact that the cabalgantes drove all the way from Hermosillo to celebrate one of their fraternity.

We climbed in the cars and headed for Fairbank on the San Pedro River. The heat of the late summer day had emptied the picnic grounds, but the restored one-room schoolhouse was still open. We walked in and met Nancy Doolittle, from the Friends of the San Pedro River, who luckily was the one person who had been doing horseback rides along the river. We explained what we had in mind, along with the history of the cabalgatas.

"I don't know about overnight with a large group," she cautioned. "The Bureau of Land Management doesn't allow camping outside of the established areas."

"How about horses overnight?" I asked.

"The Boquillas Camp has some old corrals, if they'd let you use them. You better check with the director in the Sierra Vista office."

We walked down to the river's edge and stood under the cooling shade of an enormous cottonwood tree. The water, the color of weak tea from the monsoon rains, swirled against the tree's gnarly roots. Upstream, the river meandered beneath an archway of green foliage that shimmered in the afternoon light. Above, a red-tailed hawk floated on the rising thermals. Downstream, the west bank rose up in a sheer bluff, the river undercutting its gravelly base. Diane picked up a yellowed leaf and set it adrift. We watched it disappear around the bend, riding high on the mellow current. Beyond the east bank, clumps of seep willow and walnut made a vivid green foreground to the gray mesquite thickets, where yellow warblers sang. The San Pedro River was a narrow ribbon of concentrated life in the midst of the transition zones between the Sonoran and Chihuahuan deserts. Riding horseback down its full length would be an amazing adventure, even without the historical considerations, yet the fact that we would be doing it without Oscar hung over this moment like a dark cloud.

At the Fairbank parking lot, signs on the trailhead pointed north, saying "Cemetery, Contention City, and Presidio Santa Cruz de Terranate, horses allowed." To the south, "Boquillas Ranch Headquarters, two miles."

"Kino was the first to explore the Sobaipuris Pima along the San Pedro," Enrique said. "He and Manje went all the way to the confluence with the Gila River. It would be an important ride for the cabalgata. I will send you a translation of their journals."

Part 2

The Sierra Madre Occidental: 2009

The Spanish sought to civilize the Indians by bringing them
into compact communities centered about churches.

–Edward H. Spicer, Cycles of Conquest

PLANS TO RIDE the Río San Pedro in southern Arizona had been in the making since September 2008. That fall, Diane and I made a short exploratory ride with Nancy Doolittle, riding from Fairbank, north to the ruins of Presidio Santa Cruz de Terrenate. The next step would be to get permission to camp out on the BLM Reserve with a string of horses. But the financial meltdown that began the year before worsened. With the peso and the dollar both losing value and amid all the economic uncertainty, the cabalgata decided to ride in Mexico instead.

Father Kino arrived in what would become the state of Sonora in 1687, by way of Moctezuma, the provincial capital located in the heart of the Sierra Madre Occidental. From there, he sallied forth with Father Rector Manuel Gonzales on a wide circle that encompassed the upper reaches of the both the Sonora and San Miguel Rivers. Most of the native people they encountered were part-time farmers, growing crops of corn, beans, and squash irrigated by water diverted from the rivers. On top of a hill overlooking the Upper Pima settlement of Cosari, Kino selected the site for his home church. Along the way, Kino had passed through the established mission towns of Huepac and Rayón, founded by Jesuits a half century earlier.

The cabalgata had completed most of this long loop in 1996 and 1998. That left only his trail between Huepac on the Río Sonora over the Sierra Aconchi, an immense cordillera of the Sierra Madres, to the ancient town of Rayón located on the Río San Miguel. From Rayón, we would ride downstream to where the two rivers joined at a place called Pitic, a lowland village that much later became Hermosillo, Sonora's capital.

Lea was delighted with the new route. Her Kino mission tours had not visited this area, but she and Oscar had often enjoyed the peaceful villages along the river, with their neat, irrigated farms and friendly people. In the town of Aconchi, they had commissioned several pieces of furniture for their Sonoita home. Now, Lea wanted to order a communion bench for her church. Privately, I thought that revisiting the places she and Oscar had shared together would help with the healing. Lea would stay nights in the cabalgata camps and go ahead with the supply truck. Even better, to reach the trailhead at Huepac, we would have to pass through her hometown of Magdalena de Kino. Her enthusiasm made up for my disappointment in not fulfilling Oscar's wish of showing his Sonoran friends the San Pedro River, but perhaps next year.

"So we will ride the Sonoran Sierra Madres," I murmured when I got the e-mail. I had grown up with a family legend about these dark and mysterious mountains. My father was an older man, born at the turn of the twentieth century. As a youngster, he fled his stern Pennsylvania Dutch family and went west, working on ranches and mines until he enlisted in General John "Black Jack" Pershing's army after lying about his age. When the revolutionary bandit Francisco "Pancho" Villa attacked Columbus, New Mexico, in March 1916, Pershing led the American Punitive Expedition into Chihuahua but got lost in the labyrinth of the Sierra Madres instead.

Every Friday night throughout my childhood, Dad and his cronies gathered in our living room around a poker table. My favorite of his pals, a man I called Uncle Walter (even though we were not related), had two endearing qualities to a boy of five: he smoked a pipe, and he had a wooden leg. Uncle Walter would sit down, light his curved pipe, making great billows of fragrant smoke, and then remove the peg leg. Looking at the leather-covered stump of his thigh, I wondered how he had lost the rest of it but was too timid to ask.

"Took a bullet in the knee down in the Sierra Madre chasing that damned Mexican," he growled, when my curiosity got the best of me. "I nearly died of gangrene, so they cut it off."

"Did it hurt?" I blurted out.

"'Course it hurt, son. Bit through my pipe stem. Want to touch it?"

I went to bed, rubbing my knee, and rode through the Sierra Madre with Pershing's cavalry in my dreams. The horse was white and so fast we outran the bullets.

The massive Sierra Madre cordillera was formed when the central plateau of Mexico uplifted along with the Rocky Mountains, some sixty-five million years ago. Trade winds sweeping off the Sea of Cortés collided with the mountain ramparts, creating monsoon storms that nourished a rich, subtropical landscape hundreds of miles long, extending from the state of Sinaloa northward to the sky island peaks of southern Arizona. Rivers running off the plateau dissected its western margins into a gouged, angular landscape, exposing unbelievable fortunes of silver and copper, just a few days' ride south of my ranch.

When I learned of our new route, my only request was a smooth-gaited Mexican ranch horse. I could not have guessed that on the last day, I would be riding him down Hermosillo's busy freeway, dodging bumper-to-bumper traffic and the Monster of Hermosillo.

JANUARY 28

MAGDALENA DE KINO was a pleasant town of about twenty-five thousand people, situated on the east bank of the Río Magdalena, sixty miles south of Nogales, Arizona. The town was just plain "Magdalena" until the discovery of Father Kino's tomb in 1966 beneath the old chapel of San Francisco Xavier near the central plaza. With great enthusiasm, the Sonoran authorities immediately renamed the town to commemorate their hero.

On a splendid late-January morning, wood smoke shrouded the river valley as we approached the town. Lea and I took Avenida 5 de Mayo toward Plaza Central, first passing by the larger-than-life bronze of the steely-eyed Kino, peering up the freeway exit astride a handsome horse. The priest's right hand clasped an abalone shell at his chest, while his left hand held the reins just above the saddle horn, the horse's head bowed low as if in prayer.[1]

We had two reasons for stopping in Lea's hometown. She wanted to show me the bones (*huesos*) of this man whose pathways we would follow during the next four days. But first, we attended to our second purpose in Magdalena de Kino, stopping at David Molina's internationally known saddle shop on the corner of Avenidas Juarez y Allende to order a new pair of chaps to replace my old ones, which had been shredded by the chaparral of the Canelo Hills. Molina's shop occupied a street corner with a narrow building a block long. Entering the showroom, the aroma of saddle soap and tannin perfumed the air, while the *tap-tap-tap* of craftsmen tooling leather echoed from the rear workshop. One long wall held custom saddles on racks stacked half-way to the ceiling. On the opposite side of the room, a glass case displayed spade bits with rollers and silver-inlayed shanks, replicas from the time of Spanish rule. Today, these *frenos de cuchara* bits and bridles are still used by horsemen in Mexico and California, where working cattle with a bridle horse is an art form, with its swan neck, lightning quickness, and the constant whir of the copper cricket under its tongue.

David learned his craft at an early age while working at his father's bench. The Molina family had raised saddle making to an art, saying that if you are a good craftsman, you want to make the best saddle possible. Over the decades, they had developed all the patterns for saddles and sundry items turned out in the shop. Hanging on the wall were pictures of saddles made for Mexico's former president Vicente Fox and, ironically, for Janet Napolitano, former governor of Arizona, now secretary of Homeland Security.

David made everything to custom fit. His daughter scrolled through the photos of chaps on her Apple computer until I found what I wanted: dark-brown leather, rough side out, with heavy brass zippers running down the outside seams, covered by short, leather fringes. A pocket on the outside left thigh would hold a tally book and cell phone, while the one on the inside of the right thigh would conceal a bag of jerky or a pistol.

"Perfect!" I said. "Measure me up, and we'll pick them up on our way home from Huepac next week." But David had a backlog of orders and said the job would take a month. I paid the deposit, gladly waiting for the durable piece of handcrafted leather.

Lea had been to the town plaza many times with her Padre Kino tours. We parked across from the domed crypt, next to a long sidewalk of arched entryways, or *portales*, which held her favorite ice cream shop and artisan market. Magdalena's main plaza was laid out in a large, park-like hexagon that covered fifteen acres, with a recessed fountain gurgling in the center. The massive Santa María Magdalena church anchored one corner. Inside was a life-sized image of Saint Francis Xavier, a Jesuit saint revered by Mexican and native Catholics from all over the borderlands. Kino's crypt occupied the opposite corner, covered by an arched concrete dome that looked like a Moorish tent.

Stepping through a concrete archway, I peered down through a smaller see-through plastic dome, and there lay Kino's skeleton, exactly where it had been discovered, with all the *huesos* intact, down to the final phalanx of each toe. Catholics pay homage to a multitude of icons, and here lay their Sonoran hero, reduced to his final physical essence. The murals inside the cupola, by Caborca artist Nereo Galileo de la Pena García, illustrated a pastoral diorama, with the long-haired, black-robed Jesuit in the company of naked Indian farmers with their livestock and crops. In a story of magical realism worthy of Gabriel García Márquez, Father Kino lived on here in perpetuity to inspire the faithful and astonish all the rest of us.

The contrast with the dark, reclining, robed figure of Saint Francis in the main church could not have been more striking. Father Kino's bones were, to me, more powerful, real, and immediately accessible than the Saint Francis icon modeled from wood and mortar. Perhaps that was because I was following Kino's trails over the Sonoran Desert, a landscape I considered my own, while Saint Francis Xavier came out of a time, place, and tradition I had never experienced.

Magdalena was also regionally famous for its October festival, a sacred and profane celebration that is part religious, part trade fair, and all carnival, according to the late ethno historian Henry Dobyns, the foremost authority on the event. The week-long celebration is a pilgrimage that combines piety, adoration, and party. The faithful come to the plaza to ask for divine intervention, to give thanks, to do penitence for sins, and to have household religious objects recharged for the coming year. Saint Francis is considered a very miraculous saint, one who expects to be paid for services rendered, according to folklorist Big Jim Griffith. When a worshiper asks for and receives help—for example, to cure an illness—the usual price is to walk to Magdalena from the worshiper's home village.

After the religious duties are performed, a carnival atmosphere takes over in a pandemonium trade fair that predates Christianity. The Imuris Pima once farmed the adjacent river valley and celebrated the fall harvest, trading with the O'odham, Ópata, Yoeme (Yaqui), Mayo, and other tribes. Ancient trade routes crossed Sonora's river valleys, connecting its native people with great civilizations as far south as the Aztec and Maya in Mesoamerica and exchanging goods ranging from basketry to seashells.

With the coming of the Spanish these networks began distributing more deadly exchanges. In addition to Christianity, servitude, and slavery, Hernán Cortés also served up smallpox, chicken pox, plague, whooping cough, measles, syphilis, and other diseases to which the natives had no previous exposure and therefore no immunity. Within the first decade of the Spanish arrival, "virgin-soil" epidemics raced over the native peoples of Central Mexico, severely weakening tribal structure, as mortality rates often reached 50 to 85 percent. The germs spread northward along the trade routes and preceded the arrival of the conquistadors and Jesuits into northern New Spain, inflicting havoc and misery among the people of the Pimería Alta and the Southwest. While not done intentionally, the epidemics diminished their ability to resist foreign incursions.

Nowadays, a new disease called illegal narcotics has spread from the south through Magdalena, infecting the mountain and mission towns to the north and northwest along the border. In 2009, two drug cartels, Beltrán-Leyva and Sinaloa, were battling for control of scores of immigrant and drug-smuggling routes into Arizona.

According to newspaper reports and the Drug Enforcement Agency, the Sinaloa cartel controlled the border towns, patrolling the main roads and setting up road-blocks, patiently starving out its rival, while Beltrán-Leyva gangsters stayed concealed in the mountains, striking out opportunistically. Curiously, most of the narcos (drug smugglers, also called *narcotraficantes*) arrested in the Mexican borderlands belong to

Beltrán-Leyva, suggesting to some observers that the Sinaloa cartel has ties to Mexican law enforcement.

Last year, when returning from Caborca, Lea, Oscar, and I had detoured around the conflicted areas by taking the toll road from Altar to Santa Ana and Magdalena. I asked her if she would go the October festival this year, in view of the new dangers.

"*Como no!*" she replied affirmatively without hesitation. "Magdalena is my hometown. I have always gone."

Leaving Magdalena, Lea knew of a shortcut on a paved road going east over the Sierra Torreón and joining with the Río Sonora less than fifty miles north of Huepac, where the ride would begin the following morning. Besides saving time, we stopped at the ruins of Los Santos Reyes de Cucurpe mission, founded in 1647 by the Jesuit Marcos del Rio to admire the hand-cut stone arches and the circular stone stairwells. Forty years later, when Padre Kino arrived, the Cucurpe mission was the northernmost penetration by the Jesuits into what Kino's biographer Herbert Eugene Bolton cleverly labeled the "Rim of Christendom."

The Cosari settlement and Río San Miguel were Kino's points of entry into the Pimería Alta, the land and people that would occupy his body, mind, and spirit for the next twenty-four years. He called his home mission *Nuestra Senora de los Delores*, Our Lady of Sorrows, after a painting by the Spanish artist Juan Correa de Vivar. Soon, the charismatic Kino had established smaller chapels (*visitas*) at the other rancherias surrounding Cosari, where he would occasionally preach and offer the sacraments.

Kino brought something far more important than the Raphaelite painting of our Lady of Sorrows: a royal decree from King Carlos II that exempted the Pimería Alta natives from forced labor in the Spanish-owned mines and haciendas for the next twenty years. That special dispensation placed Kino squarely on the natives' side and against the legacy of the conquistadors and Spanish settlers who were striving to profit from Indian land and forced labor.

Before the Jesuits came, tribes of the Sonoran sierras lived in *rancherías*, or clusters of brush huts, scattered alongside the rivers. Farming and gathering wild foods from the surrounding mountains formed the basis of their economies. Although they were a more settled people in comparison to the nomadic western O'odham, they did not live in compact towns in the European sense or in the multistoried Indian pueblos of the Rio Grande. Even so, this loose community structure made the Spanish policy of acculturation more acceptable.

The Spanish brought with them fixed notions of how to bring civilization to the local heathen (a process called *reducción*). Conversion to Christianity and obedience to the Catholic Church would be accomplished by bringing their far-flung rancherías into compact communities within earshot of church bells. Each community would have central plaza dominated by its church, with government buildings on the opposite side. From the plaza, a grid pattern accommodated individual houses, each one fronting the street, with a rear courtyard.

The Jesuits heartily concurred and pursued this community organization with great vigor. The missionaries could keep close watch on their proselytes, guarding against relapses to their traditional ways that were considered particularly loathsome, such as dancing naked during the summer rains. Also, the natives had a harder time escaping the constant Catholic rituals of Mass, prayers, and catechism, as well as the mandatory labor on the mission-owned farms and herds. In fairness, the paternalistic Jesuits also wanted to protect their Indians against the corrupting influences and slave-labor tactics of Spanish settlers and miners. The tradeoff for the natives included new crops, orchards, livestock, iron tools, and weapons, along with the knowledge of how to use them. Father Kino also introduced horses, mules, burros, and oxen for draft power and transport, as well as goats and sheep. The merits of the Colombian Exchange, as this swap has been called, are still debated today, but at the time, mission life must have seemed better than toiling at the bottom of a mine shaft.

Huepac (from the Ópata Indian word meaning "river grows wider") came under Jesuit influence in the mid-1600s but not without serious discussions. As elsewhere in New Spain, the arrogance and brutality of the first conquistadors left behind an atmosphere of mistrust and resentment. Francisco Vázquez de Coronado and his horde had traveled up the Río Sonora on his way to the Four Corners region, leaving a Lieutenant Alcaraz to found a Christian town along the river. After the Spanish exhibited their true colors by imposing forced labor and stealing Indian women for their pleasure, the natives attacked and killed everyone except for two they set free to put the invaders on notice.

One hundred years later, this predatory behavior was not forgotten at Huepac when the locals at first rejected Jesuit prayers and threats. Jeronimo del al Canal, with persistence typical of the Jesuit order, continued to preach, even after the headmen made it clear they wanted nothing to do with Christianity. After listening, the native leaders sat the priest down and explained that their land was created by other gods and not his Christian God. They also showed, by giving examples, that baptism cured no one and that Christian ritual did not apply to them. So telling and persistent were their arguments that de la Canal became convinced that he was conversing with the Devil Incarnate and fled. This exchange was another of the few recordings of how the indigenous people viewed Jesuit demands when their cultures first collided.

But the Jesuit handbook had no chapter on reassessing the wisdom of Catholic dogma, and de la Canal continued proselytizing in other communities. With the inducements of the Colombian Exchange and fear of hellfire, local resistance gradually declined. By 1648, several churches had been built, including San Lorenzo in Huepac, and the long acculturation process of the indigenous Americans began.

Today, the August fiesta of Moros y Cristianos de San Lorenzo, instead of commemorating Huepac's local heritage, celebrates the dim triumph of Spanish Christians over the Moors of North Africa, an event that took place six thousand miles away and six hundred years earlier. Yet Mexico was eventually to be for Mexicans. In the town hall opposite the church, we saw an original copy of the 1810 Mexican Act of Independence on display.

The sun had dropped behind the Sierra Aconchi by the time we found Arturo López's house on a well-kept street a few blocks from Huepac's plaza. Most of the cabalgantes had arrived that afternoon, and Enrique and the others were sitting around the yard. The López family had three houses, all in a row. One was rented to a retiree from Colorado who spent the winter in Huepac where, he claimed, the people were friendlier and the cost of living considerably less.

Enrique startled us with the news that he would no longer ride.

"I have a detached retina," he explained in a matter-of-fact voice. "The ophthalmologist said the jarring or a fall could cause another tear. It is not worth the risk."

Recovering from the awkward moment, I asked Enrique what he had done with his sturdy buckskin horse that I had admired last year.

"Mauro is riding him," he said, introducing us to a tall young man standing beside us.

"Your uncle's bad luck is your good fortune," I said.

"Yes, I know," Mauro replied in perfect English. "I've already taken a test ride."

José Luis asked if we'd like something to drink, and while the others turned toward the improvised cantina set up in Arturo's backyard, I headed for the pickup to unload the extra saddles and cool boxes. When I got to the gate, Arturo stopped me, saying everything would be safe on the streets of Huepac.

January 29

In the faint light of dawn, the cabalgantes began sorting out the horses at the Huepac corrals. Last year, I had mentioned my admiration for the smaller, tough-as-nails Mexican ranch horses. Now, Arturo López backed up to the loading dock in a bob-tailed truck with the last two, including mine, a shaggy, dun-colored horse that came tiptoeing down the ramp. His long, tangled tail and unruly forelock covering his eyes gave him a look of resignation. Arturo called him the Ant (*El Hormigo*) and handed me the lead rope while he proceeded to shoe him. Hormigo looked as if he'd been barefoot for quite a while as Arturo grunted, trying to force the nippers through the hoof wall.

"We usually let them go barefoot on the farm," he explained. The shoes were homemade, hammered out of rebar and shaped on a piece of railroad track.

Shoeing finished, I saddled him and stepped up. It was a short step. The Ant measured fourteen hands high (fifty-six inches) at the withers and weighed maybe nine hundred pounds soaking wet. My stirrups hung down to just a foot above the ground. Susy Salgado stood back for a better look and then laughed out loud, "Ricardo, you are riding a six-legged horse."

I countered by giving the Ant a pat on his shoulder and reminded her that ants are a hundred times stronger than horses or humans, inch for inch or pound for pound.

As we saddled, Father Santiago Varela García came whisking up on a Honda ATV. Father Varela had ridden on several cabalgatas, but a back injury forced him to exchange his horse for the Honda. A gruff-appearing man in his sixties, Varela was actually quite pleasant, often managing an open-mouthed grin when sitting around the campfire, sipping the local mescal. He would drive with us until we started up the Sierra Aconchi, and we would meet him again on the other side. Arturo Quintanar, an official of the neighboring town of San Felipe de Jesús and a prominent member of the local *ejido* community, would guide us over the Sierra Aconchi as far as Rancho Los Chinos. The Sierra Madre has been a haven for bootleggers, smugglers, and various renegades for a very long time, and nowadays, a few of its isolated valleys hid farms growing a potent new variety of Sonoran Gold. Father Varela only half-jokingly opined that we needed a guide as much to keep us from stumbling into places where we would be unwelcome as to keep us from getting lost. That said, the good father scooted back down the road to the town square for the inauguration ceremony, and we fell in behind at a trot.

San Lorenzo Church

The picturesque plaza offered a classic example of Spanish community structure taken to its best Mexican conclusion. The stark white Mudéjar façade of the church positively gleamed in the morning sun. The wooden church doorway was recessed into a tall, pointed arch with a round, open keyhole above. A low wrought-iron fence protected the church front from the walkway and street. We lined up on the street in front of the church, facing in the opposite direction toward the plaza center. José Luis passed out hand-tooled breast collars with the Caminos de Kino logo to those who had completed the 2008 cabalgata and had the *machismo* to return for 2009. Mine hung down to the Ant's knees, but it would work well on my bigger horses at home.

In the final act, the swarthy Varela removed his ball cap and clasped his hands so tightly that his shoulders pulled together. Lifting his bushy eyebrows toward the cross atop the belfry, he offered a prayer for our safe passage, wished that he too was riding, and evoked the spirit of Father Kino. As I looked over the plaza with its bright flowers, swept sidewalks, and raised bandstand, I had the feeling that for Huepac's current residents, the Spanish program of reducción had turned out for the good. The whole town had the appearance of a well-cared-for place, valued by the people who lived comfortably there. Absent was the angry scrawl of graffiti so common in border towns on both sides. The school playground next to the church had a life-sized Cessna single-engine aircraft, as if the happy pilot had landed one last time, with no intention of leaving.

San Felipe de Jesus was less than ten kilometers downstream from Huepac. Riding down the country lane, we passed the small, irrigated fields (*milpas*) that are the productive heartlands of the Sonoran Sierras. The Jesuits built their missions along the rivers because most of the natives lived there, as well as for the fertile soil and water where they planted crops of wheat, melons, sugarcane, grapes, chickpeas, fruit trees, and other European delicacies. Yet the fields we saw that day were enclosed by hedgerow fences and mostly planted to forage crops for livestock—ryegrass, alfalfa, barley, sorghum, and buffelgrass.

Wheat was introduced by Coronado nearly five hundred years ago, and the Jesuits who followed required it for communion wafers. Because wheat is a winter crop that ripens in the spring, it complemented the summer-planted New World triad of corn, beans, and squash, grown by the natives for millennia. The Spanish and Jesuits also introduced the hardy criollo cattle that thrived on the Pimería Alta's rangelands.

These two introductions eventually had more profound effects on the indigenous people than did Catholicism, according to many historians. Over time, year-round agriculture created settled, family-based subsistence communities, founded on spring wheat and fall corn and vegetables, supplemented by meat, cheese, and milk from a few cows. Water-powered mills built along the rivers ground their wheat into flour for tortillas and wafers. Household-based agriculture required community cooperation, especially at harvest and planting times, and served to strengthen family bonds. Children mostly stayed at home to help out, and the old people contributed their knowledge and handiwork.

I asked Arturo why we didn't see wheat fields today. He explained that the demand for feeder cattle in the United States had become so strong that most Sonoran farmer-ranchers had switched to growing forage in order to increase their cowherds. Over the past fifty years, as America became the "fast-food nation," with a constant craving for hamburger in all its myriad forms, the price for Mexican feeder calves soared. Today, a 350-pound Mexican steer calf is worth $500 in Arizona, where it will be pastured on grass and then fattened in feedlots. This is a huge sum in the Sierras, where wages are less than ten dollars per day. Even the old, tough, two-year-old Mexican steers, the ones with outsized horns, have become as valuable for rodeo cattle. Until recently, cows were barred from importation into the US because Mexico's breeding stock carries bovine tuberculosis and brucellosis. Nowadays, spayed heifer calves with their ovaries removed account for a quarter of all exports. This change from food crops to forage created a commodity-based, cash-crop economy, where the families back home eat the barren cows that are too old to produce a calf—when they eat beef at all. Fearful that exporting heifers may backfire when they run out of cows, Mexico's agriculture ministry now imposes export quotas on females each year.

My Subaru-driving, agrarian-minded friends in Tucson who raise a garden and hens in their suburban backyards lament the loss of Sonora's self-sufficient, agrarian communities to the international cattle market. They romanticize the small, independent family-based farmers, yet few of them know what it is like to be poor and hungry on the fringes of the modern world, without other means to properly clothe, feed, and educate their families. If the small Sonoran farmer-rancher can raise and sell twenty calves a year, that $10,000 of outside income is the difference between a modest prosperity and just getting by on beans and tortillas. Many times, a family member, usually a man, will move to the city or slip across the border to find work, sending his wages back home to support the household and keep the ranch going.

Nowadays, according to Father Varela, the drug cartels have introduced marijuana as another export crop in some isolated parts of the Sierras. While their parents grow pot, the young people, instead of learning to farm and ranch, become burreros, who backpack it across the border to the gringos who smoke it, chew it, or drink it in tea. Once the locals are hooked into the production and delivery system, escape is difficult. Pichi, who used to practice veterinary medicine in Caborca, said the cartels there entice the boys with earning money and get them hooked on drugs. By the time the boys are twenty years old, "they are dead-finished." Even so, to the landless campesino, packing drugs is a job and not a crime—more than likely the only job available in Mexico.

As a rancher and horseman, I admit my participation in the cattle export economy, having pastured Mexican-raised steers and used them for training horses and in competition. As for marijuana, I plead innocent, although I confess to a mild curiosity of what getting "stoned" feels like. The home-brewed mescal certainly packs a big thump.

In 2008, Mexico was the largest supplier of marijuana to the United States, according to the National Drug Intelligence Center. (Canada ran a distant second.) Guerrero, Michoacán, and Nayarit were the major producing states, but recently, the cartels had moved some production to the remote mountains of Sonora and neighboring Chihuahua. The chances of having the plants eradicated by the Mexican army were less here, and being closer to the border reduced transportation costs. The CIA claimed that Mexico produced 15,800 tons of marijuana in 2007, with domestic consumption pegged at no more than 500 tons. The rest was destined for the United States. About 42 percent of the total came through the Sonora-Arizona sector. The Sinaloa cartel, led by Joaquin "El Chapo" Guzman Lorea, controlled most of the routes—the so-called plazas, including the ones over my ranch in the Canelo Hills.

The flood of Mexican marijuana waxes and wanes but has shown little sign of permanent reduction. The drug is ridiculously easy to get, and its price has remained stable, according to the National Drug Intelligence Center. One reason is the extent and character of the battlefield. The Arizona-Sonora borderland is a rugged and desolate landscape, fifty to sixty miles deep on either side, spread out over fifty thousand square miles, almost the size of Mississippi. Happily for us, the Río Sonora was 110 miles south of La Línea and out of the Red Zone.

NEARING SAN FELIPE, Arturo took us alongside the racetrack, a wide, well-groomed straightaway with a starting gate at the far end and the finish line at the town limits. Horses and horseracing thrive in Sonora, another introduction that can be traced back to the good Father Kino. Nearly every town has a racetrack, and most haciendas have a prize horse or two. The horses run match races, one-to-one, over short distances of 200 to 300 meters.

Sonora also has its own version of Seabiscuit, the unlikely journeyman horse that trounced the Triple Crown winner War Admiral in a match race held in 1938. In the Mexican version, El Moro (the Dark One) was a small gray horse from the rural village of Cumpas. After rancher Pedro Frisby traded two mules for what he thought might make a good cow pony, he found that El Moro had amazing speed, easily beating all the local horses. El Moro's adversary, El Relampago (the Lightning), was a highbrow horse from California, brought to southern Arizona by Rafael Romero, a nightclub owner from the city of Agua Prieta. The match was set for March 17, 1957, for five hundred meters—long by Mexican match-race standards. Betting, according to folklorist Big Jim Griffith, totaled almost two million pesos ($200,000), in addition to private wagers of cars, farm animals, and the farm itself. El Moro broke on top, leading until the halfway mark, when El Relampago blazed ahead, winning by a length. The losers walked home, and one man lost two hundred cows. The race sparked the corrido "El Moro de Cumpas," recorded by the famous Vicente Fernandez, King of the Rancheros, lamenting the commoner's defeat by the big city ricos.

But in a rematch at a shorter distance, El Moro was victorious and became the mythical horse hero of Sonora. In April 2009, our town of Sonoita, Arizona, hosted the annual El Moro de Cumpas Stakes, a memorial race in honor of the little gray who never gave up. When we presented the owners of the winning horse with the victory trophy, a huge extended family of Mexicans, from infants in arms to grandparents in walkers, crowded around the magnificent animal for the winner's circle photograph. The man who claimed the winner's prize was draped with gold chains, a Jesus Malverde medallion, and a buxom senorita with horses painted on her two-inch-long fingernails

AFTER PASSING THE race track, we rode through San Felipe's plaza, stopping briefly to grab a cold soda at one of the *tiendas* (stores). Red, white, and purple petunias bloomed in immaculately tended gardens that occupied each of the plaza's four corners, with a small church set off to one side. As we continued down the main street, people came out of their houses and waved. An old man whisking along on a battery-operated wheelchair guided us through town, and a troop of boys ran alongside the horses, full of questions: where had we come from, and how far were we going and why? José Luis explained that we were following the footsteps of the great man Padre Francisco Eusebio Kino.

"*Quien era?*" one of the little ones asked, not recognizing the name of the famous man. José Luis pulled his horse up and delivered a brief history lesson while the boys squirmed, looking at the ground.

Leaving town, we climbed into the foothills of the Sierra Aconchi, following a broad sand wash that was treed on its margins with paloverde, hackberry, and a bushy tree with red wood that Arturo Quintanar called *palo chino*. On the rocky hillsides, organ pipe cactus raised their clustered arms. A half dozen scrawny cows watched us warily as we rode by, each one carrying a different fire brand on the hip, along with an ear tag hanging down like a wind chime. Arturo explained that the local *ejido* owned the rangeland, with each household (the *ejidatarios*) entitled to graze a certain number of cattle. Roundup could be a complicated affair, he said, because all the cattle were run together, and the calves had to be paired with their mothers before branding to decide who owned what, a process that sometimes became heated when the cow owners or the cows got confused.

In Mexico, land reforms of the twentieth century used the ejido as the vehicle for distributing lands to landless peasants. Large, privately owned haciendas—many owned by foreigners, including Americans—were seized by the Mexican government and often distributed to the very people who were working them as common laborers. In essence,

Ejido Cattle

the ejido is a corporate community-owned entity, where its household members have the right to use the land and keep what they grow (usufruct rights), whether crops or livestock, but the community-state retains ownership of the land and water.

Here, land with water is the most valuable resource, as well the most scarce. Each household holds on tightly to its allotted fields (*milpas*), passing them down over the generations as the family's inheritance. Each household manages its milpas independently, deciding what to plant, when to fertilize and harvest, and so forth. The more diligent farmers can often get two crops per year—winter barley followed by summer sorghum, for example. Irrigation water, because it comes from the river, deep wells, and from God, is managed collectively, and each household and milpa is apportioned a share.

Ejido rangeland (*agostadero*) extending into the Sierra Aconchi, on the other hand, is managed collectively. And for most of the year, each member runs his livestock in the same pastures as everyone else. This type of grazing management is not much different from that introduced by Father Kino and the Jesuits. In the spring and fall, cattle are gathered for branding, castration, and sorting, and each owner may take certain animals to his farm for fattening, milking, and to sell. During droughts, when the rangeland grows very little forage, the ejidatarios must cull their herds and graze the keepers on farm fields, else they will starve—conditions that occur more often in today's era of climate creep and the severe overstocking that has been customary for decades.

Arturo Quintanar said the ejido had about 140 members, and he guessed that most [about one hundred] of them had cattle. I wanted to know how many cattle they were running but didn't ask, because such a question would be like asking how much money they had in the bank. A recent study of ranching practices in the Río Sonora valley generally found that ejidatarios graze their ranch lands much more intensely—one cow for every six to nine acres—than on privately owned ranches. These stocking rates are five to six times greater than what government consultants recommend. The ejidatarios are well aware of the damaging effects this has on rangeland vegetation and health, but their decisions on how many cows to run are driven by the minimum number required to support the household. Given the overstocking of the agostadero, irrigated forage crops are vitally important to the San Felipe ejidatarios.[2]

The contrasting managements, independent for the milpas and communal on the agostadero, brings to mind Winston Churchill's famous comparison of capitalism, as the unequal sharing of prosperity, with socialism, as the equal sharing of misery. With over one hundred separate owners, making improvements to upgrade the rangeland or herd genetics becomes extremely difficult. Ranch management falls to the lowest common denominator, producing "a tragedy of the commons." Why, for example, would one progressive stockman pay big money for a beefier bull when it would breed his neighbor's cows for free? Getting all the cattle owners going in the same direction at the same time would be like trying to loose-herd house cats on horseback (even for the diplomatic Father Kino).

In the 1990s, the Mexican Constitution was amended to allow for sales of ejido rights. Even so, any attempt to change the ejido communal land system to a capitalistic free-for-all would probably spark a second Mexican revolution. The small landowners, both communal and private, vividly remember how it was to be landless and desperately poor, toiling under the thumbs of Mexico's ruling elite and foreign corporations.

AHEAD OF ME a little ways, I noticed that Ramón Lujan, the rancher from Chihuahua who had come with the Robles family, was riding a stallion. I hadn't noticed that before, because the horse showed none of the obnoxious stallion behavior, like squealing and biting. Ramón rode square in the saddle, leaning slightly forward, holding the reins between left thumb and forefinger just above the saddle horn, his right hand resting midthigh. His straw hat was pulled down to shade his wind-creased face and drooping gray moustache. When we rode through downtown Hermosillo four days later, he was still sitting in exactly the same place. I asked how he got the stud to be so well mannered.

"I generally buy a weanling off a mare that I like, one with the aptitude to work cattle," he replied. "Then I give it to a boy whose family has a small ranch with a few cows, where the father is an excellent horseman. The boy raises it as his own for three years, lives with it day-to-day, sometimes even taking the colt into the house. We have the understanding that I may buy the horse back, at my option. He breaks it to ride and does all the cattle work with his father. At the end of three years, I pay him the going price for such a horse."

"And how much would that be?" I asked.

"*Entre cuatro y cinco mil pesos.*"

About $400—a very good price for a well-broke stallion and a valuable apprenticeship for the boy.

We rode on. Soon the canyon narrowed, and the sandy bottom grew dark from moisture just below the surface. A hundred yards farther along, water surfaced in a freshet stream. The horses drank deeply, and the spare ponies wallowed in the wet sand. The Ant started to go to his knees until I picked his head up.

"Just put your feet down, and he will walk out from under you," Pichito said, still amused by my six-foot frame straddling the oversized pony.

We left the sand wash and started to climb in single file through boulder slides and ocotillo topped with scarlet buds. To the right, the highest ridge of the Sierra Aconchi looked like a row of molars, with our trail heading toward a gap, as if one tooth had been pulled. To the left, the ridgeline rose up sharply to a horizon punctuated by rocky bluffs, extending to the apex of the Sierra, 7,140 feet high. Father Kino had ridden this way precisely 322 years ago, a time when black bear, jaguar, wolves, and parrots graced the mountain country. The trail wove through stands of green ceanothus, a spindly bush favored by the dog-sized whitetail deer that left scattered piles of poop pellets all around. Whitetails are favorite prey for mountain lion, and according to the local vaqueros, the mountain lions occasionally kill a calf or foal, too.

Unless a lion becomes habituated to killing livestock, I don't hunt them. For me, it is a privilege to live in country that is wild and unpeopled enough to harbor both lion and bear. Rarely, jaguar will wander up from their home range in the Sierra Madre, though I have not seen one yet. Game rangers have set remote cameras in the canyons leading up from the border and occasionally photograph the splendid creature, along with more common wildlife: mountain lions, coatimundi, javelina, deer, skunks, burreros loaded with bales of pot, and the hapless immigrants that the Border Patrol and some Arizonan call "illegal aliens," as if they were creatures from outer space.

Two hours later, the Cabalgata reached the top, stopping to let our horses blow alongside the lone Mexican pine while we watched a dozen calico-colored cows hightail it over the next ridge, wild as deer. The Ant had humpety-humped up the mountain without missing a step, but I noticed that he lost the left hind shoe, so I switched to another horse and put the Ant on a lead rope. Arturo López said a horse like La Hormiga would cost around $200 on the Río Sonora. In Sonoita, he would have been a bargain at five times that price for a novice rider. In rough country, the Ant was safe and durable, like Father Varela's Honda, only the horse could go lots more places and didn't need three dollars a gallon fuel.

The gap afforded a mighty westward prospect overlooking a series of humpback ridges, stacked one behind another, each one shimmering in the blue distance. Somewhere in the invisible bottom, the Río San Miguel flowed past the towns of Rayón and Horcasitas, tomorrow's destinations. On the rising air of midday, against an indigo sky, three *zopolote* vultures sailed in lazy circles, looking for carrion. I caught the strong sense that something mysterious had once existed up here, which, even if located now, could never quite be known—the inscrutable Sierra Madre, where whole landscapes seemed alert, pensive, waiting. A day's ride east of Horcasitas was Ures, a town that twice had been the capital of Sonora and twice was sacked by the Apaches. The rugged cordillera separating the two verdant streams had been sanctuary for bands of Apache inbetween raids on the hapless villagers below.

Somewhere between the tidal waves of rock and earth and thorn scrub was the headquarters of Rancho Los Chinos, where we would make camp tonight. We left the gap through a gate marking the beginning of the privately owned ranch, one of many in the Sonoran sierras and its river valleys.[3] The crippled fence posts wedged in the rocks carried four strands of barbed wire. Immediately, one could see an improvement in the grass and general condition of the range. Land reform had been the rallying cry for the Mexican Revolution, but with Mexico's population growth, the communal lands had more and more owners with more and more livestock, and the effects on plant life and soils were severe.

The agaves had nearly disappeared too, but cattle were not to blame. In the wild Sonoran sierras, each town has its *mescaleros*—brewers with private stills for making the fermented cactus juice. Ethnobotanist Gary Nabhan says the mescaleros use mainly the narrow leaf agave (*Agave agustifolia*), although in a pinch other species will do, and I saw our guide taking note of the few big agaves we passed by. Four to five agave hearts will make one gallon of hooch, and a diligent mescalero can produce up to four hundred gallons a year. Home distilleries used to be illegal, with the fine often settled by payment in kind. Recently, the ever-practical Mexican government authorized the inevitable and labeled the local products as Bacanora, after the village in Sonora where a particularly potent mescal was produced. Our guide had a jug of home brew he was offering for the equivalent of a few dollars a liter. In the late afternoon, *un traguito* (a little sip) eased the saddle sores, he claimed.

And it did. Our winding descent of the Sierra Aconchi seemed to drag on interminably. Crossing one ridge led only to another and another, which led to another and another traguito. By the time we reached Rancho Los Chinos late that afternoon, everyone had a grin instead of a grimace and no one was feeling any pain.

Narrow Leaf Agave

That night, Enrique drove in with the supply trucks, accompanied by Lea, Mike Weber, and Father Luis Enrique Sinohui, who had often ridden the cabalgatas. He and Enrique were spearheading the campaign to have Father Kino named a saint. In fact, for the cabalgata in 2006, they traveled to the Vatican (by airplane instead of horseback) to present the formal petition and the extensive documentation of Kino's life and work, as required by the church. Father Sinohui was a smiling, bespectacled man with a full head of white hair and blue eyes that seemed to focus upward. Selection for priesthood is said to be rigorous, both intellectually and physically, and Sinohui had that athletic step of not putting much weight on the ground when he moved, like a tennis or soccer player. Although Father Sinohui would not ride with us tomorrow, he was an accomplished horseman from a childhood spent on the family ranch in Sonora.

Rancho Los Chinos had two long buildings with wide porches and a row house of adobe. The whole compound was surrounded by mesquite *retaque* fences. Digging my bedroll out of Gaspar's trailer, I settled inside a cavernous storeroom. Looking around at the floor littered with empty grain sacks, I recalled one of my mother's nightly witticisms as she tucked me into bed: "Night-night, and don't let the bedbugs bite." That, and the rustle of mice, drove me back outside. Around the campfire, the talk was about the worldwide recession and America's mountain of bad debts.

"My new chaps cost $125 in pesos," I ventured, speaking to no one in particular. "I saved a hundred bucks over the stateside price."

Rene Balderrama, the dapper lawyer from Navajoa, ventured that that was on the expensive side in Mexico.

"I tried to bargain with Molina, but the price was fixed."

"Yes, for a gringo." Rene grinned.

"Well, if the peso keeps falling, I may get them for half price," I said.

José Luis, the businessman of the Salgado clan, opined that Americans have lived on borrowed money for so long that the crisis would be long and hard. A decade of greed, waste, and war, the first of the new millennium, was grinding down.

January 30

Ding-ding-ding went the bell in the dead of night, jolting me awake. Confused, I looked around, half expecting to find Father Sinohui calling us to prayers, but it was Gaspar's alarm clock. To get away from the mice and fleas, I had made my bed on the porch near the kitchen, not knowing that the cook started banging pots at three thirty in the morning. After getting up, I stoked the fire and loaded the king-sized coffeepot with a bag of chiclero blend and set it over the flame. The night before, Gaspar had boiled a pot of beans, and now he proceeded to mash them in an iron skillet to the consistency of mortar. To this he added chopped onions and green chile and then laced the concoction with fiery chiltepins, finely ground. Next, we broke five dozen eggs in a pot. Gaspar added onions and chile with the assured demeanor of a *chef de cuisine* until he called it *perfecto*.

He set the egg, onion, and chile omelet aside to ferment while we drank coffee and chopped tomatoes and onions for salsa while waiting for the others to roll out of bed and start feeding horses. Gaspar's gastronomical salsa included lots of tomatoes, plus cilantro, green chile, garlic, onion, and lime juice, again in perfect proportions. The breakfast menu sometimes included *machaca* (a spicy dried-meat dish) and occasionally bacon but always flour tortillas and refried beans. My reward for helping Gaspar was to be first in the chow line. While the cabalgantes washed dishes and saddled up, Gaspar rolled the leftovers in tortillas, wrapping them in foil for our saddlebag lunch. Sometime during the night, a vaquero from Rancho Los Chinos had arrived to guide us through the thorn-scrub foothills to the village of Rayón. The morning air of the Sierra Aconchi foothills was still brisk as Rene Balderrama and I rode out together in the strongly slanting yellow sunlight, with La Hormiga trailing behind me on a lead rope.

The Rayón municipality boasted about 1,550 people and twelve times that number of cattle, according to the government census. The town itself was another pleasing example of Spanish reducción: central plaza with whitewashed church, clean streets, and friendly people. The church was ancient, started before Kino's time in 1638 by the Jesuit Pedro Pantoja as a mission to the Lower Pima tribe.

Here, we saw the Catholic Church in service to Sonora's pressing problems of today. Part of the church had been turned into a cooperative, producing granola and cookies, a project started by Father Claudia Murrieta, who rode on last year's cabalgata.

Rayón's local priest, Father Arnulfo Monge, gave us a tour. In one large room, the village women and their daughters mixed, baked, and packaged products for sale in local communities and in Hermosillo. The ladies wore white starched uniforms and worked on spotless tabletops while their laughter ricocheted off the whitewashed walls. Father Murrieta's vision was to make the community self-sustaining by using locally produced grains, flour, and honey, thus providing the *Rayoñeros* with more than just the spiritual nourishment of communion wafers. The project gave the women paying jobs outside the home and gave farmers a market for their crops, freeing them from government charity and giving the young people an alternative to entrapment in the narcotraficante network, just as three hundred years ago, Father Kino had freed the natives from servitude in the Spanish-owned mines and haciendas. The samples Father Monge handed out were delicious, and I bought enough to last for the rest of the trip, substituting granola for Gaspar's epicurean beans. José Luis said that in other towns where they had ridden, similar projects were being carried out by clergy of all faiths, and he hoped that other segments of Mexican society would follow Padre Murrieta's example. Cattle and farming, the historical mainstays of the local economy, could not provide a decent living for all, he believed.

But to an outsider who also was a rancher and farmer, these river towns seemed to have the raw ingredients to meet the new challenges of climate change, rising prices, and food shortages. In fact, their rich agrarian heritage has better prepared them than has the corporate agricultural economies of the United States, whose citizenry is overwhelmingly urban and has largely forgotten the connection between their food, the land, and the farmer's work.

These valleys also had water for irrigation, assuring bountiful yields for diligent farmers. The other essential ingredients included seeds and cultivation practices developed for and adapted to the local climate. As global warming proceeds, these could be crucial factors in producing enough food for Mexicans. Also, the local people still have the know-how to grow, harvest, process, and prepare their foods. Producing food and feeding families is an honorable profession, more satisfying than the bleak existence in a border ghetto, toiling in a *maquiladora* (assembly plant) or running drugs, where the burrero becomes a beast of burden, nothing more and nothing less.

Family is the most trusted institution for Mexicans, and family ties are nourished and strengthened by growing, harvesting, cooking, and eating together—a shared history rooted in family and place. In one sense, this is what the cabalgatas are about, it seemed to me. True, their Catholic faith locates them spiritually, but their sustained family ethic of living in a particular place, funded by a deep sense of its history, anchors them physically and mentally. I wondered if in addition to honoring Father Kino by riding in his footsteps, the cabalgantes could also strengthen his relevance to present-day affairs by sponsoring projects like this in other towns where their exemplary Jesuit had toiled so many years ago. I made a mental note to bring this up later with Enrique, José Luis, and Lea. Economic self-sufficiency in the Mexican sierras could go far toward reducing the uprooting of these settled people and cutting back the exodus to El Norte—more humane and more effective than the border walls and army now in place on the Arizona side.

The road toward Río San Miguel climbed a hill covered with cordon and thorn scrub. At the top, I turned and gazed over the town with its tall church, tidy homes, and lush green milpas alongside the river bottom. Except for the looming threats from the narcos, which were invisible for the moment, the idyllic scene could have been that of a small town in Utah, where the Mormons took root 150 years ago, or a village in the south of France.

Village of Rayon

Just before sundown, we arrived at El Aguajito, a small ranch not far from San Miguel de Horcasitas. Our hands and wrists were scratched from pushing through dense stands of ocotillo and thorn scrub as if we had been fighting off a pack of *onzas*, the fabled cat-like beasts alleged to roam the Sierra Madres. At the corrals, the only water was a hand-dug cistern. We unsaddled and threw the tack on the top rail of a retaque fence, scaring away the lizards that were doing pushups on their leathery chins. The water was alkaline, but the horses drank anyway. At twilight, the supply trucks arrived with Enrique, Lea, Mike Weber, and Fathers Varela and Sinohui. Gaspar did wonderful things with grilled chicken, chile casserole, and our leftover salsa, which had acquired a lofty flavor after aging for a day.

As we finished supper, an old battered pickup drove up and coasted to a stop on the edge of camp. A young man got out from behind the wheel, hurried over to the passenger's side, and opened the door. An old man unfolded, slow and stiff-like, until he stood erect against the truck. The patriarch of El Aguajito had come for a visit. His grandson guided the old man toward the campfire, where José Luis offered him a chair. Standing tall, he welcomed us formally in a soft, gravelly voice and then sat down, feeling first for the seat behind him. Pichi offered him a drink, but he replied, "*Gracias, no tomo.*"

I moved my chair closer to be able to hear him. The old man's eyes were rimmed with cataracts and sheltered by a fine-weave Panama hat, not the palm-leaf hat of a *campesino*, but the hat of a *ganadero*. I told him I was a rancher too, from Arizona, near the town of Sonoita. When I spoke, the old man swiveled around to watch my lips. He nodded as if he knew of it, a little saliva leaking out of the corner of his mouth. I asked him how the rain had been this winter, knowing that people who live on the land like to talk about the weather.

The ganadero shook his head, replying that the winter rains had not been good so far ("*Muy pobre hasta ahora*"). His weather-beaten face was deeply creased and his jug-handled earlobes brushed the clean, starched collar of the white shirt. Over the shirt, he wore a blue V-necked sweater, like golfers wear, pulled down outside over the top of his jeans.

"Now, I keep only a few goats and a couple of burros," he continued, his voice rising. "A few years ago, it made a lot of rain, but eighteen cows died. The doctor came and told us it was because of poisen weeds." His voice broke as he pushed out the words. "The very next summer it made a lot of rain again, and twelve more cows died. For this reason, I no longer have cows."

No one spoke. The ganadero fell silent also and looked down at his feet. I wanted to know more about the ejido, when it was formed, and how many ejidatarios there were, but I decided not to ask. Poison plants often grow on heavily grazed range after a wet spell, but it seemed enough for now to understand the depth of the old man's tragic losses. We gazed silently into the wind-tattered flames as if hoping for a resurrection—replacement heifers for the ganadero's dead cows, perhaps.

The conversation drifted away from cattle toward the Caminos de Kino and Enrique and Father Sinohui's efforts to have Kino named as a saint. In 2006, the formal petition for Kino's sainthood had been completed and the Catholic Church deemed him a Servant of God, the first step in the long process of canonization. The ganadero suggested that we pay a visit to the old church in Horcasitas tomorrow. As the fire dimmed, Rene and Enrique got up, stretched like cats, and left to look for their bedrolls.

The ganadero suddenly grew tired, as if the weather and years that had eroded this difficult land had also ground him down, shaping his destiny. His grandson touched his elbow, and he rose up fiercely erect, bidding us "*buenas noches.*" We in turn rose, and José Luis said, "Thank you for allowing us to stay here." The cabalgantes opened the circle to make room for them to pass. As he walked to the pickup, I had that thrill one gets when a martial band plays a revolutionary march. Before stepping in, he turned as if forgetting something.

"*Viva México!*" he cried.

I woke before dawn, thinking about the old man's losses and the cruel irony that what this bitter land needed most had killed his cows. I, too, had lost cattle after a wet spell. In the Canelo Hills, locoweed grows after a wet winter on the limestone soils around one particular water trough where cattle come to drink and lounge. One cow got an overdose and came down with the blind staggers, as if she had drunk a gallon of home-brewed mescal. The poison was a cumulative neurotoxin, and the only solution was to immediately move the cattle to a new, ungrazed pasture. But the old man didn't have another pasture in his small holding. He had only what he had.

Land reform was the battlefield for Mexico's 1910 revolution, and land distribution to millions of peasants its victory prize. But the reformers did not know—could not have known at the time—that Mexico's surging population growth and overstocking would push productive rangeland past the ecological tipping point, converting it into barren thorn scrub like Aguajito and the lower foothills we had pushed our way through that afternoon.

The sky was turning gray as I crawled out of my bedroll and walked toward the corrals, passing five cots stacked side by side, each one covered by a tarp: Lea, two Salgados, and two Ramonets. A chorus of muffled snores rose from the bedrolls, a quiet cacophony of sounds—soft growls like a truck gearing down a steep hill; another ending in a soft whistle; a horse-like snort. Just before the sun peeked over the Sierra Aconchi, a coyote joined in with its prolonged, lugubrious howl, followed by a chopped and frantic cackling, as if the little desert wolf had let fly with the first long screech and then chased it down, biting it into small pieces.

January 31

San Miguel de Horcasitas was only a few kilometers from camp, and we rode out before the morning breeze began to sweep up the river. Smoke from cook fires drifted over the village and then flattened in the cool and sinking air. I thought José Luis might ride on, so I was happy when he stopped and we all tied up to the fence around Plaza Ignacio Zaragoza, across from the small church. One of the buildings around the plaza was the office of the Asociación Ganadera. Here, cattle (approximately twenty thousand head) outnumbered people (six thousand), as in Rayón. A healthy patchwork of irrigated farms spread over the river valley. The fields seemed small, hemmed in by the Sierra, but government statistics gave a total of fourteen thousand acres under irrigation for the whole municipality, with about two-thirds privately owned and the rest belonging to several ejidos.

Although the cornerstone of Horcasitas's present-day church had been laid relatively late, in 1749, the town had been established fifty years before Kino's time and was named for the ruling viceroy of New Spain, Count Juan Francisco de Güemes y Horcasitas. As it was Saturday, the building was locked, but the caretaker kindly let us in. The whitewashed walls had been shaped by hand and splayed out at the bottom, forming a sturdy foundation at least two feet thick. Plain white arches supported the interior ceiling, with the altar stage holding three glass cabinets, each one containing the carved and painted figure of a saint. For such a large population, the building seemed small in comparison to the churches in Rayón and Huepac. Even so, this was a Catholic municipality with a strong Indian heritage. The 2005 census showed it was 88 percent Catholic and that 15 percent still spoke an indigenous language, probably lower Pima and Ópata.

We followed our new guide—a small, stout man wearing a new palm-leaf hat—out of town on the back road toward the river. His physique matched that of his horse, a short, black mare (*yegua*) that traveled quickly along, with a swinging, side-to-side gait. He trotted down a fence line into a wooded, swampy area ahead of José Luis but suddenly disappeared with a yelp. All I could see was his hat floating on top of the swamp and the horse floundering, over its belly in mud. José Luis leaped in and grabbed the man's flailing arm, pulling him to the fence. By this time, Pichi had a loop around the horse's neck. José Luis wallowed back in and jerked the saddle off while

Vaquero Guide

Pichito got another rope around her neck. Don Ramón took several turns around the saddle horn and pulled tight. For a moment, it looked as if nothing was going to give. Then the *yegua* came out with a loud sucking noise and scrambled to the bank. Retreating, we took the main road out of town, stopping beneath a grove of cottonwoods by the river. Here, the water ran clear over round stones, and José Luis and our intrepid guide waded in to wash off the San Miguel mud.

For the rest of the morning, we rode through a multicolored mosaic of well-tended fields—wavy fields of rye; grain sorghum stubble, dotted with cows; new sprouted barley; and brownish buffelgrass, a pesky plant native to Africa. In Arizona, buffelgrass is considered a dangerous weed, as it crowds out the native grasses, but in Sonora, some ranchers like it because it can withstand heavy grazing and grows on poor soils. Living hedgerow fences of mesquite and thorn scrub surrounded each field, the brush thickets swarming with birds, from feisty wrens to bushtits. A roadrunner darted across the road in front of me, intent on spearing a lizard. The margins of the farms looked messy but alive and protective. Near the river, the hedgerows changed to willow and cottonwood, apparently planted for flood control and firewood.

In a large corral alongside the road, a dozen scimitar-horned cows with floppy ears lounged in the shade, their jaws milling sideways, as if discussing some wet and fleshy herd scandal. Over the fence, another cow with wide-set eyes was tied to a post, while a boy sat beneath her flank on a three-legged stool. Jets of milk struck the tin pail with the rhythm of a snare drum while her lop-eared calf, tethered to a nearby post, bawled for its turn. Seeing us, the boy stood up to watch the procession, his eyes wide more with curiosity than alarm. A straw-colored cur raced to the edge of the road, barking furiously, with its hair roached up like porcupine quills. The boy spoke to it sharply, and the dog slunk away after dousing a fence post with squirts of pee.

At the next house, a teenage girl was pounding her clothes, rub-a-dub-dub, up and down on a corrugated scrub board in a suds-filled galvanized tub. I wondered if she had a date tonight, and if so, what would they do? Perhaps go to a formal dance at the Asociación Ganadera, chaperoned by grandmothers, and afterward, a promenade around the plaza? *That's how it was a hundred years ago,* I mused. Even so, such courtly customs might still be honored here today, although we were only thirty miles from the outskirts of Hermosillo, with its shopping malls, discothèques, movie theaters, cafés, and bars.

We came to a crossroads, and a man on a bicycle whisked by. His seat was padded with carpet, and his basket overflowed with oranges. A little way down the road, he stopped and did a double-take, looking back at all the horses coming toward him. When José Luis pulled alongside, he asked where we had ridden from.

"Huepac," José Luis replied. *"Somos del cabalgata de Kino."*

"So far!" the man exclaimed, shaking his head in disbelief. He smiled and pushed off, peddling furiously toward the next town. In the countryside over which we rode, no one passed without a friendly greeting.

The dirt road meandered out of the irrigated farmland and back into desert thorn scrub. Where the river disappeared into a forest of mesquite, we passed an abandoned flour mill, its *acequia* (canal) dry. Once, the canal had diverted river water to turn the wheel that powered the mill, grinding wheat into flour. The two-story brick building stood on the riverbank, with the water wheel in the upper level. The grinding stones had disappeared, but they must have been on the lower floor, where the milling platform opened out to a loading dock. In the days before Bimbo bread and factory tortillas, each farmer in the community brought his grain here to be milled, returning home with his own flour, minus the "miller's tithing." I asked Ricardo how long the mills had been abandoned.

"When the farmers started growing more wheat than they needed for themselves," he said. "With the new varieties, production increased so much that the farmers started selling their wheat to the big commercial mills in Hermosillo."

Norman Borlaug, a plant breeder working in the Yaqui River basin of southern Sonora, developed high-yielding, disease-resistant wheat adapted to low elevations and high temperatures. By 1963, Mexico had increased its production sixfold and had become a net exporter of wheat. Borlaug moved on to Pakistan and India, repeating the development of superior, higher-yielding varieties of rice for those countries where the population explosion had produced widespread hunger. The Green Revolution, as it became known, saved a billion people from starvation worldwide. Borlaug was awarded the Nobel Peace Prize in 1970 and became a Padre Kino–like figure to many Mexican farmers.

Even so, I had seen widespread hunger and malnutrition in El Salvador and Guatemala in the 1980s when the Green Revolution was supposed to have provided plenty of food for all. Somehow, the people who needed food the most didn't have money to buy it, or it might have been that waste, corruption, and inefficiency prevented the food chain from connecting with the rural villages where I worked. The best-nourished poor people had been those who had land on which to grow their own food, and I suspected that might be true in rural Sonora as well.

By early afternoon the last cool air from the river had disappeared, and the river itself vanished into dense mesquite thickets. The air was hot and dry, and the sun beat down on the hard-packed road, the heat reflecting upward. The dry clop of hooves echoed on the sun-heated gravel, and the horses began to sweat. Just ahead of me, I noticed that Pichito had switched horses and was riding the bay and leading his paint. They had been racehorses, and Pichito was using the cabalgata to get the run out of their systems. Both were wide-bodied steeds with muscular hindquarters and bulging gaskins. Even so, Pichito was wider still than the backs of his horses.

The road led to a sandy river bottom, marked Zacaton on the maps, and we crossed over as the evening shadows lengthened. An hour later, we entered the suburb settlement of San Pedro where Pancho and Nancy Almada had a small acreage in a subdivision surrounded by other such homes. We had arrived on the outskirts of Hermosillo at eight o'clock on Saturday night, and all around us, weekend festivities were getting underway.

We unsaddled and watered the horses, feeding them hay out of Pancho's barn. The corrals were cramped, and the pecking order took a while to sort out so every horse got its fill. Gaspar had set up the cook shack at the end of a long table under a patio and was grilling scallions. But Nancy Almada had already prepared the main dish: menudo, a lovely stew with hominy, onions, and chiles in a clear, oily broth, with ribbons of tripe swimming on the bottom like slow planarians.

"Very good for curing hangovers," Pichi opined. But nobody was drunk yet.

I took my bowl and tortilla and sat next to Ramón Lujan, who was still dressed for the trail. He rolled the tortilla up like a cigar, dipping it in a bowl of salsa and then spooning up the menudo, following with a bite of tortilla. Don Ramón had said little the whole trip, and except for telling me about his stallion, we hadn't talked much. Intent on eating, I stayed with the food as the table around me burst with chatter and laughter. All the families had come to dinner: spouses, nieces, nephews, boyfriends, and girlfriends. Ramón leaned back in his chair as he finished the menudo, a satisfied smile breaking out below his drooping gray mustache.

"Muy rico," he sighed, taking off his hat at last.

There was no place to bed down in the busy house, so I went out into the yard under a small grove of orange trees. The ride from the old man's ranchito to the suburbs of Hermosillo took only twelve hours, but it felt as if we had moved at least a century forward in time. Norteño music blasted from a nearby house, where another party had commenced, and from behind the orange trees, another celebration was underway with a Sinaloa band. Both were playing *narcocorridos,* glorifying the drug trade and vilifying the *federales* (federal police) and gringo Border Patrol. The lyrics portrayed violence as just retribution to authority in the same way rap music does for disenfranchised youth in America's ghettos. The deep basso and polka-like rhythms made the ground shake and would have been hypnotic, if they had not been so loud.

At five in the morning, after the music had finally stopped, another chorus began. Across the street from Pancho's house was a farm that raised fighting cocks. In a large grassy yard, each rooster was tethered to a stake under a small, peaked shelter, open on both ends. The tethers were long enough so the belligerent roosters could swagger toward each other without making physical contact. Flapping their resplendent wings and crowing, each one sang its own praises and threatened its neighbors, exactly like the narco musicians had done.

HERMOSILLO, WHERE THE ride would end, was the capital of Sonora, a city only slightly smaller than Tucson, with busy streets and a freeway bypass for interstate traffic bound for Mexico City. At the base of two hills not far from the confluence of the Sonora and San Miguel Rivers, Father Kino had written of an Indian mission called Pitic. Here, Kino's contemporary, Father Adam Gilg, had tried unsuccessfully to convert the Seri Indians into farmers. A coastal tribe of nomads, the Seri lived by hunting, fishing, turtling, and raiding, and they rejected the settled life required by the missionaries. Enrique and José Luis had pinpointed the exact coordinates of the old church, *Iglesia Vieja*, by searching historical documents with the help of the municipality of Hermosillo. But their discovery had been buried by a hundred feet of silt backed up behind the now-dry Abelardo L. Rodriguez dam.

We rode out of the brush thickets and into the hazy, midmorning light, a ragtag, mismatched and calico-colored cabalgata of forty Mexicans and one gringo. The dry expanse of the lake bed spread out before us to the base of the Pitic Hills, a mile to the west. A towering dust devil swept over the dusty lake bed, suddenly cutting our view down to hundred meters. Then stepping out of the haze, three horned cows appeared like ghosts, trudging in single file toward the windmill at the edge of the dam, each one trailed by its calf, like an automaton on a string.

At the church's precise location, we were met by historians, curious onlookers, and reporters from Univision. Enrique gave them the Father Kino story and the background of the cabalgatas, saying this ride completed the cycle of Kino's travels in Sonora. One asked me why I had come along.

Why indeed? To see the Sierra Madre and feel the culture and traditions of Sonora rising up out of its history, the land, and its people; to demonstrate that Sonora and Arizona have much in common, in spite of the recent turmoil on the border. The river trails and villages had been a peaceful diorama of Sonora's past and present, cemented in memory by the *compañerismo* (good fellowship) of the cabalgantes, as well as the friendly locals. And the ride had kept me in touch with Oscar and Lea.

We rode on. José Luis set out toward the freeway, cutting past the base of the hills. A pair of municipal police cars blocked traffic, allowing the riders to cross unimpeded. Silenced by a hoofed procession that belonged to another century, not a single car tooted. We climbed to a saddle between the hills, where we could look out over the sprawling city. Below was a cemetery where Enrique, Lea, and others waited. Ricardo Ramonet, riding beside me with his entire family, pointed to the central plaza and cathedral in the heart of the city a mile or so on the other side of the cemetery.

"That is where the ceremony will be," he said.

Suddenly, I remembered all of my perilous taxi rides, dodging through Mexican traffic.

"We're not riding through the city, are we?" I asked.

"*Como no,*" he replied evenly. Of course.

We lined up in front of the magnificent Central Cathedral facing the Plaza de Armas. At one end of the cabalgata stood a larger-than-life statue of Cowboy Kino— mounted, of course; cassocked and caped, bareheaded, hands on the reins, feet booted with spurs, and legs protected by leather armas. Unlike the statue at the entrance to Magdalena de Kino, this horse's head was up, ears pinned back, attentive to the rider. Early this morning at Pancho's house, extra horses had been trailered in, so that all the families now sat proudly on their horses as Fathers Varela and Sinohui proceeded with the invocations. Jesus Enrique was honored as the founder of Los Caminos de Kino, along with previous riders who no longer could make the journey. Lea darted around the plaza with her camera, getting shots from different angles. She was without Oscar but surrounded by an adopted family who had shared important moments in their lives together. The *Hermosillo Expreso* newspaper took photographs in a panoramic view of the cathedral, Kino's statue, and all the riders, with Father Sinohui in the center, splashed over the front page the next day. On Sunday afternoon, the tree-lined park overflowed with churchgoers and children on Rollerblades and scooters. Hungry pigeons waddled by, snatching bits of popcorn from old men slouched on wrought-iron benches.

The highway to the Salgado farm on the western edge of Hermosillo followed what was left of the river, now a steep-sided canal encased in concrete. After the cathedral, our police escort had vanished. Even so, forty riders on a busy paved street made their own wake, and we stayed bunched up so no one got separated. Once out of downtown by a couple of miles, we entered the suburbs, passing strip malls and auto dealerships, grocery stores and Mexican delis, all on the right side of our one-way street. To the left loomed the concrete river. At a traffic light, a crossroads led to Costco and Walmart *supertiendas.*

Ahead on the right, a tall, wind-driven tube—a scarlet-colored monster complete with arms and painted face that leered at the passing traffic—writhed and collapsed and filled again, whistling loudly above the din of the traffic. B. F. Goodrich was advertising a tire sale, and a stampede seemed like a dead certainty. I looked for a way to circle around and go behind the monster, but storefronts completely lined the avenue. Traffic was bumper-to-bumper, passing so close that cars scraped my left stirrup now and then. One by one, the leading riders passed by cautiously. Then Alejandro Robles's stallion arched his neck and sidestepped into the slipstream of traffic. As cars screeched to a halt, he danced back in line to the angry blast of horns. Ramón Lujan's stallion passed by, paying no more attention to the monster than Don Ramón had done. Suddenly, the light turned red and we had to stop. I held my horse back, hiding behind Pichito's broad back for what seemed like an hour. When the light turned green, I took a tight rein and eased him forward. That good bay horse took it all in stride, a Spanish Barb carrying its rider safely through Hermosillo's modern-day battlefield.

After that, the last two miles to the Salgado farm was a cakewalk. As we approached the Salgados' farm, the teenagers called for a race and disappeared in a cloud of dust. Daisy and María José won by four lengths. Unsaddling, we hosed off the sweaty horses and turned them into a big corral, where they dropped to the ground for a mud bath. In truth, I was more than a little smelly myself. The good Gaspar had the usual carne asada prepared with salsa, guacamole, tortillas, and icy Negra Modelo beer, good enough to die for. Had we been riding through Hermosillo on my rough-edged ranch horses, there would have been a real funeral.

The next morning, Lea and I took the direct route home, going up Highway 15 to Nogales. This time I was driving. As we passed the Kino statue at the entrance to Magdalena, she looked out the window wistfully. The Cabalgata had served to cushion the absence of Oscar and reconnected her spiritually with her Padre Kino mission tours. And the cabalgantes had adopted this remarkable woman, now approaching her eighth decade, as their matriarch—a modern-day persona of the historical borderlands.

Part 3

Discovering the Sobaipuris: 2010

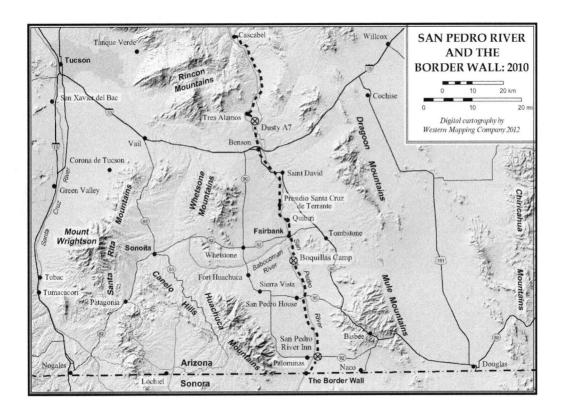

November 2, 1697. We set out from Dolores, taking three pack loads of provisions, the usual Mass kit, thirty horses, and gifts to win over the Sobaipuris, whom we were going to see and discover.

–Manje's journal of the fourth expedition

THE WINTER OF 2009–10 blessed the borderlands with abundant moisture, and the mountains surrounding Sonoita glistened with snow, even into March when the cabalgata finally decided to ride the San Pedro River in Arizona. Although the US economy was still mired in recession, the Mexican peso had strengthened against the dollar. Many economists attributed its rise to the billions of dollars Mexican workers in the United States remitted back home to support their families; also, the American purchase of illegal narcotics under the table, said to be between $25 billion and $40 billion annually, had some positive trickle-down effect.

Over the past twenty-two years, the Los Caminos de Kino riders had covered most of Father Kino's trails that meandered over Sonora and the western part of the Pimería Alta. That left his expeditions into northeast to win over the Sobaipuris, a separate band of O'odham-speaking natives who lived precariously along the San Pedro River. Just east and north of the river, the Chiricahua and western Apaches (and their allies) claimed the rugged mountains of what today is southeastern Arizona as their sacred homeland.

Though previous trips had started and ended in Mexico, this one presented an additional challenge for the riders. First, Mexican horses are barred from entering the United States without a long quarantine period. Second, Gaspar did not have a green card, so we had to manage without our regular cook. Rental horses cost a lot of money, so José Luis and I made a deal: if he would take care of the food, I would find horses. I thought I could get them from local ranchers for a reasonable price, and the horses would be better than rental nags.

The cabalgantes arrived at the Collins C6 Ranch in Sonoita on Thursday evening, April 6. It was the beginning of Easter holiday in Sonora, so that the foot soldiers who didn't ride came along as ground support and for shopping in Tucson's malls. Lea and Enrique agreed to drive the supply truck, while Pichi volunteered to be the designated cook. As Pichi was a veterinarian, I wondered what might end up in the stewpot, but my Mexican friends had it all arranged, as I discovered the first night on the river.

April 7

THE DAWN AIR was crisp and damp from an overnight shower as I walked to the barn to feed. Pichi and Pichito were already up and looking over the horses milling about in the arena. To have enough horses to go around, I had to use my two fillies, Frosty and Cranberry—both the color of ripe cherries, both five years old, and both still a little green. Stabling mares overnight with strange geldings was a recipe for kicks, bites, and wire cuts, but I hoped to find separate corrals along the way or tie them to trees at our campsites. If we had to throw them all together, at least we had no stallions to deal with as we did on the last two rides.

All horses seem more or less crazy, but it's not something they try to hide. As a prey species evolved on open savanna, they come by their high startle reflex honestly. The same qualities we admire—alertness, speed, strength, stamina, and keen eyesight— protect them from predators. Horses in general hate surprises, especially the younger ones. A few months ago, Frosty had rudely reminded me of this when I lifted my jacket off a fence post, and she wheeled out from under me, leaving me flapping my arms like a rooster looking for a roost. Now, the whites of her eyes rolled suspiciously as we walked behind her. After two rides with the cabalgantes, I had a pretty good idea of their horsemanship—the better to pair up horse with rider. Ricardo Ramonet rode with the balance and precision that would give Frosty the confidence she needed. I put a hand on her flank and walked to the rail, pulling her lead rope free.

"Ricardo, you take Frosty," I said, handing him the lead. "She's got an easy way of going, but don't wave your bandana at her. She's pretty watchy." I turned to David and said, "Cranberry's my pick of the fillies. She's gentle but quick. Sometimes she'll get bored and toss her head a little, but the fillies are stable mates, and you and your dad can ride together."

A small, stocky gelding with a mallet-shaped head lounged against the far fence, his eyes closed and one hind hoof cocked over. "Ricky, you take Hammer," I said, pointing to the gelding. Ricky did not ride as much as David. In fact, this would be his first cabalgata, and Hammer came equipped with a built-in set of training wheels. The pony had no ego whatsoever and would be content to poke along with the fillies behind the other geldings.

Pichi and Pichito were big men, going toward fat, but they both rode well. I paired them with two gray geldings weighing 1,300 pounds each.

"El Moro de Sonoita." Pichi smiled when Diane handed him TJ's lead rope.

"The cook gets the best horse." She smiled back.

Pichi bowed graciously. "What means this—TJ?" he asked.

"His sire was TJ Blue Cowboy, a ranch horse stallion in South Dakota where we bought him," she said. "But I call him Marvie for his marvelous gait and mellow disposition."

"But…but…you are not going to ride with us?" he stammered.

"Not this time. I'll trailer the horses to the river and pick you up at Cascabel at the end," she replied.

The other riders selected their horses out of the remuda, all short-backed, strong-boned geldings accustomed to rough country. I rode a lined-backed dun-colored gelding, the color Pichito called *perlino*. Lacey was just four years old, but he hadn't made any big mistakes so far. And he had a soft mouth, responsive to my hands on the reins. His only fault was that he didn't like walking in water or having wet sand suck at his hooves, a problem that saved us some embarrassment when we got to the quicksand ford.

We unloaded the horses where the San Pedro River crossed under Highway 92 at the village of Palominas. In 1987, the Department of Interior had purchased the lower San Pedro corridor for a nature reserve, recognizing its ecological importance as a free-flowing desert river. The reserve started at the border and extended northward forty-two miles, protecting this rare river bottomland from the surging development of nearby Sierra Vista and Fort Huachuca. At the end of the nineteenth century, Palominas had been a prosperous railroad town, but today, little remained except the school, a feed store, and scattered ranchettes.

A short river, the San Pedro nevertheless qualified for dual citizenship. Starting in Sonora about thirty miles south of the border, it ran northward for 140 miles to join with the Gila River at the Arizona town of Winkleman. When Spanish explorer Francisco Vásquez de Coronado first saw the river in 1540, it flowed as a broad, shallow stream through a tawny sea of grass, sprinkled with cottonwood, willow, and walnut.

In November 2, 1697, Father Kino left his home mission of Dolores for the eastern and northern boundaries of the Pimería Alta. He was fifty-two years old and eager to explore the native settlements on the San Pedro River and *El Río del Norte*, the Gila River. Reports and rumors had reached Dolores that these new people, numbering many thousands, were farmers ripe to harvest for the Lord. Also, Kino had a strate-

At The Trailhead

gic vision for the protection of Sonoran settlements from Apache depredations. By bringing the Sobaipuris and the other O'odham-speaking clans into the ecumenical fold, they would form a defensive line for the Pimería Alta against the Apache raiding parties. Already deadly enemies of the Apache, the Sobaipuris would gladly seize any opportunity to settle scores.

Lieutenant Juan Mateo Manje, as usual, accompanied the priest. A compulsive journalist, Manje took head counts at each village, recording the crops the Indians grew and noting whether they had horses and cattle and if they had Spanish brands. Even though Father Kino had vouched for the Sobaipuris, the Spanish military still doubted their true allegiance. General Domingo Jironza, Manje's uncle, ordered Captain Cristóbal Bernal and twenty-two well-armed soldiers from the presidio of Fronteras to accompany the two explorers just in case. The two parties would meet up at Gaybanipitia, a Sobaipuris settlement at the confluence of the Babocomari and San Pedro rivers. From there, they rode downstream together along the fringes of Apache territory. Their ultimate goal was the large Casa Grande ruins on the Gila River, near the present-day farming town of Coolidge, Arizona.

Kino and Manje had entered the San Pedro River basin at Gaybanipitia which lay downstream a day's ride from Palominas, but the Salgados, for symbolic reasons, insisted on starting our ride at the border wall. By 2010, the wall had become the most conspicuous symbol of America's nativism and Arizona's fear of Mexican immigrants and drug smugglers. The snow-capped Huachuca Mountains gleamed in the midday sun when Enrique lined us up at the trailhead for photos and the benediction.

"Everybody better take their visas," I called out before leaving. "Chances are good the Border Patrol will check us." We mounted our horses and roweled them forward like a band of slow marauders, following a rude dirt track that ran parallel to the river that lay one-half mile to our west. Between our road and the river, giant sacaton bunchgrass covered a wide expanse of abandoned farmland, so deeply cut by arroyos that a man could walk down them to the river bottoms without being seen. We climbed a low hill, and the border wall appeared ominously on the horizon, coming toward us out of the east through mesquite thickets and thorn scrub. On the hilltop, radar towers scanned the countryside for alien movement, the sort of vigilance usually reserved for demilitarized zones between nations at war, like North and South Korea.

Seeing the towers made me uneasy. Just ten days before, Rob Krentz, a rancher, was murdered fifty miles east of here, possibly by a drug smuggler he had surprised while checking on fences and waters. The thirty-five-thousand-acre Krentz ranch was established over one hundred years ago, and Rob was the fourth generation of his family to live on the borderlands. Shortly before the murder, Krentz's brother had alerted the Border Patrol to a load of marijuana he found stashed in a mesquite thicket—a common occurrence on borderland ranches these days. Perhaps the killing had been retribution, perhaps not. Rob managed to flee in his ATV but died a short distance from the ambush. His cow dog, a Queensland Heeler, was by his side but so badly wounded that he had to be euthanized. The killer was tracked to the border, where the police had to stop, barred by international law from crossing over into another sovereign nation. Krentz was well known and well liked, and the senseless killing sent shock waves over the state and even the nation.

"We can't stop you from going, but stick together and keep to higher ground out of the river bottom," the Border Patrol cautioned when I called them the week before the ride, explaining our trip. I didn't mention our nationalities, because in addition to the immigrants and drug mules we might bump into, vigilante violence was possible, given the tension building over Krentz's murder.

We rode on. Soon, the ramparts of Coronado National Memorial rose up in the distance beyond the river to the west. A mile farther south, we came to an abandoned ranch headquarters split by the wall itself, leaving splintered corrals on our side and a few crumbling adobe buildings in Sonora.

These tumbledown corrals had a legacy. A bronze plaque erected by the Bureau of Land Management read "William C. Greene Historic Corrals." A hard-rock miner, Greene struck it big-time while prospecting for copper. As early as 1780, the headwaters of the San Pedro had been declared an official mining district, *Real de Mina*, by the Spanish. In the late 1800s, the crafty Greene gained control of the best properties and built a smelter with investor money from Wall Street. Worldwide demand for copper made him fantastically rich, and he built up a three-million-acre ranching empire, including the upper reaches of the Río Sonora where we had ridden last year, as well as most of the San Pedro River basin. The corrals had been the shipping point where Greene had loaded railroad cars with beef destined for American markets and where he imported blooded stock to upgrade his Mexican herds. Greene died in 1911, but his Cananea Cattle and Greene Cattle Companies operated for another half century. In the 1950s, land reform swept over Mexico, and President Adolfo López Mateos seized Greene's ranches, breaking them up into ejido communal properties distributed among Mexico's landless peasants, along with thirty thousand head of his cattle and one thousand horses.

West of the corrals, we came up hard against the twenty foot-high wall made of slotted steel panels sunk in concrete. Each panel was slightly offset to the next, allowing the wall to climb the clean, grassy hillside like a bad suture, the wall rising and falling with the undulating landscape. The narrow slots in the panels created shafts of sunlight and shadow over the ground, creating the effect of bars in an open-air prison. On the top, the panels were solid to eliminate handholds. On the Arizona side, a graded dirt road ran parallel to the wall. The Border Patrol pulled chain gangs of old tires to erase any footprints, so that they might see where anyone who scaled the wall had dropped down and walked away. The border wall exuded an unnerving, sinister aspect, as if a barbarian giant had cauterized the land with a hot iron to stop a great hemorrhage.

"*Foto, foto!*" José Luis yelled, grabbing a camera out of his saddlebag.

"*Foto, foto!*" someone else echoed, and the Mexicans lined up against the wall like a bunch of happy tourists at the Grand Canyon. José Luis motioned me over for a group picture.

The Border Wall

"No, thanks," I replied, sitting on my horse just out of camera range and waiting until they finished the photo op. A Border Patrol truck parked on the hill just above the corrals surveyed the scene. The afternoon sun winked back from their binoculars. From the Mexican side, I sensed that other eyes were keeping watch as well.

At the river's edge, Normandy-style vehicle barriers made from railroad track jack-knifed down to the running water, replacing the steel plates. In the river channel itself, a single long bar spanned the gap, with a loose barbed-wire gate to keep cows from passing through. The whole contraption was connected to more barriers on the other side, where the wall started up again, climbing steadily toward Montezuma Peak in the Coronado National Monument. The barricades and water gap allowed the river to flow, but it also created an open funnel (*El Embudo*) where northbound drug mules and immigrants could slip through.

"Why you no want your picture of the fence, Ricardo?" José Luis asked as we rode back toward the trailhead.

"Two reasons," I replied. "First, it's an eyesore, and I'd just as soon remember the country without the scars. Second, the drug runners still get through, so it doesn't solve the problem. It makes us, the United States and Mexico, into adversaries when we ought to be allies."

"Already they are selling twenty-foot ladders along the border," José Luis quipped, mimicking Janet Napolitano, Arizona's governor before she became secretary of Homeland Security.

"How much are you getting for them?" I asked.

"We are not selling them . . . yet," he replied.

"What do Mexicans think of the wall?"

"For us, it is unnecessary. I suppose the wall makes it harder for Americans to buy illegal drugs."

"I'm old enough to remember Ronald Reagan scolding the Russians for separating German families with the Berlin Wall during the Cold War. It seems hypocritical for the United States to do the same thing here on the borderlands. The hell of it is that once it's done, there's no going back. A hundred years from now, people will look at this mess and ask what were people thinking when we did this to the land. Maybe by then it'll be a tourist attraction, like the Great Wall of China—which, by the way, didn't protect the Chinese from the Mongol hordes."

José Luis managed the Salgado family business in Hermosillo, which manufactured pipe and concrete products for the construction industry in both countries. Their business had thrived during the building boom of the last decades. At the same time, illegal immigration had surged, with Mexicans filling jobs in construction, food processing, and service industries, as well as agriculture. By 2009, eleven to twelve million lived and worked illegally in the United States, with a half million in Arizona.[1]

The present-day immigration problems go back at least as far as World War II, when the Bracero Program brought Mexican farm workers in to fill the labor gap left by the military draft (*bracero* is Spanish for one who lends a hand). When they returned home, the word of paying jobs spread throughout rural Mexico, and the exodus began.

In 1986, Congress passed immigration laws allowing those who had lived and worked in the United States and kept out of trouble to choose between a path to citizenship or a green card that allowed them to keep working, provided they returned home to Mexico each year. These common-sense laws recognized that many Mexicans were needed and contributed positively to the US economy and culture. Miguel, an irrigator on my farm, chose a green card, returning to his home village in the Sierra Madre every Christmas. Even so, some people have labeled this as amnesty for criminals. Lately, they have been clamoring for more Border Patrol, Army National Guard troops, and more walls.

The sun was hovering just above Miller Peak on the Huachuca Mountains on the way back to the trailhead when Ricardo Ramonet trotted up between José Luis and me.

"What we don't understand in Mexico," he said, "is why you don't want some of these people. It is impossible to farm without good workers." Ricardo, himself a farm owner, understood this reality in spades.

"You're right," I replied. "Ask any farmer in the western United States, and he will tell you he can't farm without labor from Mexico. Americans won't do farm work unless they own the place. Most jobs in town pay better, and the work is easier. Sometimes I think people who oppose a guest worker program are clueless about the connection between their food and the work needed to produce it."

In the 1990s, America's push for free trade in the global marketplace, an economic paradigm that was supposed to raise all ships, rich and poor, forced many small Mexican farmers from their homes and fields. The 1994 North American Free Trade Agreement (NAFTA) was crammed down the people's throats by Mexico's ruling class, backed up by the economic might of the United States. NAFTA phased out tariffs on basic foods that protected the small Mexican farmer from low-priced commodities imported by US agribusiness giants, the same commodities produced with massive government subsidies to American farmers. Unable to feed, clothe, or educate their families, thousands of Mexican farmers lost both the dignity of their work and self-reliance, and they fled to *El Norte* for paying jobs.

For many rural Mexicans, NAFTA meant that the rich and powerful were "free" to trade to the disadvantage of the poor and weak. The result has been that millions have been disinherited, further widening the already wide gap between Mexico's "haves and have-nots." An entirely new form of poverty and servitude was invented and imposed, augmenting the colonial system of *repartiemento*. This new order is called "globalization and free market economics," a predatory arrangement championed in the United States by academic economists and politicians who serve the interests of multinational corporations. Ironically, NAFTA intensified the exodus that America now fears and struggles to halt with a border wall and army, while those who live on the borderland suffer the consequences.

BACK AT THE trailhead, Diane had already left for home and the cabalgata made its way in the twilight to the San Pedro River Inn, located five miles north on the east side of the river. The inn was a dairy farm in the 1890s that produced milk for the miners in nearby Bisbee, but now the cows had been replaced by bird-watchers, flocking to the San Pedro River basin to add its rare species to their life lists. The congenial owner, Walter Kolbe, allowed us to camp and corral our horses on his property. Towering cottonwoods shaded the inn's spacious lawns, several of which had boreholes occupied by great horned owls. A spring-fed pond harbored coots, a pair of mallards, and enormous, multicolored carp that surfaced to slurp up pieces of Pichi's tortillas. The grounds, all neatly enclosed by a white board fence, sloped gently toward the river a quarter mile to the west.

That night, Pichi whipped up a delicious stew he called *caldo de vaquero*, with braised oxtails simmering in a broth of hominy, green chiles, onions, and potatoes. When I asked him about his recipe, he said it was simple. "First you light the stove and then take the frozen stew from the cooler and heat for thirty minutes. The hard part was driving all the way to Cecilia Ramonet's house to pick it up." He chuckled.

"Pichi's caldo goes best with this special mescal." José Luis grinned, thrusting a dark bottle into my hands. A swirl produced oily pillars that cascaded down its sides. In the bottom, a pale worm circled like a pathology specimen.

"*Hijole!*" I gagged after taking a swig. I shoved the bottle toward Pancho Almada, who was standing next to me. The courtly Pancho was more circumspect. He rolled a sip around with his tongue, smiling through his full beard for a minute or two before gently swallowing. And so it went around the fire, until Ricardo Ramonet intercepted it on the way to his teenage sons.

"Pichi, you get those oxtails from your patients?" I croaked.

"Ha-ha-ha, Ricardo, very funny." Pichi guffawed. "I only work on dogs and cats and once in a while, snakes and lizards."

"Worse come to worse, Pichi, you can light the cook fire with this stuff," I said. Liquor flowed easily—brandy, mescal, and fine tequilas. Each rider carried a leather-covered flask hung on the saddle horn to ease the saddle sores toward the end of the day, an "aide-de-camp" of which Kino might have disapproved, as Manje and others wrote that the good father never touched liquor, except for altar wine during Mass.

That night, I pitched my bedroll alongside the horse corrals, lulled by the horses' steady munching. One by one, the bright stars came alive in the cold, blue dusk, and Venus twinkled in the western sky. A pair of owls calling in the river woods suddenly fell silent, and I wondered if the Mexicans who slipped through the funnel today were now making their way up the riverside trail, northward toward Interstate 10. How many were hopeful immigrants who had risked everything to make the journey, and how many would be carrying cocaine, marijuana, or crystal meth?

APRIL 8

AT DAYBREAK, DEW covered my bedroll. On the western horizon, the snow-covered tops of the Huachuca Mountains gleamed in the first light. The smell of coffee and clatter of pans from the cook fire promised that Pichi was working his magic again. I pulled on my clothes and boots and walked to the corrals with Pichito, who grabbed the twine on the hay bale before I could get my pocketknife open and raised up with his three hundred pounds until the string broke. We tossed a flake of hay (Pichito called them "tacos") to each horse and sprinkled grain on top. In the rising light of the coppery sun, the fillies' coats gleamed like new-struck pennies.

"They are very pretty, the fillies," Pichito mused, casting his expert eye over the horses from the top fence rail.

"They're making first-rate cow horses, especially Cranberry," I said. "And they'll raise good foals too, bred to the right stallion."

"Así es," Pichito agreed.

"Personally, I've always thought the horse ought to be our national symbol. I mean, what has the bald eagle ever done for us?"

After saddling, we presented Walter Kolbe with a bottle of store-bought mescal and said our good-byes. I started toward the river, riding next to a hedgerow fence where a vermillion flycatcher perched, waiting for the sun to bring out insects. The male of this species was the signature totem of the San Pedro reserve, and its appearance so early in our trip was a good omen. The river looked dark and syrupy, and Lacey balked at entering the water but then gathered himself and cleared the gap in a single bound.

A dirt road led out of the river bottoms and up onto a mesa covered with bright green Lehmann lovegrass. A mile or so along, the trail led to the mouth of a deep arroyo that angled back toward the river. Here, a Bureau of Land Management (BLM) sign pointed us toward the Lehner Mammoth-Kill site, discovered by a local rancher, Ed Lehner, who noticed large pieces of what turned out to be mammoth bones exposed in the eroding vertical walls of the arroyo.

At the end of the last Ice Age, 10-12,000 years ago, the climate was cooler and wetter and much of the San Pedro River was marshland. Paleo-Indian hunters had slaughtered mammoths and other big game here, including horses, giant ground sloths, and camels. The BLM diorama pictured gigantic elephant-like beasts with recurved tusks ten feet long. The mammoth and other large mammals became extinct as the climate warmed and became drier, and human hunters thinned out their populations. We dropped down into the arroyo riding single file, excited about seeing elephant bone and stone-age Clovis spear points. Instead, we rode into a vacant burrero camp, littered with the usual trash, plus mattresses, brassieres, ragged blankets, and an open latrine with rosettes of stained toilet paper.

Regrettably, dumping grounds like these are common on most borderland ranches these days. On mine, a long wooded ridge tumbles off of Mount Hughes where the immigrants and drug mules camp under juniper thickets while hidden from Border Patrol helicopters. One morning as I was pushing a dozen cows off the ridge, they suddenly spooked and scattered like quail. The cow dog, instead of running to get around the cows, heeled up behind my horse and whined. Fifty yards below us, a band of burreros trudged by, each one carrying a bale of marijuana wrapped in black plastic. They ducked under the pasture fence one by one, when the last in line turned, looked up, and shouted. The leader put binoculars on me while talking into a handheld radio. Thrusting his fist in my general direction, he said something short but not loud and then turned and walked on, with the others following quickly behind.

"A la tuya," I called back. Their lookout on top of Mount Hughes had cleared me. They knew who I was, where I lived, the color of my horses, and the blue-eyed dog. They also knew the road-bound Border Patrol did not get this far back into the mountains. The lead burrero had no interest in drawing attention by picking a fight, nor did I. This was not a situation to be rectified by individual heroics; not at this moment, anyway.

Until recently, the drug mules stashed their loads in a highway culvert and then walked out on the road to wait for the Border Patrol to give them a free ride back to the trampoline cities of Ambos Nogales. Turned loose in Mexico, the burreros collected their pay (said to be $1,000 per load) and then went home to wait for the next load of Sonoran Gold for delivery to the drug dealers from Tucson. But the Border Patrol recently wised up and started taking fingerprints and photographs. Adapting quickly to the new tactics, the drug mules now walk back to Sonora after dropping their loads. Clever mice never entrust their lives to only one hole.

An hour later, the cabalgata rode under the Hereford Road bridge spanning the river, disturbing small birds roosting in the undercarriage. Their flutter made Lacey squat, and I too bent over, grateful that a truck did not rumble over the bridge at that moment. On a dead cottonwood rooted at the river's margin, a few vultures perched in sepulchral arrangement; the new arrivals from the south spread their gruesome wings toward the pale sun for warmth. *Be thankful for nature's brooms*, I thought.

Our trail meandered through seep willows rooted in the stream bank and then climbed onto a bench covered by grass so tall and green that it swallowed Hammer and Ricky. The land for the next eight miles had been irrigated pasture when the Kern County Land Company owned it, but the BLM had eliminated grazing in 1987. The giant sacaton grass covered up rotting sprinkler pipe and barbed-wire fences that were dangerous traps for horses and hikers. The BLM had conveniently cleared a trail, but it was some distance from the river. Where we could see a clear path to water, we took it, hoping to glimpse sign of beaver that had been recently reintroduced. In the bottoms, cottonwoods, pale green and shimmering, hovered over the spring-budding willows and leafless mesquite. The beaver seemed to be thriving once more, judging from the many chiseled stumps and gnawed limbs, although we did not see one. Biologists who study beaver behavior say they build dams to increase safe habitat, but only beavers know why they work so hard.

In the foreground plain, northern harriers skimmed over the rolling grassland, riding the springtime thermals with only an occasional wing beat. One suddenly rose up to hover over a grassy clump, and then dropped like a feather bomb with claws outstretched. The hawk did not rise again, so it probably caught some unlucky mouse, vole, or rabbit that we could not see. Harriers, like owls, have excellent hearing and hunt as much by sound as by sight. A paradise for raptors, the grassy San Pedro River corridor teems with prey, and the birds use its trees for hunting perches and nesting sites. This morning we had already seen a mating pair of red-tailed hawks shrieking in high, twisting flight, as well as the elegantly colored American kestrel, the smallest falcon.

In November 1697, Kino and Manje would have ridden through a golden, belly-high grassland, unencumbered by border walls, pipes, or fences. The cottonwoods, ash, walnut, and willows in the river bottoms would have started giving up their leaves, green fading to golden yellow and brown. The end branches of mesquites would have turned brown too, not because of frost but because the mesquite girdler beetles had "girdled" the twigs. The explorers must have seen antelope and mule deer, but their journals seldom mentioned wildlife. The weather in early November would have been balmy—warm days and cool nights, with little rain and no snow, except in the high surrounding mountains. The river itself would have been wide and shallow, meandering between heavily sodded banks, harboring beaver and muskrat. In 1824, when trapper

James Ohio Pattie traveled the San Pedro southward from its confluence with the Gila River, he caught so many beaver that he called the San Pedro "Beaver River," a name that soon disappeared along with the big rodents. Kino and Manje saw the landscape not as naturalists, but with the eyes and attitudes of ranchers and farmers. Here was an agrarian paradise with deep, fertile soil, a mild climate with two reliable wet seasons, and rainfall averaging fifteen inches a year.

It still looked that way to Ignacio Elías González and his partner, Nepomuceno Felíx, one hundred twenty years later, when they petitioned the Mexican government for two land grants that straddled both sides of the river, extending from about Palominas northward toward Saint David. Spain and later, Mexico, granted or sold enormous tracts of land to reward its elite soldiers, creating a frontier-ranching aristocracy that survives in Sonora today. Thousands of Elías González cattle and horses had grazed here until the Apaches killed two of the brothers and most of their vaqueros. The Mexicans fled back to Sonora, leaving their livestock behind, to the delight of the hungry natives.

"Yippee, you guys made it already," Lea chirped as we rode into the parking lot of the San Pedro House. By the time we had dismounted and tied the horses, Lea and Enrique had the tailgate down on the supply truck and the ice chest open. The 1930s ranch house had recently been converted into a bookstore and picnic area by the Friends of the San Pedro River, a volunteer group that included Oscar and Lea as charter members. Already, the gregarious Lea had engaged a visiting couple from France in the full history of the cabalgata, including the fact that most of its members were Mexicans. Indeed, we looked like a Pancho Villa patrol: full-bearded men with gleaming white teeth, leather leggings decorated with silver conchos, and broad-brimmed hats secured against the wind by stampede strings under the chin. While they talked and posed for photos, I went inside to pay the user's fee and made a donation to the Friends in the name of the cabalgata. Outside, Marvie slipped his bridle and strolled into the picnic area, begging for potato chips and depositing a fragrant pile of horse apples in exchange.

Leaving the tourists behind, we crossed a paved road and rode north toward the ghost town of Charleston with Tombstone and Sierra Vista. In the 1880s, mule-drawn wagons hauled silver ore from Tombstone to Charleston's stamp mills along the river. The refining process required huge amounts water and firewood, denuding the river bottoms of cottonwoods and mesquite, as well as the oak and pine from the surrounding mountains. Sepia photographs dating from the mining era show a barren and badly eroded landscape right up to the water's edge.

An hour later, we reached Escapule Wash, an outsized example of a *boquilla*, which means "the mouth of a tributary stream where it empties into the main river." The first Spanish explorers had been impressed by the many boquillas, as well as the thick stands of *nogales*, or walnut trees in this part of the river, and gave the land grant its name— "San Juan de las Boquillas y Nogales."

Alongside the deep sandy beach, beneath the delicious shade of cottonwood, the San Pedro River ran clear over gravel flecked with mica that sparkled in the dappled sunlight. The far-side bank was heavy sod and deeply undercut by the current; beyond, mesquite and catclaw covered the river bench. Above the bench, layers of rock and cinders rose up fifty feet to an abandoned railroad grade.

"This looks like a good place to eat lunch," I said, stepping down from Lacey. I pulled off his saddle and spread the blankets to dry over a huge cottonwood limb. Leaning against the trunk, I slid down to the sand and took a deep breath.

Pancho Almada squatted in the sand at the edge of the river, gazing at the patches of shadows and splotches of sunlight playing over the rippling water. "*Muy bonito este lugar*," he murmured.

"Yes," I agreed, "this is a very nice place."

"How do we go from here?" José Luis asked.

"I didn't scout this part," I replied. "We'll just have to feel our way along. Right now, it's time for that great Mexican tradition, the siesta," I said, pulling my hat over my eyes and staring into the sweat-stained crown. Down the creek, the three teenagers, David and Ricky Ramonet and Chepo Salgado, sprawled on the sand. For now, the only sounds were birdsong, the gurgle of water, soft snores, and the rustle of cotton-wood leaves, as if people were whispering without words.

A half hour later, José Luis spread the map out on the tree trunk. "It looks to be about a mile to the Charleston Road Bridge," he muttered, impatient to get moving again.

"Sounds about right," I mumbled into my hat.

"Maybe if we cross here and take the railroad, it will be faster," Ricardo Ramonet added.

"Could be bad footing for the horses," I replied, sitting up and looking at my watch. "It's two o'clock now. Say we've got one mile to the bridge and then another eight to the Boquillas Ranch. That's a couple of more hours, and it's getting dark about six thirty."

I turned and faced the log, pulling myself erect. "The old maps show a *vado* [ford] over the river a little way upstream. We'll have to backtrack some."

"Those maps are over a hundred years old," José Luis said as he mounted up. "Why we don't try here to save time?"

I rode Lacey to the water. He stepped in a few feet and then balked, the water breaking in flumes around his legs. The usually lazy San Pedro carried a swift flood of water fed by this year's wet winter and lingering snow atop the Huachuca Mountains. As Lacey sank into the deep sand of Escapule Boquilla, I stared at the deeper water along the undercut bank on the far side.

"Here, I go first," José Luis said, pushing his big gelding forward. "Your horse no likes to go in water."

True, Lacey had refused the river twice already today. "That far bank looks treacherous," I said. "Maybe we should look—" But it was too late; José Luis, with Ricardo Ramonet following, were already halfway across. José Luis was nothing if not decisive. When he made a decision, he followed through quickly, as I had learned during the past two rides with him. I backed Lacey up and watched. Nearing the far bank, the horses did what horses do in deep water, they tried to swim the doggy paddle. But the water was only half deep, the bottom half was Boquillas sand. Then they lunged forward, kicking at the soupy bottom, trying to find traction as the water rose up above their bellies.

"Quicksand!" I yelled.

José Luis slid off on the upstream side, going in up to his shoulders. Grabbing onto some willows, he pulled himself to the bank, still clutching the reins. Ricardo swung forward in the stirrups over the saddle horn, grasping a hank of Frosty's mane. The filly got her front feet up on the bank for leverage and lurched forward, dragging herself and Ricardo out of the river. José Luis crouched on the bank and pulled on the reins while his horse floundered downstream, the current drifting the gelding against the solid bank where he scrambled out. José Luis looked the hail fellow, all dirty and wet, dumping water and sand out of his soggy boots. The two horses shook themselves like dogs and started grazing on the green grass as if nothing out of the ordinary had happened.

The rest of us rode south, crossing the water where we could see rock bottom the whole way. Pichi went first on Marvie, while I brought up the rear. Lacey watched the others, gaining confidence. He still didn't like it, but he liked even less being left behind.

When we caught up with José Luis, he was off his horse, bushwhacking through the mesquite thicket and scrambling up the rocky bank with his shirt torn half off. We followed on foot, leading our horses.

"That got a little gnarly back there," I muttered, looking back down the steep riprap bank to the river. I thought about last year when our guide and his mare had disappeared in the Río San Miguel swamp.

José Luis had his saddle off and was shaking out the wet blankets. "Yes, but we made it." He grinned.

"Lacey gets an extra taco tonight for saving the rest of us," Pichito added merrily.

"That we did," I agreed, thankful that it was not the guide who screwed up this time.

Before long, we came to the Charleston Road bridge. As we rode into the parking lot, an old man sitting beside his motor home pulled out a cell phone. Minutes later, three border patrol pickups careened into the parking lot, red lights flashing. Enrique and Lea had just arrived in José Luis's supply truck with Sonora license plates, and the Border Patrol trucks pulled around them, blocking their exit. The smiling Lea jumped down to intercept the grim-looking officers, explaining the cabalgata business one more time. After checking the registration of the pickup and Enrique's visa, they piled back into their trucks and left without further to-do. So far, we had led a charmed life with the Border Patrol, and we would need that luck again that night in Boquillas Camp.

Beyond the Charleston Road bridge, the trail veered east away from the river, looping past Millville, another ghost town, and then circled north around the base of three sharp-pointed volcanic hills. At the north brow of the fall hill, we looked down a long narrow sand wash as it angled westward back toward the river. In the distant valley beyond, a linear band of green bulged up from the gray background of the leafless mesquite bosque. The sand wash funneled into a one-track road leading north and back into the river bottoms. Lacey and I were content to bring up the rear behind Hammer and the two fillies. We had been in the lead most of the day, and the youngster had handled it well.

We rode on. The river meandered through a wide floodplain, but it was impossible to know if we were within a hundred feet of the river or a half mile because the land was so overgrown with brush and mesquite, the upshot of much human meddling in nature's dynamic equilibrium. Weather in the Pimería Alta has two wet seasons: the slow, winter *equipatas* rains from the Pacific Ocean and the violent summer *chubasco* storms boiling up from Mexico. As the summer monsoon approaches, thunderheads generate fierce electrical storms, igniting grass fires that flash over the land—violent and lyrical but swiftly over. Grass plants, because they grow from their roots and crowns, usually survive and flourish afterward in the monsoon rains. But fire kills mesquite and brush seedlings because they grow from the tips of their stems. Fire severely damages the mature plants as well. Also, the archaeological record confirms that native people used fire for centuries as a tool for hunting game.

Large-scale grass fires all but disappeared at the beginning of the twentieth century with advent of the Smokey the Bear character and the supposedly enlightened notion that all fire is evil, ugly, and unnatural. By removing fire from the grassland ecosystem, we allowed the mesquites and thorn scrub to thrive and hijack the river bottoms and much of the upland range. Severe overgrazing by cattle, coupled with drought in the 1890s, amplified this process. Cattle were removed from the reserve in 1987, but the San Pedro landscape still needs a good burn. That may be politically unacceptable today, because the birders would squawk, and everyone would mourn the loss of the magnificent cottonwoods.

Ricardo Ramonet dropped back alongside me, pointing out the old telephone poles that came off the mesa from the east. In a few places, a single wire still was connected the poles, and we listened in silence for the dot-dash-dot-dash of the telegraph's Morse code. In the old days, a telegram meant something important was in the works—an Apache raid or a train wreck, perhaps.

"We must be getting close to where the Babocomari River dumps in," I said.

"Where is this Babocomari?" Ricardo asked.

"You remember after Oscar's memorial, we came down from Sonoita and crossed the San Pedro River? The Babocomari joins it just south of the bridge."

Just ahead, David and Ricky Ramonet rode side by side. David's mare tossed her head, anxious for the day to be over, while Hammer trudged quietly along, eyes drooping and nearly asleep with the soporific motion.

"Nice that your sons want to ride with you," I said.

"This is Ricky's first cabalgata. He is not so much interested in horses as David," Ricardo replied. Both boys attended school in Hermosillo, where their mother was the administrator. The family lived in town, and Ricardo drove to the farm every day.

"The Babocomari was a Mexican land grant," I said, "like the two on the San Pedro we've been riding through—to the same family, Elías González."

"That is a famous name in Sonora," Ricardo replied. "An Elías is governor of the state at this moment."

In 1827, José Ignacio Elías González and his sister, Eulalia, petitioned the government for eight *sitios* of land, five miles wide and twenty miles long, following the Babocomari River east from the Canelo Hills, almost to its confluence with the San Pedro River, a tract of thirty-five thousand acres for which they paid $380. With the Gadsden Purchase, the United States agreed to honor all legitimate Spanish and Mexican land grants. In 1877, Elías González sold the Babocomari to Dr. Edward B. Perrin, one of the first of Arizona's many land speculators. Under Perrin, the ranch had been severely overgrazed and in poor condition, when Frank Cullen Brophy, a copper mogul and banker from Bisbee, bought it in 1936.

The Brophy family still owns it today, operating a cattle ranch that uses controlled burns and sustainable grazing practices, restoring the magnificent grasslands to their near-original state. Each fall for the past several years, I had sold my calves to Ben Brophy and the famous Babocomari. Not by accident, the named saint of the Babocomari Ranch is the Saint Ignacio of Loyola, founder of the Jesuit order.

We were strung out over a half mile, riding singly or in pairs down the sandy road, as the sun dropped below the mesquite bosque. A dull ache in my left foot registered the miles we had ridden, when José Luis, in the lead, called out, "*Llegamos a Las Boquillas!*"

We also had reached what Kino believed was the southern edge of Sobaipuris territory, the village of Santa Cruz de Gaybanipitea, which lay just across the river from Boquillas Camp. On Thursday, November 7, 1697, Manje recorded twenty-five houses [brush huts] and one hundred inhabitants, noting their prosperous gardens irrigated by river water. On an earlier visit, Kino had left a few cows and promised to send a missionary father to live among them. The natives had built an adobe house with beams and an earth-covered roof as a residence where they lodged Kino and his companions. For the next two days, Kino and the Captain preached the gospel, explaining to them the key articles of the faith. Here, Capitan Bernal and twenty-two soldiers joined the expedition, and the explorers butchered two beeves for them. The observant Manje noted that Kino's few cows had multiplied to one hundred head.[2]

Our cabalgata entered Boquillas Camp from the south, passing in front of a two-

Boquillas Camp

story, rusty tin barn and a sagging set of corrals on the north side of the large clearing. On the south side, two empty clapboard houses stood side by side, windows and doors protected by iron bars and surrounded by low chain-link fences. The parking area in front had two Port-A-Johns, one for the handicapped—incongruous reminders of the social conventions we had left behind for a brief interlude. The road going north to Fairbank and Highway 82 entered the compound on the east side of the clearing, passing between the houses and a shady picnic area that was conveniently equipped with a table and fire ring. Enrique and Lea had left the supply truck and trailer parked beside the table and returned to Sonoita because the park ranger locked the entry gate at sundown.

In the twilight, Pichito and I watered and fed the horses, watched by a pair of barn owls perched in the hayloft. Lacey was dead last in the pecking order, and the older geldings kept chasing him away from the hay, pinning their ears and baring their yellowed teeth, so I put him alone in a small corral. We had been out in front most of the day, and the colt had handled it well. Once, he had wheeled around and whinnied, his herd instinct momentarily overcoming his natural inclination to be in front. I scooped a double handful of grain, and the colt nibbled at it with soft, blunt lips until there was nothing left but slobber.

Pichito had finished checking the other horses for gall marks and loose shoes and left the corral. I followed him through the gate, hobbling toward the picnic area where the others stood around the campfire. The dark-colored bottle was making the rounds again.

"Hey, Ricardo," Pichi called out. "You want some medicine for your back?"

"Only on the doctor's orders," I grunted, taking a tiny sip of the gusano mescal and rolling it cautiously around with my tongue this time.

"I prescribe this for all my patients after a twenty-five-mile ride." Pichi grinned.

"I thought you only worked on dogs and cats," I squeaked.

"*Pues, si*," he agreed. "Except that once I worked on a *culebra*. It was a big boa constrictor. A narco's girlfriend brought it to the clinic because it had quit eating."

This was beginning to sound interesting. "So what did you do?" I prodded, sitting down and stretching out my legs to the fire.

"I checked its temperature, and of course, I listened to its lungs." Pichi was heating up supper, and he paused to reach down and flip the tortillas warming on a piece of tin over the coals. "It was too cold," he said.

"So what?" I answered. "Snakes are cold-blooded anyhow."

"*Así es*. But this one was *muy fría*. So I kept it overnight for observation. That evening I put a live rat in its cage, and the next morning the snake had a big lump in the middle, and its temperature was back to normal. When the lady came in, the snake smiled when I told her not to feed it tacos anymore." Pichi erupted in great gusts of laughter.

"A hungry snake with a low temperature and a grin." I tipped my hat to Dr. Pichi's brilliant diagnosis. "But tell me something. How did you know the lady was a girlfriend of a narco?"

"She was dripping with gold—rings, bracelets, necklaces, around her ankles, too. And the Jesús Malverde medallion, right here," he said, poking at his chest.

"Seriously now, how do ordinary people in Hermosillo avoid getting tangled up with the narcos?" I asked. "Not that you're ordinary, Pichi."

"Well, we generally know who they are," Pichi replied. "If they bring an animal to the clinic, I treat them like anybody else. But I keep it on a professional basis. We don't become friendly."

Pichito spoke up. "For me, the only difference is that I work on horses, so I have to make farm calls; go to the haciendas."

"¡Óigame!" José Luis stirred out of his seat in the truck where he was scraping mud off his boots and came striding over. "We don't have so many users as you do in the States. Most Mexicans are too poor to buy the expensive drugs, except maybe some glue sniffing and meth in the barrios."

I glanced over to Chepo, who was studying at the university while working in the Salgado family business. He shrugged.

"We read in the States that the Mexican police are working for the narcos lots of times," I said.

"When I come to the States, I hear all the time about how Mexico is too corrupt, the police are working for the drug cartels, the cartel peoples are killing each other, and the soldiers are killing the narcos." José Luis had worked up a head of steam. "Yes, we have corruption," he continued, "but so do you, especially along the border. If it was not for the Americans buying so many drugs, Mexico would not have a drug problem. The gringo drug addicts are America's form of corruption. It is your problem as much as ours, maybe even more."

Ricardo Ramonet, the usually soft-spoken farmer, jumped into the fray. "The cartels use the dollars from American drug addicts to buy guns from American gun dealers and then use them to kill Mexicans. Pretty soon, the cartels will be shooting Americans with their own guns," he said.

I chewed on the double irony that Mexico was fighting America's "War on Drugs" while the United States was supplying the enemy with money and weapons. I could think of nothing more to add, except that neither country had a monopoly on bad guys. And $40 billion a year in illegal drug sales draws the bad guys like flies on stink. The conversation died when Pichi called for dinner—*carne con chili colorado*, salsa, and refried beans, with warm tortillas thin as egg shells.

Just before sundown, a helicopter began circling Boquillas Camp, not a green Border Patrol mosquito but a bigger, blue-and-white craft with side windows and doors. The pilot tipped into the turn, and we saw a man in the doorway, looking down. The entire Cabalgata ran out in the clearing and watched back.

"Hey," I yelled, waving my hat.

"Who is that?" Pichi asked, hands on hips as he tilted back for a better view.

"Not sure," I replied. "It could be ICE."

"*Hielo?*" Pancho asked.

"Not that kind of ice. ICE means Immigration and Customs Enforcement," I replied. "They are like the Border Patrol on steroids."

The helicopter started flying in wider circles over the mesquite bosque and then zipped south down the road in the direction from which we had come.

"Maybe we tripped sensors when we rode in," I muttered. The Border Patrol's electronics couldn't tell the difference between harmless horseback riders and drug mules, or between bird-watchers and illegal immigrants.

Minutes later, a green-and-white pickup careened through the east entrance to Boquillas Camp and sped by us without so much as a wave. The Border Patrol driver was hunched over the wheel, and the passenger was bracing with both hands on the dashboard. At the south edge of the clearing, the pickup skidded into a hard left turn, and disappeared down the road into the darkening mesquite forest.

We ate standing around the campfire as twilight deepened, listening to the faint whap-whap-whap of the helicopter to the south of our camp. Suddenly, the noise became louder—*whap-whap-whap*—and the aircraft circled the clearing again. Now, its spotlight cast eerie shadows over the corrals, where the horses jerked up their heads in wild-eyed confusion.

"If he lands, we'll have a stampede!" I yelled, sprinting toward the corrals. But the helicopter made only one circle before disappearing again, this time going west toward the river.

"I hear more trucks coming," Chepo warned, looking toward the main entrance. This time there were two. One kept going south past the entrance; the other sped by us and followed the first one out of the clearing.

"Something big must be going down," I said. "It costs a thousand dollars an hour to operate that bird."

We had ridden twenty-five miles that day, escaping from quicksand at the river ford. We dined on Pichi's carne con chili colorado and congratulated ourselves with gentle sips of cactus juice. Each of us chose a spot and unrolled blankets. José Luis erected his tent and vanished inside. As if to say good night, a Border Patrol truck alarm went off up the road—not a siren but like an all-clear signal, rising and falling in pitch. Much later, I learned that the patrolmen leave it on at night so they can find their way back to the truck, like pigeons honing in on the roost. I crawled into my sleeping bag and gave thanks that I was an American citizen and in my homeland. Still tense over the raid, I closed my eyes and lay back, puzzling over why the Border Patrol didn't stop and say something to us. Were they chasing a drug deal going down? Or were they after illegal immigrants? Or both? With ICE involved, it had to be something big.

THE BLITZ BROUGHT a vivid collage of images out of my distant past. The first was two men running toward me as I looked out of my office window on the American School campus early one morning in Guatemala City—short, thickset men who moved crab-like and close to the ground. I could see white rags tied around their upper arms. They came across the school's baseball infield and straight over second base and into the outfield, where our small laboratory building perched on the edge of a steep ravine. I remembered thinking, *If they are wearing ski masks, this is not a ball game.*

The next image was of them breaking through my door, pistols at ready, grenades hanging from their shirt loops.

"Get to the ground!" one of them shouted.

I don't remember how I ended up crouched beneath my desk, but the next image was pure sound, a deafening blast that flattened me against the cold cement. Two more blasts followed in rapid succession. The concussions sucked the air out of my lungs. Blood trickled from my ears and nose as I lay there, stunned.

As my mind cleared, another fear struck, so intense that it erased the tincture-of-blood taste. My daughter, at this hour, would have been in the classroom just across the baseball field from where the assassins had come, and Diane should be arriving at the main gate with Richard West for morning preschool. The final images were more sounds—the shattering blast of cannon, the ping of sniper fire. I saw the house in the ravine below our office explode, pieces of splintered wood airborne in a mushroom cloud of cement dust. The men who had been inside fled in terror down the ravine as they were executed one by one.

But I could not have actually seen those last two images because I ran in the opposite direction, looking for Jennifer, and found her safe in the classroom. My mind filled in the blanks out of what I was later told at the American embassy. In 1981, Guatemala was locked in a civil war, pitting a ruthless coalition of Guatemalan military and civilian oligarchy against peasant farmers and labor unions. The army had located a rebel safe house next to the university and brought in civilian guerilla fighters to take it out. The white rags tied around their upper arms were for identification, so they would not be shot by army snipers. A tank had been parked to block the school entrance, and soldiers had surrounded the perimeter fence. I was told by the military attaché that the two men crossing the ball field had been sent to protect me in case the guerillas tried to take hostages.

Perhaps that was true. Or perhaps I was under suspicion because I worked in the countryside with campesinos and Mayan villagers. In Guatemala, a told truth was often a masquerade for another kind of truth.

Guatemala's civil war raged until 1996. Two hundred thousand were murdered, mostly unarmed Mayan Indians; fifty thousand disappeared; and more than one million fled their ancestral villages to refugee camps in southern Mexico. Thousands worked their way up to the US border, including one who showed up at the ranch one afternoon several years after I had left Guatemala—a short, sturdy man with nut-brown skin and flat face of the highland Maya. He had waded across the Suchiate River on the Guatemala-Mexico border, carrying a bicycle on his shoulders. Months later, he sold it in the village of Santa Cruz and started walking north. After he had rested and eaten a little, he asked me the short way to North Carolina, where he had family working in poultry processing plants. I filled his water bottle and pointed him toward the Greyhound Bus station in Benson. America could use that kind of grit in its gene pool.

Throughout the long course of the war, the US government, fearful of the spread of Communism from Cuba and Nicaragua, cynically deemed it a "low intensity conflict" and continued supporting the Guatemalan military with money, weapons, advisors, and intelligence—and in the process, unwittingly abetted the flood of immigrants to

American's heartland. Later, a United Nations investigation labeled the war "genocide," and in 1999, President Bill Clinton made a formal apology for the United States' role.

SOMETIME AFTER MIDNIGHT, we woke to the high-pitched whine of a drone circling Boquillas Camp. The truck alarm was silent, so the patrolmen must have found their way home. I got up to make water, and José Luis popped out of his tent and walked to the edge of the clearing, where we sniggered about how in some dim cubicle on Fort Huachuca, a computer screen voyeur was snooping in on our toilet.

Snuggled back in my bedroll, I lay back and watched the throbbing red light circle and circle beneath the bright stars. I wondered again about the forces that shape the trajectory of an individual life—how, by the mere accident of birth, I lay here in a warm, soft bed instead of shivering under a mesquite thicket with the modern-day Pilgrims. And how on that deadly day in Guatemala City, my five-year-old son had been kept home from school as punishment for wandering off campus the day before to pet the horses grazing in that same ravine.

Father Kino would have claimed divine intervention and given thanks to God for his salvation. But why me, instead of the unlucky immigrants? Why Richard West and not the murdered insurgents?

April 9

Dawn in Boquillas Camp. Doves calling from the mesquite thickets in the gray beginnings of day. The warm smells of damp earth and horse dung.

When the light hit my bed, I burrowed in deeper to shut out the day for a while longer, pulling the stocking cap down over my ears. After the Border Patrol ruckus ended, I had finally slept, but it had been a short night, and I wasn't ready for it to be over. But my alarm went off, so obnoxious it might have been a call to bear arms. My hand, which an instant before had been asleep, darted out snakelike and banged the off button.

What a great place to linger for a day, I mused. Fifty yards from our camp, the river sashayed along in broad, tawny pools, held back by a beaver dam. A newly constructed lodge of cottonwood and willow branches slouched close to the riverbank. At dawn, the beaver might be still in the river, and with stealth and a little patience, maybe we could see one.

A flock of Chihuahua ravens broke my trance, squabbling over oaty bits of horse manure in the corrals. I sat up and looked around. Pichito had rolled over on his belly by the fire, scooting up on his hands and knees inside his sleeping bag. He looked like a gigantic inchworm emerging from a blue chrysalis. I pulled on my clothes and walked to the corrals. The ravens hopped up into the morning breeze, exposing their light-colored neck feathers. One landed on the top rail, cocked its head, and glared at me for interrupting its breakfast.

While Pichito fed the geldings, I tossed hay to Lacey and the fillies and walked inside the barn to see if the owls had returned. In a far dark corner of the loft, I could just make out their broad faces and fierce eyes. Their presence brightened the morning, and I started back to the cook fire, where the others were beginning to stir.

"*Café?*" Pichi asked.

"Yes, thanks," I replied, extending my coffee cup. I loved these early Cabalgata mornings: the plain food, the friendship and simplicity, the contentment of doing only one thing at a time. There was no good reason to hurry that I could comprehend at that moment.

"What time for breakfast?" I asked.

"*A las siete,*" Pichi replied.

The entrance gate to Boquillas Camp on Highway 82 opened at six thirty. This morning, Pichi waited to cook breakfast so the others could join us. Julia, José Luis's wife, and his daughters, Juliana and María José, had spent yesterday shopping in Tucson, while Cecilia Ramonet visited Pima Community College, where her daughter planned to study next fall. After breakfast, I hitched a ride with Enrique and Lea, loaning Lacey to María José so she could ride with her dad. Salvatore, Enrique's six-year-old grandson, rode too, his dark eyes sparkling with excitement while clinging to the saddle horn in front of his uncle.

Fairbank was the only ghost-less ghost town left on the San Pedro. Most of the mining towns scattered up and down the river had been little more than tarpaper and tin shacks, with saloons, brothels, and rooming houses that lasted only a decade or two before the silver ran out. But Fairbank had been a railroad hub, serving the bigger mines in Tombstone, Douglas, and Bisbee, and hung on until the 1970s. All the buildings were crumbling when the BLM took it over in 1987. While the others looked over the town and its picnic grounds, I went in search of the camp host to asked about last night's raid.

"It happens more than you'd think," he said. "Especially when the checkpoint is open on Highway 90 going to I-10. The drug packers and illegals take the abandoned railroad on the west side of the river to get around it. The track goes all the way to Benson on the freeway."

"Do they ever bother you?"

"Not so far, but Rob Krentz's murder over toward Douglas two weeks ago has us worried. Up to now, the illegals have pretty much avoided us, and the Border Patrol keeps a truck close by at night. The highway is a pickup point for the drug dealers from Tucson."

"I wonder why they didn't stop and talk to us last night."

"Don't know for sure. Maybe because the BLM knew who you were. They told me to expect you. By the way, how far did you go yesterday?"

"Twenty-five miles, I reckon. We plan on making Terrenate and St. David Cienega today."

"Be sure to see Contention City, too," he recommended, getting into his golf cart.

"How about Quiburi?" I queried.

"You'll ride by there first, but there's nothing much to see." He whisked away with a load of trash bags for the Dumpster.

Quiburi, once a thriving Sobaipuris settlement, and Santa Cruz de Terrenate, a

Spanish *presidio*, or fort, were both located on the west bank of the San Pedro River a little way north of Fairbank. The recorded histories of these two settlements—one indigenous, the other foreign—revealed much about how Spain and the Catholic Church hoped to control northern New Spain and its people and how the Apache knocked the Spanish back on their Iberian arses when their cultures first collided there.

Perhaps of all the sights on this Cabalgata, we were most intent on seeing the presidio because of its tangible ruins. By walking amid the crumbling walls, we might come to some comprehension of the isolation and fear the Spanish felt here in the Pimería Alta's Heart of Darkness, where the Apache took full advantage of the Spanish intrusion. But first, we had to pass by Quiburi, an O'odham word meaning "Many Houses," where Kino made peaceful contact with the Sobaipuris and their headman, Capitan Coro, eighty years before the presidio was built.

From the parking lot, our trail led northward on the east side of the river. A half mile later, we came to a sign: "Cemetery. No Horses Allowed."

"Aha!" Pichi cackled. "It says that we no can bury Ricardo's horses in this *cementerio*!" We tied the horses up to mesquite trees and followed him to the top of the ridge, where we counted ten piles of rock—a few with crosses but none with names. While the others scrambled over the mute stones, I paused to look east at the rose-colored monoliths of China Peaks that thrust up on the south flank of the Dragoon Mountains, marking the entrance to Cochise Stronghold, an ancient Apache sanctuary.

Quiburi appeared as a black dot on Father Kino's maps, just north of the confluence of the Babocomari and San Pedro Rivers. Kino first passed through here in 1692 and immediately sent his vaqueros back with cattle and a small drove of mares to start a ranch. In 1697, the herd had grown to several hundred cows. On November 9, 1697, Kino and his entire party continued downstream from Gaybanipitia a short distance to Quiburi. Here, Manje counted one hundred houses and five hundred people, tending their irrigated crops of corn, beans, squash and cotton from which they wove cloth. Kino was already known to their headman, Capitan Coro, as the Jesuit had brokered an uneasy peace between Spanish soldiers and the natives two years earlier, caused in part by the summary execution of three Sobaipuris accused of stealing horses. The Indians had been caught roasting meat that the Spaniards thought was their horseflesh, but Coro showed them it was venison instead. The soldiers admitted their mistake and apologized, but the three natives remained dead nevertheless.

Kino's expedition had sent word ahead of their arrival, because surprise visits on the fringes of Apache territory were ill advised. Coro had prepared a magnificent reception, lodging Kino's entourage in an adobe house constructed just for that purpose, giving them reed mats to sleep on. The welcome fiesta included a scalp dance, celebrating a recent victory over the Apaches, recorded by the observant Manje: "All day long they celebrated by dancing in a circle around a high pole decorated with thirteen scalps…taken from as many slain hostile Apaches."[3]

The Spanish soldiers still harbored doubts about the loyalty of the Sobaipuris, despite Kino's assurances, and this finally convinced them that Coro and his people were allies. The visitors were also delighted to see the Sobaipuris had not accumulated the hundreds of horses and cattle stolen by the Apache from Spanish ranches and missions. Manje also noted that "the soldiers, too, took part in the dance, delighted in being undeceived."[4]

Capitan Coro and the Sobaipuris again proved their allegiance a few months later. On February 25, 1698, Apaches sacked and burned the nearby Cocospera mission, running off their horses. Kino summoned his Pima allies to join the Sonoran garrison in pursuit. They ran the thieves to the ground in the Chiricahua Mountains, killing thirty of the enemy and recovering their mounts. While this was going on, six hundred other Apaches, reinforced by Jocome, Janos, and Suma warriors, attacked Gaybanipitia, burning the village and killing three mares, which they immediately began to roast. Three miles downstream at Quiburi, Capitan Coro got word and hurried to the scene with five hundred warriors. A standoff ensued, with each headman choosing ten of his best warriors to settle their differences. The Sobaipuris prevailed, mainly because they were expert archers who could also dodge the enemy's arrows. The Apache headman was thrown to the ground, and Capitan Coro beat his head in with a rock. The Apaches broke ranks and ran, with the Pima archers in hot pursuit. When Kino and the Spanish soldiers tallied the final count a few days later, three hundred of the enemy had been killed, most of them by poison arrows. A church dignitary—none other than the Father Visitor of Sonora—gave "a thousand thanks to his Divine Majesty for the very fortunate event," but it was the Sobaipuris Pima who did the job. Kino's confidence in them had been vindicated.[5]

Manje's journal entries on the meetings between Kino and Coro suggested that the priest's uncritical acceptance of the native culture had much to do with the trust and affection they afforded him. His first order of business was preaching the Christian gospel, aided by two Pima interpreters, who were also trained catechists. This went on all day, with Kino also insisting on peace with the neighboring Sobaipuris living downriver. After delivering the precepts, Kino sat around all night with Coro and the other headmen, discussing matters and enjoying the give-and-take, as any other leader was expected to do. In fact, Kino's journals and biographies often make mention of these long exchanges with natives wherever he traveled, so the Jesuit must have been a good communicator and listener. He was interested in the people as individuals and not in their tribal customs, which engaged the attention of many other missionaries.[6]

The O'odham made important decisions collectively during such meetings, where the unanimous consent of all adult men was required. Perhaps Kino had perceived this from his many close interactions with O'odham people, or perhaps he just instinctively understood how fellow humans ought to act toward one another. But he clearly recognized the importance of the Indian grapevine. An oral culture, the O'odham immediately broadcast to others whatever they perceived about the missionaries, good or bad. Kino admonished his Jesuit brethren, "Hence it is so imperative not to offend or displease any one of them."[7] Scholars have also noted that Kino seldom criticized native customs or attempted to destroy what they already had. This, along with gifts of livestock, seeds, tools, and the knowledge of how to use them, made Kino beloved and welcome throughout the Pimería Alta.

But other Jesuits complained mightily about the ignorance, ingratitude, and laziness of all native people, one writing of his displeasure when the O'odham celebrated the end of a long drought by dancing naked in the first monsoon rain (an urge that any borderland rancher has felt). The moralist was apparently offended by clean, bare skin. If the natives had had a written language, they might have reciprocated their disgust at the smell of the unwashed priest, wrapped in his black robes despite the fierce desert heat.

Another Jesuit, Ignaz Pfefferkorn, expressed his astonishment at the complete tranquility of the indigenous Sonoran at death. He wrote: "At a time when circumstances of death are wont to weigh upon the heart…and glimpses into the future to excite horror and shuddering, the Sonoran gives not a single sign of an inner fear or disquietude."[8]

A cursory look at their two creation myths suggests an answer to the missionary's quandary. The Jesuit worshipped a perfect God who resided in the heavens and held absolute power over the earth and all its creatures. If—and it was this "if" that worried Pfefferkorn—if the Catholic Christian lived a good enough life, he or she would ascend to heaven and live in everlasting comfort. By contrast, the O'odham venerated I'itoi, an earthly god who lived in a cave, chased girls, made mistakes, and sometimes got lost. When the O'odham died, they returned to earth; death was a homecoming.

The cabalgantes make these rides to honor the memory and accomplishments of

Father Eusebio Francisco Kino, hoping to convince the Catholic Church that he is deserving of being canonized as a saint. I know nothing of the requirements for sainthood and so can offer no opinion, but Kino was clearly ahead of his time, rising above his peers in words and deeds— a praiseworthy example of what it meant to be a humanitarian in the context of the land, people, and times of the Pimería Alta.

THE PRESIDIO OF Santa Cruz Terrenate lay downriver about three miles from Fairbank on the river's west bank. The ford was not marked, but I had tied a white cloth on a willow branch where I crossed on a scouting trip a few weeks before. Lacey splashed across, and we scrambled up a faint trail leading to a high bench overlooking the river. The BLM had made hitching rails where we tied up the horses and entered the ruins on foot.

"The Spaniards were like sitting ducks," I mused out loud. Enrique, Pancho, Rene, and I stood alongside the crumbling adobe wall, looking east over the river to China Peaks.

"Reminds me a little of how the British colonials hunted tigers in India," I said.

"How's that?" Rene asked.

"They'd take a goat into the forest and tether it under a big tree. Then they'd break its leg so it bleated all night, while the gentleman hunters sat in the tree until the tiger came."

"So the goat was *cebo*—bait for the tiger," Enrique said. "And here, the soldiers were bait for the Apaches."

"Yes and no," I replied. "The Apaches were mostly after horses, at least in the beginning. They liked horses with lots of color, like the buckskin you rode in 2008."

"My last ride, Sonoyta to Caborca," Enrique mused wistfully.

Santa Cruz de Terrenate had been the northernmost bastion protecting Spain's hegemony over the Pimería Alta from Apache depredation. Starting in the 1600s, the Spaniards built a great arc of presidios, starting at El Paso on the east, then looping southwest down into Chihuahua at Buenaventura and Janos, and on to Sonora at Fronteras, Terrenate, and Tubac. The Compañía Presidial cavalry garrisoned these fixed fortifications, patrolling the adjacent countryside to intercept hostile invaders coming from the north. Behind the presidial lines, Compañías Volantes—the flying cavalries—lived in towns as emergency responders to confront raiding parties who had already penetrated the forward defenses.

I had been to Terrenate's original location twenty years ago, a peaceful village called

Santa Cruz, located a few miles south of the present-day border. By 2010, it had become a staging area for the Sinaloa cartel, smuggling marijuana and immigrants into Arizona. During the Spanish-Jesuit era, the wily Apaches still slipped by the presidios, raiding the rich settlements deep in Sonora and Chihuahua. Multiple atrocities were committed by both sides, reinforcing the mutual thirst for revenge. By 1772, King Carlos III had become fed up with the constant pilfering of his properties. He ordered his military governor, Hugh O'Conor, an Irishman with flaming red hair, to review the presidios and move them to more effective locations.

By the 1750s, the Spanish had figured out that the mountains ringing the San Pedro and Gila Rivers were strongholds for the Western and Chiricahua Apache bands. On August 22, 1775, O'Conor selected a site seventy miles north of Santa Cruz along the San Pedro to block the river trail into Sonora, confidently claiming that it would "effectively close the Apache frontier." Just two days before, he had ordered the Tubac Presidio to the present location of Tucson, Arizona; in so doing, he became the "founder" of Arizona's second-largest city.

While the Irishman rode off to become the governor of Yucatan, the Spanish soldiers of Terrenate packed up and rode northward—fifty-six elite leather-jacketed cavalry, each with six horses and one mule, two pistols, and one musket, sword, and lance. These were battle-hardened veterans, as tough and brave as any foreign frontier fighters the Southwest would ever see. But they were not native to this difficult land. Behind them trailed an unknown number of settlers and Christianized Indians, driving their oxen, cattle, wagons, and four hundred horses.

The new presidio would never be completed but became instead a death trap for the soldiers and a supply depot for their enemies. Construction began in early 1776 on this bluff fifty feet above the river's west bank, with walls of adobe brick laid on top of a low rock foundation, one hundred meters square. The main gate faced the river, with only a few yards of freeboard between it and the sheer cliff. Below, the river flowed as a broad, shallow stream, lined with cottonwood, willow, and ash—too far away, it seemed to me. From the front gate, I had to ride nearly a quarter mile to reach it, climbing down a steep arroyo, all the while exposed like a snail on a plank. On the opposite bank, cottonwoods and brush provided cover for the enemy.

Yet on the surface, the site appeared to be well chosen. Protected from frontal assault by the cliff overlooking the river, the north and south sides were flanked by arroyos, making it harder for the enemy to approach. The wide floodplain below had good soil and water for crops. To the west, rolling scablands of creosote bush and whitethorn reached clear to the Whetstone Mountains. To cover that open prospect, the Spanish plan included a raised bastion with cannon in the southwest corner. But the lack of a well within its perimeter would prove to be calamitous. Also, the huge horse herd had to be pastured miles away from the fort, and then driven back to the river to drink. Directly across the river from the presidio, a broad hill covered up the enemy's approach from their stronghold in the easterly Dragoon Mountains.

As soon as the Spanish arrived, the Apache began probing their defenses, running off a few horses. Then, at daylight on July 7, 1776, they attacked in force; two hundred warriors stormed the half-built main gate. Taken by surprise, Capitan Francisco Tovar and over half of his company were slain before the enemy faded back into the desert.

Next to where we stood, an iron plaque summarized Terrenate's brief history: three captains, ninety-five soldiers, and an untold number of settlers and tame Indians slain in less than five years.

Real Presidio de la Santa Cruz de Terrenate
1776–1780
Muerto en Batalla

7 julio 1776
Capitán Francisco Tovar
29 soldados

24 septiembre 1778
Capitán Francisco Trespalacios
27 soldados

nov 1778–feb 1779
39 soldados

Capitán Luis del Castillo
mayo 1779

Although reinforced several times, by the end of 1779, only twenty-six soldiers survived, and they were starving. All but four of the Christianized Indians had deserted, and less than one hundred horses remained. The Spanish abandoned the unfinished fort and limped back into Sonora.

By the time the Spanish started building the new presidio, the Apaches had had two hundred years to perfect their cavalry-based raiding tactics, often referring to the Spanish and later Mexicans as their "shepherds and flocks." They became the most prolific horse thieves in New World history, equals to the Mongols of the Asian steppes. The Apaches rode them, milked the mares, used them as pack animals, and ate them, but never established breeding herds like most tribes of the Great Plains. Perhaps they preferred the adrenaline rush of the raid over the day-to-day drudgery of husbandry.

The BLM erected placards in the Terrenate ruins, written in Spanish and English, labeling the parts of the unfinished fort: chapel, commander's quarters, main gate, barracks, and bastion. The cabalgantes spent most of the morning walking slowly around it, silent or speaking in hushed tones, as if afraid of waking some guardian chimera from beneath the hardened mud—a quiet intensified by the apprehended presence of ghosts. Even Lea, who had walked in from the road with Enrique, was subdued. The morning wind had a raw edge to it, sawing through the low acacia. In the riverbed, cottonwood leaves loped and skittered over dry stones. The midday sun was beating down when at last we turned to our horses to leave.

I took a last look eastward over the bajada and could sense the isolation and terror that had tortured these hapless people in the long ago. From beneath the ramparts of China Peaks, I pictured a legion of Apache warriors riding full gallop toward the flimsy sanctuary, where for nearly five years there had not been a single morning when the people of Terrenate awoke with the assurance that they would be alive the next day. The Spanish made the fatal error of trying to defeat a ruthless, mobile enemy, fighting on their native soil with a stationary fortification manned by an enclave of foreigners who were bewildered by their surroundings. For good reason, the Chiricahua Apache were called "the tiger of the human species" by General George Crook, America's most tenacious Indian fighter.

Back at Quiburi, on November 11, 1697, as Kino and Manje prepared to continue northward into the fringes of Apache territory, Capitan Bernal and the other soldiers balked, as they had been told that two hundred soldiers would be needed for this excursion. But Kino replied that they would be safe among the Sobaipuris, and Capitan Coro was going along with thirty of his best warriors as reinforcements. Even so, before starting, Father Kino said Mass (as he did each day), and the soldiers, including Manje, confessed and received communion, just in case things went wrong.

I LED THE cabalgantes off the bluff, taking the north trail, where our horses skidded down the sandy bank on their hocks until we reached the bottom of the deep arroyo. We stayed in single file, as the canyon was so narrow we could reach out and touch both sides at the same time. At the old railroad bed, we crossed under a trestle made of timbers dark with age. On the edge of the sun-sparkled river, Lacey spread his front legs like a giraffe and drank deeply from a quiet eddy, while small fish studied his nose.

A dead skunk lay on its side between the roots of a cottonwood, its black fur still shiny and its lips pulled back over needle teeth in a bloodless snarl. I couldn't see any marks on its body and started to dismount to have a look. But the veterinarians cautioned against it, saying skunks often die of rabies.

We splashed across the river shallows toward a water gauging station. So far, the river had maintained a healthy flow, fed by a wet winter and lingering mountain snow. But the San Pedro was a desert creature and in-stream water an ephemeral blessing. In the arid pre-monsoon months of May and June, when all the trees were fully leafed out, they sucked up so much water for photosynthesis that the river went dry by midday. After dark when the plants shut down, the water slowly retuned to the surface. Harking back to the new presidio's beleaguered history, the Spanish must have felt that they were dealing with the Devil incarnate, forcing them to fetch water at daybreak while Apache warriors waited in ambush.

We meandered alongside the river through mesquite brush and Bermuda grass, freshly grazed by cattle, judging from the spoor. A mile downriver, we came to Contention City, another ephemeral creature. Contention's shaky claim to prominence came from a silver lode discovered by a pair of mules—the four-legged variety. The mules broke loose one night and went in search of water, dragging their chains. Their owners, Ed Williams and Jack Friday, tracked them the next morning and noticed the gleam of silver where the chains had scraped the overlying dirt.

After recovering their mules at the nearby camp of rival prospector, Ed Schieffelin, Williams and Friday then raced to the claims office and filed their official papers. Schieffelin bitterly contested this as an infringement on his territory. To keep the peace, the claims officer played King Solomon and split the claim, awarding the north end to the two mule skinners and the south end to the irascible Schieffelin, who named it "Contention City."

Silver extraction required lots of water, and Schieffelin had to build the stamp mill on the river a dozen miles west of the mine. Established in 1879, Contention City became at first a tent and tin-shack ghetto, but the Tucson newspaper declared it would soon rival Tombstone. Two land promoters, D. T. Smith and John McDermott, surveyed the town site and started selling lots for $150 each. The post office was opened on April 6, 1880. The enterprising McDermott opened a saloon; a fleabag hotel soon followed, and then a blacksmith, butcher shop, and Chinese laundry. The 1882 census counted the population at 150 souls.

Milling was dangerous, dirty work. Mules hauled wagonloads of fist-sized chunks of ore from the mine. The mill itself perched on a hillside in three levels, to use gravity to move the ore through the processing. Ore dropped in the crusher at the top was reduced to chunks the size of apricots. Mixed with water, the coarse gravel was then pulverized at the next level by stamp mills made of heavy metal rods, dropped in rapid sequence by rotating camshafts, which created an ear-splitting din. The resulting slurry was then mixed with mercury. Silver adhered to the toxic heavy metal and the worthless, leftover tailings floated off. Heating the silver-mercury amalgam removed the mercury as a poisonous vapor, leaving purified silver. Each ton of ore required three tons of water, which was returned to the river—toxic to fish, livestock, and humans.

Contention City died a rapid death after the silver vein ran out in 1888. All we could see today was the three-tiered rock foundation scaling the hillside. In the quiet afternoon, the river gurgled along, unaware and uncaring of the small, dirty drama in which it had played a major part.

This was as far as I had scouted the route, but the BLM maps showed a trail to Saint David Cienega that followed the old railroad bed on the west side of the river. We crossed the river again and started a long, hot slog of a ride that took up the rest of the afternoon. As the horses plodded along, their hooves crunched into the loose black cinders. We had dropped almost a thousand feet in elevation from Palominas, and our horses began to sweat in the glare of the afternoon sun. The railroad track showed heavy use by ATVs and pickups—drug runners and Border Patrol chasing them toward Interstate 10.

The barbed-wire fence on the left side of the railroad marked the eastern boundary of the Sands Ranch, where I had rented four of our horses, including the hammer-headed small gelding that Ricky rode. Their land sloped down to the river from the Whetstone Mountains, cut here and there by deep, brushy arroyos that flooded during rainy season. Travis, their young foreman, told me they lost cattle every year in the river bottoms, when thunderstorms washed out their water-gap fences or when immigrants, drug packers, or Border Patrol cut the wires or left gates ajar. Every year he had to make a roundup from Contention City, driving the cattle north to Saint David corrals. Even so, some escaped and went feral. Travis was a Mormon cowboy from Graham County who loved the ranching life and was not given to exaggeration or cursing, but he hated the river bottom and its feral bovines—"wilder than the shit house mouse." Once, he lost a horse in the quicksand. The only way to work it is with cow dogs, he said. Nicko-lette, his wife, didn't like it either. The mesquite brush and whitethorn ate Travis's shirts like a paper shredder. She planned to talk to the ranch owner about a clothing allowance.

Sands Ranch cows were not the first example of wild, cloven-footed animals in the San Pedro River valley. Paleo-camels, now extinct, wandered the area during the ice age, thirteen thousand years ago. In the 1850s, camels returned, imported by the army for pack animals. Turned loose during the Civil War, they were spotted occasionally until the early 1900s.

Mexican cattle by the thousands had grazed the valley until the 1830s. After the Apache drove the Mexican ranchers back to Sonora, their cattle ran free. The natives hunted them like any other wild game, killing mostly the cows and calves. Before long, the herds had been reduced to large and lonely bulls. When the Mormon Battalion trekked down the river in December 1846, the bulls attacked and the Latter-day Saints fought their only battle of the 1846 war with Mexico, not against Mexican soldiers but against Mexican bulls, enormous in size, black in color, with "horns like unicorns" only double. The bulls gored several mules in the guts and one Mormon in the groin before retreating to look for their beloved lost cows.

TWO HOURS LATER, the water tower at the Apache Powder Company plant at Saint David appeared over the mesquite bosque. Across the river to the east, the bajada sloped down from the Dragoon Mountains and then broke off sharply in eroding cliffs that fell into the river bottoms. Soon, the river trees shrank back to the far eastern edge, and the bottom opened up into heavy bunchgrass meadows, marking the beginning of the Saint David Cienega.

Philemon C. Merrill, a survivor of the Battle of the Bulls, returned in 1877 and founded the town of Saint David. The Mormons tried farming at first, but the marsh-bred mosquitoes carried malarial fever, the same disease that later drove the soldiers out of Camp Crittenden a few miles southwest of Sonoita. The Mormons fled to the Huachuca Mountains, where they eked out a living by cutting timber for the mines and military. But the Latter-day Saints had been ordered by Brigham Young, their supreme leader, "to make the desert bloom like a rose." They returned to the river and dug an irrigation canal, draining the marshland. In 1880, the Southern Pacific Railroad pushed across the San Pedro River, giving birth to the town of Benson as a transportation hub. The hardworking Latter-day Saints prospered, their farms supplying produce to as far away as Tucson.

Saint David Cienega had another connection with Mexico in addition to the river's headwaters in Sonora: the monarch butterfly. During the summer, the marshy Cienega produces a sea of milkweed that is the only host plant for larval monarchs. The adults feed on milkweed nectar and lay their eggs on the underside of leaves, where the larvae hatch and feed for a month and then pupate and emerge as the stunning orange-and-black butterflies. In the fall, the adults migrate by the millions to winter in the Mexican state of Michoacán (as well as to California). Perhaps Kino would have seen them on one of his trips, but his diaries are silent on this morsel of natural history. His attention was focused on celestial matters.

A few hundred yards ahead, our trucks and trailers came into view at the Saint David Cienega corrals, marking the end of the San Pedro River Reserve. I, for one, was sad that it was over and would have gladly turned around and repeated the ride. We had seen the San Pedro not in the best of times—it was overgrown with mesquite and thorn scrub—nor in the worst of times, which was in the 1890s, when mining, drought, and cattle had reduced its grasslands and trees to bare dirt. But we had seen it in our time, under our terms, the desert river healthy with flowing water. And I had experienced it with a congenial, historically literate people with a strong connection to its landscape.

Today, the biggest threat to the river is not the illegal immigrants, or mining, or grazing, or farming, where the water is returned to the soil, but the surging urban/suburban development in Sierra Vista, Fort Huachuca, and Benson, which sucks down the water table, in effect killing the San Pedro's Corúa, the O'odham water serpent, like the city of Tucson has already done on the Santa Cruz River, fifty miles to the west.

Early on, I had decided to trailer the horses around Saint David and Benson. Marsh, quicksand, and farmers' fences made the riverbed impassable. We could have followed US Highway 80 north to Interstate 10, but my horses were not town-broke like the ones we rode in Hermosillo, and I didn't have spares. So we loaded up and trailered to the Dusty A7 Ranch, located six miles north of the freeway on the river's east side.

At the Dusty A7 Ranch, Shelby and Bonnie Twaits farmed several hundred acres of alfalfa and grass, irrigating their pastures with circular pivot sprinklers. A well-matched pair, Bonnie practiced veterinary medicine, specializing in horse reproduction, and Shelby trained quarter horses for cow work, while a herd of Angus cows completed their operation.

We unloaded next to the corrals and took an excursion over the farm, looking for the picnic area by the river where Shelby said we could camp. But his sprinklers had soaked it overnight. On the way back, we dropped into the riverbed, sliding down a steep bank of silt. North of Interstate 10, the character of the river changed. The once broad, shallow stream became a deep ditch, down-cut through the alluvial soil with vertical banks that were twenty and thirty feet high. Riding in the sandy bottom made us feel as if we had entered a vast, dry tunnel. The afternoon sun beat down on the white river sand, creating a convection oven that made the horses sweat as we labored along. We rode as far north as the confluence of Tres Alamos Wash, where tomorrow Shelby would take us to the ruins of a Sobaipuris settlement. Turning back, we scrambled up the riverbank and rode back through verdant fields that seemed out of place against the grays and browns of the surrounding desert.

At the corral gate, left-handed Pichi tried to side-pass Marvie to open it, but he kept turning away. He tried again, but Marvie still refused. "What's this?" Pichi muttered.

"Switch hands with your reins," I suggested.

Pichi changed reins to his other hand, and Marvie side-passed to the right, giving Pichi an easy reach to the latch, and then gave the gate a nudge with his nose to open it.

"The horse is a creature of habit, just like you and me. I've ridden Marvie for ten years, and he has never seen a left-handed rider until today." I grinned.

When we got to the corrals, Deb, the other gray horse, started kicking at his belly even before Pichito unsaddled. Pichito led him to water but only allowed him a few sips. We hadn't watered the horses since Terrenate, and the afternoon had been long and hot.

The horse has fifty feet of unsupported intestine that can get blocked by a hay bolus if dehydrated, causing intense pain. The trick was to get Deb out of pain and back to pooping again. Pichito quickly injected a drug to relax the smooth muscles in his gut and then poured two liters of mineral oil down a stomach tube. We took turns walking Deb around the corral for an hour until he let loose with a cannon shot over the top rail and pissed almost at the same time. Pichito followed up with electrolytes as a precaution. We gave him a drink and put him in a separate corral so he couldn't overeat and colic again.

"My fault," I said. "Deb's been turned out, and I didn't have time to get him in condition for the trip. He's so fat that rainwater would puddle on his backbone."

"Good thing he decided to colic now, when we could see it," Pichito said. "Colic's easy to treat if you catch it early—like a tummy ache in kids."

That night we had guests for dinner: Bonnie and Shelby Twaits and Tyler and April Bassinger, who had loaned us the horse that José Luis was riding. Tyler was a master farrier—the best in southern Arizona—and had been at it for so long that he walked with a stoop and had forearms as big as his thighs. José Luis asked him how many horses he had shod. Doing some quick math, Tyler figured a dozen horses a day, times five days a week, times fifty weeks, times thirty years.

"'Bout ninety thousand," he said. "Gonna quit when I get to a hundred grand."

"Figure ninety dollars each," I added.

"*Hijole!*" José Luis cried after a minute doing the math. "That's over twenty thousand dollars a month!"

"That's way more than I make on the ranch," I added. "Twenty grand a year's more like it, if I'm lucky."

"Oh yeah!" Tyler growled. "When I retire, I'm gonna do what you do. I'm gonna ride and never look back. I'll ride to where I can't even find a single day where I was shoeing horses." He took another sip of the Agave Azul and shook his head as if it had bugs in it. Then he passed it to April.

"Get that stuff away from me." She grinned, holding up both hands flat.

"Excuse her; she's one of those Saint David Mormons," Tyler said, taking another sip.

"But she puts a good handle on a colt. Man could drive the wheels off a new pickup and not find a better hand." Tyler took another sip, gripping the bottle with gnarly hands that could choke the life out of a bear.

April smiled back. "Stop your sweet talking, honey."

Pichi handed April a plate with beans, carne asada, and tossed salad. "Ladies first," he said. Pichi's cooking had a ceremonial sense of order, even though we had only one burner and not enough plates for our guests.

"You fellers sure do eat good. How do I get invited on one of these here rides?" Tyler asked.

"You are invited," José Luis jumped in. "Just bring me that good sorrel horse."

"You're ridin' Marshall?" Tyler asked.

"*Pues, sí.* He is very good in the quicksand. How did he get the name Marshall?"

"Fella named Marshall Ashcraft gave him to me for a bunch of shoeing I did. That honyocker didn't tell me Marshall had web feet."

We hadn't brought any extra plates, so we ate in shifts. Lea and Mike Weber drove up about then and got in line. I gave up my dishes and walked over to check on Deb. He was sleeping standing up, a good sign. I got back to the cook table in time to see Tyler get up.

"Well, people, it's time for me and April to go. We've got work to do tomorrow," Tyler said. "If your horses stumble, fall, or throw a shoe, call me, and I'll come fix it. Otherwise, I'll see you next year."

Lea brought a bag of pistachios, and we all sat around cracking them and tossing the shells in the fire. Bonnie was scheduled to do embryo transplants at a horse farm in Tucson the next week, and she invited Pichito and Pichi to go along. The technique involved flushing a mature ovum from a high-value mare and fertilizing it in a petri dish with sperm collected artificially from a chosen sire. The in vitro fertilized egg is then transplanted into a recipient mare. Mares have an eleven-month gestation period, and embryo transplantation allows several foals to be raised from the high-grade dam each year. This seemed like cheating Mother Nature, but breeders like it because the technique gives them more foals to sell.

On the downside, it dilutes the value of each consecutive foal. Also, there is no way to tell how much nurture is lost from the high-value mare by having her genetic offspring raised by a surrogate mother. Breeders brag to hell and back about the sire's influence, but the dam contributes way more than half, because the foal will have her disposition, in addition to her genes.

People who ride and use horses a lot will tell you that grit is priceless, and most of this "try harder" attitude comes from the dam. I'm kind of old-fashioned myself and prefer pasture breeding au natural. But then, I also think that women should rule the world. They don't let overloaded egos get in the way, like men so often do—except for the good Father Kino, of course. He, too, would have opposed artificial breeding, as the church regards it as sinful. But when science perfected the process for childless couples, the pope still couldn't see it in any other light.

SHELBY BROKE THE news that he couldn't show us the ruins at Alamos in the morning as planned. The memorial service for Rob Krentz would be tomorrow in Douglas, Arizona. Scarcely two weeks had passed since Rob's murder, and the borderlands were in an uproar over this senseless killing. I would have liked to have paid my respects also, but that would wait until November, when I went to see Wendy Glenn, Rob's neighbor, who had monitored his last radio transmission. Later, when I did visit, they still hadn't caught the killer, who had been tracked to the border on the day of Rob's murder. And he won't be found either, the Cochise County sheriff said, unless someone talks in Mexico. Given the massive Border Patrol and National Guard buildup afterward, chances were good that the killer was already toast. Increased publicity and law enforcement were the last things the cartel thugs wanted to see.

APRIL 10

WE RODE UP the river that morning to the confluence of Tres Alamos Wash, Ash Creek, and the San Pedro River. Shelby had said the ruins were on a bench on the east side of the river, just north of the confluence. We scrambled up an old road and spread out, riding northeast looking for signs. Cholla thickets made riding treacherous at first, but soon the vegetation changed to creosote bush, ocotillo, burroweed, and prickly pear, with scattered paloverde and mesquite. Following a dirt track, I came to a cross fence and signaled the others to the wire gate. Comparing findings, we had a few pottery shards, lots of shiny gun brass, beer cans, and a couple of broken coffee mugs. The bench may have been a Sobaipuris ruin, but lately, it had been a shooting range. The lack of usual immigrant-burrero trash meant that most of the traffic got picked up in Benson or on I-10.

"Well, people, let's go through the gate and give it another couple of hours. I could kick myself for not getting a map from Shelby," I said. "Archaeology is not my strong suit."

Three hundred thirteen years earlier, Kino's entourage proceeded downstream from Quiburi more cautiously, putting scouts ahead and sending messengers forward to the other Sobaipuris villages that the great Black Robe was coming. Everywhere, they entered settlements on roads swept clean and arches and crosses erected in his honor. Kino dispensed Christian instruction and baptized children, while the military officers harangued the villagers about loyalty and duty to the king, especially about the necessity of making the war on the Apaches. Twenty-five miles north of Quiburi, they arrived safely at Tres Alamos before dark. Manje noted the many shady cottonwoods (*los álamos*) and willows along the riverbank where they camped, along with good water, land suitable for cultivation, and excellent grazing. But his report said nothing about the down-cutting we had seen.

The following day, they reached a place in the river where cliffs came down on either side, narrowing the channel into a gap a few hundred yards wide. Here, Bernal and his soldiers balked again. This was the northernmost penetration by the Spanish military, a place where past patrols had turned back because of the threat of Apache ambush. Kino and Manje chided them, saying that these were not the Straits of Gibraltar, and they had little to fear. They rode on without mishap, after first putting a scouting party through the funnel.

The cabalgata, on the other hand, turned back after failing to locate the Los Alamos ruins. Our original plan had been to ride to the ranching settlement of Cascabel that lay some ten miles north of Los Alamos and beyond the narrows, and then trailer back to the ranch in Sonoita for the night. Failing to locate the Los Alamos ruins, we decided instead to return to the Dusty A7 and cut the ride short by a half day. Tomorrow was Sunday, and most of the riders had to return to Hermosillo. José Luis and Enrique were disappointed, but it seemed like the best option.

At home in Sonoita, we uncovered another miscue, as sometimes happens when dealing in a second language. When José Luis and I made the deal about horses and food, he understood that they would bring the *cena de despidida*–the farewell dinner. But Diane and I had intended to feed the whole crew at our house, along with Rich and Jackie and a few neighbors. As it turned out, everyone ate enough for two, so nothing went to waste.

Jesus Enrique gave a short talk about how Kino and Manje had continued on to the confluence of the San Pedro and Gila Rivers, opening up the eastern boundaries of the Pimería Alta. Riding west along the Gila, they were astonished by the four-story-tall Casa Grande, a mud adobe city that the ancient Hohokam abandoned in the thirteenth century. On the day of their arrival, Father Kino neither drank nor ate, in order to be pure when he offered Mass inside the ruins. The nearby villages had hundreds of friendly native farmers, ripe to harvest for the Lord and eager for the horses, cattle, and seeds that came with conversion. Enrique hoped that on future rides, we too would be able to complete the same long circle. Kino and Manje returned from the Casa Grande ruins by way the Santa Cruz River past Tucson, Ambos Nogales, San Lázaro, and down the San Miguel River to Dolores mission. All told, they rode 650 miles in twenty-nine days, while taking time to census 4,700 persons in 920 houses and baptizing eighty-nine, explaining the Catholic faith to all with whom they came in contact and making the maps and geographic observations of landscapes and peoples previously unknown to Europeans. And they lost not a single man during their trip.

José Luis made an accounting of our expenses and discovered that we had an $800 surplus. Looking at me, he said, "I suggest two options. We can give this to Ricardo for the extra expenses he had—use of the trucks and trailers, sleeping here, and so forth—or we can use it to pay for Enrique's journal." Enrique had kept a journal on each of the twenty-three rides, showing the routes taken, along with many photographs. His goal was to have copies printed by the end of the year.

No one said anything, but they all looked my way.

"You mean that money is mine?" I asked.

"Of course," José Luis said.

"Thank you very much," I said, taking the wad of twenty-dollar bills from his hand and counting it as I walked slowly toward Enrique. "Since it is mine, I give it to Enrique for the Cabalgata journal. It has been our pleasure to do this."

MONTHS LATER, WHEN I read José Luis's account of our ride in the official cabalgata journal, he pointed out two major differences between riding in Mexico and the United States. First, in the States, we could not ride in the nature reserves, towns, highways, or private property without first getting permission, and sometimes permission was withheld for various reasons—or for no apparent reason. In Mexico, the cabalgata was welcomed everywhere, and rancher owners and ejidatarios gladly offered their cow camps and other facilities for our use and comfort. And we rode through the towns and state capital without any fuss by the authorities.

Second, the ride in the United States was more relaxed, with time to explore and appreciate the natural and cultural history of the landscape and to get acquainted to the local people. In Mexico, the routine was to leave camp at seven-thirty and stop at six in the evening, in order to make the thirty to thirty-five miles per day that Father Kino averaged during most of his trips. At our speed on the San Pedro River, José Luis opined that we would need another twenty-two years to cover the distance Kino and Manje rode in a month going straight through.

Matching Kino's speed no doubt gives my friends a closer feeling of kinship with their exemplar Jesuit. But I wondered if the Catholic tradition of penance, the voluntary self-punishment to make amendment for sin, also figured into their motivation. Manje noted in his journal that Kino practiced self-flagellation to purify his soul, a common practice by priests of the medieval era. Perhaps for the Catholic cabalgantes, the daylight-to-dark routine amounted to wearing a hair shirt.

Part 4

Cerro El Nazareno: 2011

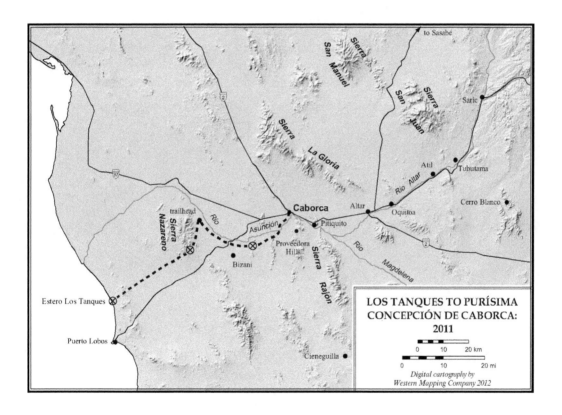

LOS TANQUES TO PURÍSIMA CONCEPCIÓN DE CABORCA:
2011

0   10   20 km

0   10   20 mi

Digital cartography by
Western Mapping Company 2012

Father Kino had the Apaches, while we have
the *sicarios* [assassins] to worry about.

—José Luis Salgado

After failing to reach Cascabel in 2010, our goal on the upper San Pedro River, I decided to spend more time scouting the possible routes to Casa Grande Ruins National Monument for 2011. Two problems were immediately apparent from looking at the maps and Manje's 1697 travelogue. First, the distance by river miles amounted to thirty-five miles per day for five days. Second, Kino and Manje took seven days to reach the ruins, with time out for negotiating a truce between Captains Coro and Humari on the lower San Pedro and for connecting with the other Pima-speaking tribes farming along the Gila River. Distance-wise, this reach divided better into two three-day rides—the first from Cascabel to Winkelman; the second from Winkelman to the Casa Grande Ruins.

Also, the river bottom was deep sugar sand in places, according to Tyler Bassinger, and farmers and ranchers had cross-fences we would have to navigate around. That left the option of riding the state highway right-of-way to Winkelman and the confluence of the Gila River. The most historically interesting part of this route would be Aravaipa Creek, where in November 1697, Kino and Manje linked up with Chief Humari and where in 1871, the infamous Camp Grant massacre took place.

When I sent this information to the Salgados, the reply was that 2011 was the three hundredth anniversary of Father Kino's death in Magdalena and riding in Sonora this year would be a more fitting tribute. I heartily agreed. Not only would Sonora be more appropriate, but riding the highway right-of-ways in Pinal County would be a butt-numbing event, even for the most ardent Kinophile. Instead, we would place a cross on top of Cerro Nazareno, where in 1693, Kino had first looked across the narrow beginnings of the Sea of Cortés. That mighty panorama so fired his curiosity that during the next years, the explorer pushed overland to the confluence of the Gila and Colorado Rivers, traveling down the latter all the way to the sea.

Kino's many arduous journeys to the coastal regions of the Pimería Alta produced irrefutable evidence that Baja California was a finger-like peninsula sticking out from the fist of mainland California, rather than an island. His enthusiasm for geography and exploration made me rather suspect that Kino's true calling was not that of a mission priest, but that the trail was his real home, and his life was one long horseback journey into the unknown. Even so, our ride would end at the elegant Caborca church that he founded in 1692.

That church was a favorite on the Kino mission tours, Lea had told me on our return from the 2008 ride. I was keen to see it, so much so that the month before the 2011 ride, I went to see San Xavier del Bac with Lea and a group from Tucson. Dr. Bernard Fontana, who had lived alongside the O'odham for decades, led the tour. Until then, I hadn't realized that the "White Dove of the Desert" had been completed by the Franciscan order after the Jesuits were expelled from New Spain in 1767, even though Father Kino had started its construction in 1700. The splendid exterior soared into the clear morning sky, but the baroque interior seemed garish and overly ornate. I preferred the simplicity of clean, white, handmade walls like those of the smaller churches in the Sierra Madre and wanted to see Caborca to make a comparison. After three cabalgatas and a ton of reading, I had developed a mental picture of Father Kino as an energetic, no-frills man of action who liked to get things done so that he could move on to the next new thing.

Lea was delighted. She had many friends in Caborca, including the Venegas family, who owned the motel where her tours stayed and a ranch where Carlos Venegas celebrated a traditional *churrasco* (barbeque) for her guests. By now, the cabalgantes had become Lea's extended family and a strong connection to her shared past with Oscar and the mission tours. José Luis and Enrique always included her in the e-mails and deliberations about dates and locations. Lea continued with her tradition of bringing a fine brandy to ward off our saddle sores at the end of the day. This year she added trail mix and pistachios for horseback cocktail snacks.

Our ride would start at an estuary called Los Tanques, just south of El Desemboque, where the Rio Concepción empties into the Sea of Cortés. This was near the place where Kino and Manje had planned to launch a homemade boat to resupply the Jesuit mission of Loreto, across the gulf in Baja California. Kino's stalwart Jesuit colleague, friend, and fellow Italian, Juan María Salvatierra had founded the mission in 1697, and he was in desperate need of cattle and other supplies from the mainland. The voyage never came to fruition, fortunately perhaps, because neither Kino, Manje, nor their Pima carpenters had any experience with building ships. And the cottonwood, which was the only large tree available, was too soft and porous for an ocean-going vessel.

February 3

Lea and I arrived midday at the Salgado farm on the outskirts of Hermosillo. José Luis and the other riders had left earlier, following the eighteen-wheeler that was carrying thirty-five horses. At the farm, we met up with Enrique and Ricardo Ramonet, who had a van stuffed with duffel bags and food. We stacked the saddles and tack in my pickup bed and secured the load with a tarp. A hard freeze had been forecast for the next two nights, so I included extra horse blankets.

Heading west out of Hermosillo toward the Sea of Cortés, Ricardo guided us to a broken asphalt road that linked up with the new highway north to Libertad, Puerto Lobos, and Puerto Peñasco. We passed through miles of barren farmland, abandoned when the underground aquifer was depleted. Ricardo's farm was several miles southwest of here, and he too had had to deepen his wells and was converting to a water-saving drip irrigation system. Ricardo grew pecans, oranges, and melons, as well as chickpeas (garbanzos), a drought-tolerant crop adapted to Sonora's climate.

"We export them to Europe," he said.

"How much longer do you think you can farm where you are?" I asked.

"Twenty years, I hope, with new technologies of irrigation," he replied.

"Do you still grow those delicious navel oranges?" I asked, remembering the luscious fruit from the 2008 ride.

"We replaced them with garbanzos to use less water."

"*Lastima!*" I groaned. "I've been hungry for one ever since we left home this morning."

Ricardo hoped that within twenty years' time, desalination of seawater would be economically feasible. The coastal area of Sonora from here south to the Ríos Yaqui and Mayo and on into Sinaloa supplied most of the winter vegetables and spring melons for the United States. He also had faith that genetic engineering would develop high-value crops that used less water and that would be more salt-tolerant. Ricardo has lectured at the University of Sonora on the value of transgenic crops, but he said a small group of academics with no practical farming experience opposed their use.

"On what grounds?" I asked.

"That they will take over the traditional varieties and lead to monocultures," he replied. "Like corn and alfalfa or the dwarf, disease-resistant wheat."

"Those are already monocultures in the United States, except for a few artisan farmers who grow for niche markets."

"Mexico must continue to produce enough to feed itself. Those who say no to transgenic crops have never been hungry," Ricardo replied.

"Norman Borlaug called the artisan farmers elitists," I said, "but I think they have a valid point when talking about subsistence farming. The old varieties grow better where they were developed. Have a better taste, too."

"We have a saying," Ricardo replied. "*Si tiene hambre, no hay pan duro.* I will translate: if you are hungry, there is no such thing as hard bread."

Just ahead, the road T-boned into the coastal highway. As we approached the intersection, a squad of men stepped out of the brush, wearing camouflage and bristling with automatic rifles.

"Stop and do what they say," Ricardo cautioned in a low voice. "I'll do the talking."

The man with sergeant stripes came to my side of the truck, a machine gun slung loosely over his shoulder. Our interrogator was a short, thickset man with a pockmarked face. Wraparound sunglasses and a camouflaged cap shaded his eyes. Behind him and a little to his left, a soldier stood with an assault rifle held at the ready, balanced against his hip. Backing them up were four other men, two on either side of the road, their rifles pointed toward our trucks. Looking in the cab, the sergeant asked where we were going. Ricardo explained the cabalgata, mentioning the truck that had passed by here earlier with horses and that we were carrying the saddles and food. The sergeant looked at my Arizona vehicle registration upside down and asked to see the Mexican insurance that Lea and I had fortunately purchased that morning in Nogales. He pulled up the edge of the tarp and peered at the saddles, wrote down my license plate number, and then walked to Enrique's van and repeated the check.

"Mexican army," Ricardo said, exhaling. "It should be no problem."

Stepping back, he waved to the other soldiers, and we turned north on the newly paved road. A few months ago, Puerto Peñasco's police chief and bodyguard had been gunned down. The State Department issued warnings that the Sinaloa cartel had increased its presence there, as well as along the border from Sonoyta and all the way to Agua Prieta.

"They are looking for drugs going north to Sonoyta. On the road to my farm, they also have checkpoints," Ricardo said.

"It reminded me of my days in Guatemala. Those guys looked like Mayan Indians."

"Many of Calderón's troops here are from the south. The army sends them to the opposite end of the country so they are not operating in their homelands, fighting against their own people."

"The Border Patrol has checkpoints on our side too," I said, "but they don't look nearly as serious as those guys."

"Calderón has a war on his hands," Ricardo said. "You have only burreros and drug addicts to worry about."

Approaching Libertad, my pickup announced its need for gas with a ding, and we stopped at a Pemex station beside the ocean. The air was still, and the temperature readout on the dashboard had plunged to below freezing; the low sun over the water offered no warmth. Above the quiet waves, *pangas* (fishing boats) lay on their sides like beached whales. In 1694, Juan Mateo Manje called Libertad "a little port shaped like a sack…inhabited by an infinity of fishes."[1] Red lights blinked on the towers of the electrical generating plant on the far point of the cove; the odor of diesel smoke coated the town. I turned over the keys to Ricardo. In case of another roadblock, it would be better if he were driving, especially after dark.

We drove on for twenty miles without passing another vehicle, until a police car waved us over to a side road. Enrique had arranged an escort of off-duty police, and we followed his pickup into the Estero Los Tanques camp. Enrique said that the armed guards would serve notice to the local gangs that we were not a bunch of pushover tourists.

"We are learning to adapt to the violence," he added.

José Luis quipped, "Father Kino had the Apaches, while we have the *sicarios* [assassins] to worry about."

The campsite was on damp sand a few hundred yards from the sea, where the other vehicles had circled the trailers. Gaspar had a big fire going under a pot of menudo, and we tumbled out of the truck to greet Pichi, Rene, Father Sinohui, and other friends from past cabalgatas. Pichi had a brace on and said he was driving a supply truck this trip because of back surgery a few weeks before.

This was a big crowd, and the new faces included Domingo Pesqueira, from the town of Altar, and Marco Antonio Martínez, Patricia O'Daly de Martínez, and a professional photographer, all three from Nogales, Sonora. To accommodate everyone, José Luis had hauled in extra horses, although Pesqueira and a few others had brought their own personal mounts. Pichito and Daniel Sotelo were scattering tacos of hay around the perimeter of a large portable corral made with steel T posts and yellow rope. María José took my extra blankets and put them on her thin-haired barrel horses.

After checking the weather report last week, I had rushed to Tucson and invested in a wool stocking cap, heavy gloves, and mountaineering underwear. I had decided against the tent, as there was no rain in the forecast. They cost a lot, and I already had a tarpaulin to throw over my lovely, luxurious one-piece cot that I unfolded in the last light of the day. The blood-red sun throbbed in the freezing haze as it dropped smoothly below the ocean horizon.

AT DAWN THE next morning, the temperature had sunk to six degrees below zero. The tents looked like a cluster of igloos from the moist ocean air that had frozen on the outsides. Ricardo got a text message from the farm, saying his garbanzos had frozen, but the watermelons had survived. A black plastic cover over the rows kept the heat in. Our ranks thinned out when Alejandro Robles and his son from Chihuahua had to hurry home to take care of cattle caught in the blizzard. Before they left, I asked about Ramón Lujan, the rancher who rode with us in the Sierra Madres. Killed in a horse wreck last year, Alejandro replied. The horse he was riding flipped over backwards on top of him. Not riding that good natured stallion, I asked. Alejandro said he didn't see the wreck but heard that Lujan was on a different horse gathering cattle in the mountains when it happened.

In the rising sun, we caught the horses by using buckets of grain as chum; the holdouts had to be roped one by one. Rene Balderrama stood in the center of the pen, throwing his overhand loop while the last few horses circled the corral like dizzy fish in a bowl. We led them to Los Tanques, breaking through the ice with Gaspar's axe, but they refused to drink the brackish water. Cinching up, the cold-backed horses got froggy and hopped around the corral, but the sand was a soft landing for the riders who bailed off. Today, we would ride thirty miles, the last part across a ranch belonging to the Pesqueira family. Domingo Pesqueira had hauled his own horse, a stocky, red roan gelding with foxy ears and hard black feet. With his steep-angled hocks and easygoing disposition, the horse seemed as close to the Spanish Barb as one could find.

The name Pesqueira runs through Sonoran-Mexican military-political history like Andrew Jackson does in the United States. Ignacio Pesqueira was born in Arizpe, just north of Huepac, in 1820, where his father served as captain in the Spanish cavalry before Mexican independence. Ignacio, at the age of twenty-four, commanded militia forces, protecting towns on the Río Sonora against the Apaches. Later, he took on the French Imperial Army when Napoleon III tried to annex the whole country. Pesqueira's armies routed the French and forced them to sail from the port of Guaymas in disgrace. Elevated to the post of interim governor in 1856, Ignacio Pesqueira became the *caudillo* (strongman) of Sonora after beating back multiple challenges from Manuel Gándara, who had occupied the post for the previous twenty years. In 1857, Pesqueira extinguished a threat from California freebooters who sought to annex Sonora, meting out a form of frontier justice that has been reenacted in a dozen Hollywood grade-B movies.

Riding horses through the surf would have been fun, except for the freezing temperature. Also, a Seri Indian camp was nearby, but I knew that José Luis and Enrique's goals were ecumenical, not anthropological. We struck out northeast through a sparse landscape of brittlebush, creosote, fourwinged saltbush, and wisps of galleta grass, each plant with great spaces of red sand in between. Mists of breath flared from the horses' nostrils as they nodded their heads and tossed their bridles, impatient to go. I got lucky and drew a smooth-gaited, rangy sorrel gelding that slow-trotted on a loose rein. Even so, after hearing about Lujan, I warmed the gelding up by lunging him on the ground until he relaxed and licked his lips. As the sorrel circled around me, I wondered what had gone bad that day in the mountains. Don Ramón was a prudent horseman born to the saddle, and about my age as well.

We crossed the Santa Rosa Wash, draining the southern flank of the Cerros Blancos hills, where a few starveling trees grew on its margins. As we climbed the rugged volcanic slopes, ironwood, cholla, and cordon appeared, along with a tortured ocotillo species with twisted stems. Ricardo pointed out indigo bush, saying the Seri Indians used the branches for thatching their brush huts. The morning sun cut through the chill, but the sky was empty and no wind blew. A curve-billed thrasher burst forth in song, proclaiming ownership of the solitary ironwood tree against all others of his kind.

The thickened brush gave off musty smells from cow dung that had accumulated beneath trees pruned up by hungry cattle. We came into a clearing of sorts, with a concrete *abrevadero* (drinking trough) in the center of mesquite wood corrals, with a windmill hanging lifeless in the cold air. We dismounted and skimmed off the ice, and the horses drank deeply from the sweet water.

"Papolote Santa Rosa," José Luis said, looking at his Google-generated map. "Now we start to climb."

Leaving the corral, we passed a lone black Angus cow, waiting to drink. She had a yellow ear tag with the number three, which gave her an impression of refinement all out of proportion to the landscape. The trail, such as it was, turned into shards of volcanic rock, angular and sharp-edged, yet Domingo Pesqueira and his vaquero picked their way along sure-footedly, with the cabalgata strung out behind.

A group of O'odham had roamed this landscape from the Sea of Cortés, northeast toward Caborca, when Kino first encountered them in December 1693. Their leader,

El Soba, was a renowned warrior who had long been feuding with the Eastern Pima. A decade before, El Soba had, in fact, killed the headman of the Cosari Pima, who lived close by to Kino's home mission of Dolores. Following the standard operating procedure of how church and state worked together, Kino reported these new people (numbering perhaps four thousand) to General Domingo Jironza, requesting his participation in taking care of military and political affairs, while Kino administered to their souls. The general assigned his nephew, Lieutenant Juan Mateo Manje, who made this the first of nine expeditions as Kino's close partner in the coming years.

Kino also had two other able helpers: Francisco Cantor, an interpreter (Kino did not understand Pima, at least in the beginning), and Coxi, a Pima headman whom Kino baptized as Carlos. Coxi was well known in the area and forged ahead to the rancherías with the news that the great missionary was coming. A trained catechist, the bilingual Cantor made Kino's messages clear to the natives and helped form local church groups.

The men came back together in February 1694, retracing Kino's previous steps. Manje was also favorably impressed with the new country, noting the fertile land, water, and abundant pasture. During their stay, Kino preached the gospel, baptized infants, and passed out meat, flour, and other presents. The Sobas begged him to come back and bring a missionary to stay among them. Looking back on the earliest contacts between priest and native, one might conclude that the O'odham, at first, understood this as a windfall in addition to a revelation: water sprinkled on the baby's head and a new creation myth in exchange for horses, cattle, food, and tools. But they soon discovered that more strings were attached to the exchange.

Even in the dead of winter, the hardy Sobas appeared in their natural state, including the valiant El Soba. Manje described him "as poor as he was naked, without any other ornament than innocence."[2] Taking pity, the two explorers gave him a pack load of pinole flour. With nothing to carry it in, El Soba took two deerskins from his women and made sacks while the two Christians looked on, noting the Indian's lack of shame at being unclothed. Shivering in my canvas saddle coat and long johns, I marveled at their cold-hardiness, walking around in their birthday suits in the middle of winter.

TWO PARALLEL RIDGES separated by a narrow, brush-filled valley ran southward downhill from the summit of Cerro Blanco. We crossed over the first ridge, through a low saddle treed with ironwood, saguaro, cordon, and jojoba bush, a plant much valued for cattle browse. As early as 1716, missionaries were sending jojoba oil back to the

Vatican, as it was thought to cure baldness among the cardinals. Descending into the valley, we came up on the lee side of a small dam crossing a deep arroyo. A cave on one side of the canyon showed signs of recent habitation, with a neat, small hearth at the entrance. Peering in, I could see a candle stuck in a crevasse and a tattered jacket that someone had hung on a spike. A barbed-wire fence encircled the dam and pond behind it, and I thought maybe the cave was where the vaquero camped when he worked this side of the range.

"*Yo no.* The Papagos walk this way," the vaquero said. If so, then the cave may have been used long before the dam was built. The O'odham had long foraged over these coastal mountains, hunting bighorn sheep. Sheep had been a regular part of their diet for millennia, as well as a totemic creature whose horns and skulls required special disposal. In one village along the Gila River, Manje reported a two-story-tall mound of sheep horns ritually left out in the desert, far away from the O'odham rancherias.

The O'odham also had a tradition of making winter pilgrimages to the Sea of Cortés to collect salt and dreams. These journeys served as coming-of-age tests for young men, who followed their elders to the ocean where they bathed and fasted for days, waiting for the surf to bring them a dream song that would guide them for the rest of their lives. Perhaps Kino and Manje had bumped into El Soba returning from such a pilgrimage. Today, O'odham poet Ofelia Zepeda speaks of the O'odham pull to the sea, recording the fervent desires of O'odham elders to see the ocean before death. Old habits die hard, especially if recorded in song. Perhaps this explained the absence of the Papagos in Quitovac during our stopover in 2008; perhaps not. But it gives me pleasure to think that their cultural traditions could still be strong.

We entered the campsite from the rear, a ramshackle frame house with strips of dried meat hanging from a clothesline. The dwelling looked abandoned except for the packrats nesting in the oven of the propane stove and in the corner of the outhouse. In the bottom of a deep arroyo, Pichito and José Luis began bailing water from a hand-dug well with a bucket and pulley, while rest of us set up the rope corral around the well and then scattered hay around. Enrique, Lea, and Pichi had already arrived, and Gaspar, as usual, had the cook trailer set up and a big fire going. The busy Father Kino must have had several Gaspars!

Kino and Manje usually traveled with a dozen or more servants, as well as the herdsmen and muleteers necessary to manage the thirty to one hundred horses that needed pasture and water each day. Even so, their journals sometimes made note of dry camps. Without native guides to lead them to water, the explorers surely would have perished. José Luis wisely followed Kino's example by using a local vaquero as a guide to water holes, and our supply truck carried hay and grain.

During their expeditions to the western deserts, Kino and Manje often sent relays of spare horses and supplies ahead to way stations like Sonoyta. Yet their journals had little to say about what they rode. Given the mileage they covered, twenty to fifty miles a day, they had to have extra mounts. A short-coupled horse like the Spanish Barb could walk four miles per hour and faster at a running walk or a trot. Along the way, Kino was occupied with ecclesiastical chores, as well as making maps and journal entries, so he must have hurried his horse or mule right along. When Kino made mention of his mount, it was often a mule (a hybrid cross between a jack burro and a mare). A mule would make sense, because it is narrower over the rib cage and therefore easier on the hips and knees. Also, a mule can carry 25 percent more weight than the average horse and get by on less food and water. Since the priest plowed straight ahead and didn't need the coordinated spins, turns, side-passes, and stops of a fighting horse or a cow horse, mules were the better choice, provided his vaqueros could find one or two that didn't kick or bite.

Much of what we know about Sonoran horses of the Jesuit/Spanish era comes from the German Jesuit Ignaz Pfefferkorn, who worked in the Pimería Alta forty-five years after Kino's death. With typical Germanic thoroughness, Pfefferkorn described the many fine qualities of the Spanish Barb: relatively small, sturdy and strong boned, proud and fiery, swift and gritty, yet easily tamed. The one preferred for everyday road travel, the *caballo de camino* had a speedy yet comfortable gait, so comfortable in fact that Pfefferkorn claimed he could ride right along, holding a cup of water without spilling a drop.

But the soldiers and vaqueros preferred the field horse, both in battle and for everyday work like roundups on the haciendas. Indeed, early descriptions of roundups in Sonora sounded a lot like warfare. Field horses were raised in rough country and trained from an early age to run at top speed over the rugged terrain without the benefit of shoes, a conditioning process that made the survivors swift, sure-footed, and durable. Each Spanish soldier had a string of five to six such horses and one mule for carrying provisions. To bolster the resolve of his newly arrived missionaries, Caballero Kino compared the tedious task of converting natives to the making of such a durable mount: "The more spirited the horse, the harder to convert, but the wild horse once broken in, made a better and more spirited charger."[3]

Later on, the sturdy Spanish Barb became the foundation horse for most of the

Indian ponies bred by native people in the Americas, not only on the Great Plains but also by tribes east of the Mississippi River. In Texas, the Spanish horse was crossed with English breeds like the Thoroughbred and others, and became the foundation stock for the Quarter Horse breed used today on western ranches, as well as for horse shows, rodeos, and cutting contests. But the show horse and ranch horse can differ by a country mile. Show people look for pretty, fat, and slick; the rancher, vaquero, and cowboy look first at the feet, legs, and back for soundness. One of my better ranch horses had a head shaped like an ironing board, and hair like rusty wire. His big, black hooves never lost a shoe, he never needed the vet, never missed a day's work, and never became friendly.

The early version of the ranch horse also conspired with the landscape to produce today's icon of western Americana, the cowboy. Historically on farms, the cowherd was often a mentally defective adult or child, good for little else except ensuring that the cows grazed where they should and bringing them home safely to the barn at night. The vast spaces of the American West required a different sort of husbandry—wilder and more free-ranging. To do the job, the cowherd needed a horse, rope, spurs, gun, and big hat, trappings that normally belonged to the upper class. The cowboy became the "Image of the Worker in Glory," according to writer Marilynn Robinson. The horse made him mobile, free, and fast, and the ways in which he went about his daily chores evolved into equestrian art forms imitated today in horse shows and rodeos all over the West. The well-trained cow horse operates by sight and feel—the slightest shift of the rider's weight or a gossamer touch of the reins. The sensation of speed and unity between horse and rider is exhilarating, an ecstasy that has inspired a thousand horsey legends as far back as the mythical winged horse, Pegasus that carried the Greek god Zeus seven centuries before the birth of Kino's Christ Child.

In the twenty-first century, ranches on either side of the border still require horses to work cattle efficiently. An ATV, helicopter, pickup, or person afoot cannot sift through mesquite thickets or climb down the canyons to ferret out the cattle, or rope a bagged-up cow five miles from the corrals to milk her out and save the calf, or drive a herd of cantankerous cows for miles over rolling scablands, or cut off the calves from their mamas in the corral. All the same, the Mexican vaqueros first developed the skills that were later adopted by America's working cowboys. Witness his vocabulary peppered with words corrupted from Spanish: "dally" roping where the roper takes a turn around the saddle horn comes from *dar la vuelta*; chaps, the leather leggings from *chaparreras*; lasso, to rope something from *lazar*; latigo, from *latiguera*, the leather strap that tightens the cinch girth; McCarty from *mecate*, meaning reins braided from horse hair used on hackamores. And corrupted place names, too. My favorite one is Monkey Springs, from *Agua de Monje*, the main source of Sonoita Creek near my home, discovered by Juan Mateo Manje, Kino's soldier sidekick.

Today's ranch horse still runs on solar power—the sun's energy stored in grass—with no recharge necessary or gas tank to refill, a virtue increasingly important as we run short of fossil fuels. The problem these days is finding a cowboy with a string of good horses who knows how to do the work. One advantage of ranching on the borderlands used to be the pool of handy vaqueros from Sonora. Now, the old vaqueros with work papers have retired, and getting new work permits for the younger ones has become next to impossible.

On ranches today, cowboys ride eight hours a day, more or less. The rule of thumb is that a horse gets three days off for every day worked, so each rider needs a string of four horses, sound and shod. Kino's trails were easier than gathering cattle; even so, the Jesuit must have had a favorite quartet. An average day's ride on the cabalgata was twelve hours in order to match Kino's distances. Even for a seasoned rider, four straight days of this can be arduous; for those who don't ride at all, even one day can be hell. The mistake new riders often make is to tense up, fighting against the horse's movement instead of relaxing into its stride.

At the end of the day, you are acutely aware of the horse's step, the tiredness in your bones, the terrain immediately ahead, and the friends around you.

AROUND THE CAMPFIRE that evening, I asked about the narcotics problem in Sonora. One of the cabalgantes had been a rancher but now lived in Nogales, Sonora, where he owned a business. In his opinion, the news media had exaggerated the amount of violence.

"Yes, the drug people are killing each other," he said, "but that has not changed our lives very much. Nowadays, people just have to be more careful about where they go and when." When I asked about the legalization of drugs, he replied thoughtfully, "Laws should reflect the reality of society."

In 2009, Mexico decriminalized the possession of small amounts of narcotics for personal use, recognizing the reality that small-time users are almost never prosecuted. Others thought the United States should have legalized drugs first; otherwise, the demand would continue to drive competition between cartels, provoking violent clashes between rivals and with Mexican law enforcement.

Mexican Vaquero

José Luis again said that Hermosillo does not have a drug violence problem because there are few users and one group is in control—the Sinaloa cartel—so they don't have competitors trying to cut into their business. But if and when the demand for narcotics drops off, either through legalization or the United States securing the border, would not the cartels diversify into other crime, like kidnapping, robbery, human trafficking, and protection rackets? In fact, they already have in other places like Tijuana, Ciudad Juárez, Monterrey, and Nuevo Laredo, where they have become nearly as powerful as the Mexican government. Another business owner in the cabalgata said that if the cartel starts with the extortion/protection racket, the only option would be to immediately close down. "Once you start paying off, there will be no end to it," he said.

Another rider, who was also a schoolteacher, had a more alarming perspective. He had done his public-service teaching in the Sierra Madre near the border with Chihuahua, where some families grow marijuana as a cash crop. In these small towns, most people, especially children, live in situations of chronic scarcity—jobs, food, money, health care, and education—everything except family and church. So when a narco comes around and gives them a chance to earn money, many are tempted to join up. They look at drugs as job opportunities, not as crimes. But the pushers are like pharmaceutical reps, giving out free samples to increase consumption, he said. Pot and meth make them feel good at first, and peer pressure to experiment is strong.

His view was that the drug threat in Hermosillo was on the rise. He told the story of the recent capture of Edgar Valdez Villarreal, "La Barbie," of the Beltrán-Leyva cartel. Villarreal, a former football star in a Laredo, Texas, high school, had drifted across the border and became a cartel enforcer and cocaine trafficker. Following the death of his boss, Arturo Beltrán-Leyva, in 2009, Villarreal waged a vicious war for control of the cartel, using torture and decapitation of his competitors to terrorize the competition and enforce control. Arrested by Mexican troops in August 2010, he was paraded before the cameras wearing a green polo shirt. The next week, all the students came to school wearing that same shirt, and the department stores had completely sold out of it. In short order, a *corrido* folk song featuring "La Barbie" appeared on YouTube, glorifying his lifestyle with live video of murder, decapitated bodies, bales of money and narcotics, AK-47s, beautiful women, and fast cars. The feature quickly accumulated a half-million hits.

"How can I teach my students anything when this is their hero?" the teacher asked.

FEBRUARY 5

At breakfast the next morning, the Salgados outlined a plan to ride the final fifteen miles to the trailhead for the Cerro El Nazareno summit, climb to the top on foot, and plant the cross in a rock cairn overlooking the Sea of Cortés. José Luis figured the ascent would take two hours, with one hour allotted for the return, and he had arranged for a guide from Caborca to show us the trail. Afterward, we would ride another eighteen miles to the last campsite, an abandoned farm near the O'odham graveyard of San Valentin del Bizani, first visited by Kino in 1694. Bizani had been an ancient meeting place for the Papago, and Kino erected a chapel there in 1706. The mission church of Caborca, our final destination, lay fifteen miles farther east. Chepo Salgado, who had arrived last night after finishing his exams in Hermosillo, needed an extra horse to ride with his girlfriend, so I gave him mine, and I drove the supply truck.

At the trailhead to the summit, we met the caretaker family, who lived next door in an adobe hut with a saguaro-ribbed ramada out front. While the others raced for the top, I pulled up a lawn chair and sat in the shade of the ramada, like a tourist on the beach, except here there was no surf, only sand. An old back injury was acting up, and I didn't want to slow up the other climbers. The rugged bluffs of Nazareno looked like a half-day's climb at a minimum, and already the sun had reached its zenith. Pancho Almada had also declined to make the ascent because his feet had been broken riding motorcycles.

Pancho was one of the happiest men I've known on either side of the border. His neatly trimmed beard spread with a smile that seemed to broaden as the day went on. Pancho's perspective on the cabalgatas was "the possibility of adventure on horseback while in the company of good people." Starting in 2001, Pancho had been on every cabalgata except the one to the Vatican, and he would have gone on that trip too, if he could have ridden his horse.

Pancho and Nancy own and operate an auto parts business in Hermosillo, where they have made impressive advances in equal opportunity and local community trust. They sell to large fleets, like the Coca-Cola distributor, but also to the mom-and-pop businesses and to individuals, on credit.

"Working people are good credit risks," Pancho said. "They make the payments every payday, and we lose less than 1 percent." Taxi drivers owning a single cab are some of his best customers.

The Almadas prefer to hire women in the store so Pancho and Nancy can train them to do things their way. Women learn faster, Pancho said, because they don't pretend to know something when they really don't. In fact, over half of his employees are women. They are grateful for the chance to earn money outside the house, and they make fewer mistakes than men. He gives them equal pay, maternity leave, and regular benefits.

"It took time for the men to adjust to women as equals on the job because auto mechanics are thought of as a male thing in Mexico. Some never could get used to it and quit. My walk-in customers also wrestled with the idea of women knowing car parts, but most of them are okay with it now. Still, a few always wait for the man at the counter."

A dented truck rumbled up to the side of ramada, with two boys riding precariously atop a load of firewood. The caretaker, a thin man with rheumy eyes and a sunken chest, got out and hurried over.

"We beg your pardon," Pancho said. "We have invaded your home."

"*No, no, al contrario.* This is your house," he sputtered, apologizing profusely that his wife was sick and could not attend to our needs (not that we had any). The two boys jumped down and began stacking the wood under the shade. The man pulled aside the tarp over the doorway and disappeared inside.

The boys finished unloading and sat down, leaning against the mesquite posts, eyeing us curiously. I had filched a couple of PayDay candy bars from Gaspar's food wagon this morning and gave them each one. Bryon, who looked about ten years old, broke his in two and put one part in his pocket. A small hairless dog popped out of the house and wheedled up to the boys, wagging its rat-like tail, but Byron shooed it away.

Hector, half Byron's size, ripped the paper off his and also saved half. The man returned with two barefoot girls, each one carrying a glass of *horchata*, a drink made from rice water, honey, cinnamon, and vanilla. I was about to get up and look for more PayDays when Byron and Hector gave their halves to their sisters. I got up anyway and went to Gaspar's wagon and filled a bag with apples, oranges, trail mix, and pistachios and gave it to Byron. We all sat around nibbling until the foot soldiers suddenly came down from the mountain in a rush.

José Luis and the other Salgados were fit to be tied. The guide, instead of waiting for them at the trailhead, had already gone up with some other Kino fans from Caborca, and our group couldn't find the trail. Failure to place the cross on the top rated as a serious ecumenical fiasco. Pichi, Enrique, and José Luis huddled to discuss what could be done, while the rest of us packed up. Finally, they decided to return later. The three hundredth anniversary of Kino's death fell on March 11, so they had plenty of time. That old corn pone that "all's well that ends well" could not have been truer. We found out later that the hike took a half day instead of the three hours that José Luis had plotted on his GPS. The Jesuit had done it in three hours, but he was Father Kino and had the help of angels.

KINO'S OBSESSION WITH the peninsularity of Lower California was much more than a cartographer's curiosity. Father Salvatierra's missions in Baja California were in desperate need. Supplies and livestock had to come across the Sea of Cortés, and ships were few, expensive, and unreliable. If Lower California was connected by land to the Pimería Alta, pack trains and cattle might be driven down the peninsula. Also, Kino envisioned his mission farms and ranches as crucial for the extension of Spanish and church influence into mainland California by supplying livestock, seeds, and tools, as well as seasoned missionaries and soldiers. The Spanish crown wanted missions and presidios on the Pacific Coast to thwart British and Russian designs on the territory. Spanish galleons sailing from Manila, loaded with treasure for the Spanish crown, needed a safe harbor where they could resupply and let their crews recover from the scurvy that inevitably accompanied long voyages.

In early 1701, Kino, Salvatierra, and Manje set out to finally answer the question of island or peninsula. They left Caborca with forty pack loads of provisions and thirty-eight men riding in relays behind them, because of the scarcity of water on the way. Kino wrote of riding in high spirits through the desert covered with spring wildflowers, while singing psalms in Latin, Castilian, and Italian. Manje, the practical-minded soldier, saw it differently. Two days without water, the caravan limped into Quitovac, with the pack animals crazed with thirst. Several mules died.[4] After resting a day, they moved to Sonoyta, where they replenished their supplies from cattle and wheat that Kino had left with the natives a few years earlier.

Now the explorers had to choose which route to take to the mouth of the Colorado River. The little-known route, from Sonoyta south toward the Gulf and then west-northwest, looped underneath the volcanic Pinacate Mountain and generally followed the coastline up the Gulf. Slag heaps, lava flows, and deep sand barred the way, and water holes were few and poorly known. Still, it seemed to be the more direct route. El

Camino del Diablo skirted around the north side of the volcano and followed established trails to the Gila River and downstream to its confluence with the Colorado near the present-day town of Yuma, Arizona. From Yuma, they could ride down the river until it emptied into the Gulf. Manje voted for Camino del Diablo, because it was known and had water. The priests wanted to take the shorter route despite the uncertainty. Faith prevailed over reason, and they took the shortcut. Along the way, the natives (probably Hia C-ed O'odham) got cagey about the location of the few scarce water holes, as well they might. Kino's huge caravan used a lot of water, and the O'odhams' lives depended on the meager supply.

Seven days later, the caravan came to its final halt against massive sand dunes. The explorers descended to the sea, where they calculated their location at 31 degrees 30 minutes north latitude. Here, the Gulf was about thirty miles across, due west, to the Baja side. The coastline ran from south to north and then circled to the northeast, out of their sight. At that point, the head of the Gulf had narrowed to seven miles. The Jesuits were jubilant, concluding that the Sea of Cortés ended there and that the continent of New Spain and California were joined. Manje was not convinced, saying that he could not testify to something he had not actually seen. But they could go no farther, as their guides pointed out that the Colorado River was seventy miles to the northwest, an area covered by sand and without pasture or water.

Back in Sonoyta to recuperate, Manje proposed another solution. Traveling light with the best horses, the three men rode north-northwest for two days and climbed Cerro Santa Clara (today's Sierra Pinacate volcano). From this vantage point, they could see that the Gulf continued to narrow northward until it seemed to disappear into the land. Manje wanted to ride all the way to the Colorado River and down to the Gulf to actually see its termination, but once again, the land in between where they stood and the Gulf was waterless.

In November of the same year, Kino returned without Manje or Salvatierra to the Colorado River, traveling via El Camino del Diablo. From Yuma, Kino and his pack train and cowboys went downriver on the east side of the Colorado, until he reached the villages of the Quiquima tribe. The Quiquimas were astonished by Kino's horses and refused to believe that they could outrun their fleet-footed warriors. So Kino organized a race. The Pima vaquero gave the natives a head start and then left them behind to eat his dust at the finish line. Two days later, the natives built a raft and placed a large basket on it, where Kino rode high, dry, and alone, as they swam across the high volume Colorado to the California side. Kino strolled into the interior of the river delta accompanied by throngs of complete strangers (who did not speak Pima) and spent the night in a small house they prepared for him. That night, he learned by sign language that the South Sea (Pacific Ocean) was only a ten day journey to the west.

The adventurer in Kino must have been sorely tempted to go see it. The natives seemed to know the route. He could have ferried his supplies across the river, and the Pima vaqueros could have swum the horses across. But he turned back toward Dolores and his responsibilities to the Pimería Alta instead. By following his explorer's instincts, first aroused eight years earlier by the view from the top of Cerro El Nazareno, Kino had proven beyond doubt that Lower California was not an island, as the rest of the world had thought. He had discovered the new land route between New Spain and the Pacific Ocean.

LEA AND I left the Nazareno trailhead behind the riders, creeping down a rude dirt track toward the Caborca plain in one of the supply trucks. Ahead, Pichi led the way, followed by Gaspar, the hay truck, and a shiny SUV. The sports car belonged to Heriberto Robles, who drove it from his home in Los Angeles to Hermosillo, where he traded it in for a horse. One of the Salgados had ferried it to last night's camp, but the road was so broken and rough that Heriberto worried for its safety, so he traded back again.

Breaking out of the foothills, we came up against a deep sand wash, where Gaspar buried his truck and trailer to the axles. Luckily, Pichi's four-wheel-drive truck made it across first. After digging Gaspar's axles free, we rigged up a chain and towed him to high ground. Jesus let some air out of the hay truck's tires and eased across with a steady tug from Pichi's Toyota Tundra 4x4. Heriberto was up next and looked worried. The SUV was slung low, and I thought he might drag its guts out on the sand, but the tires were wide and driven by an all-wheel-drive transmission. The chain would wreck the chrome bumper, so Heriberto backed up and took a run. The beast took flight and skimmed over the sand, fishtailing like a kite. Lea and I were pulling the heaviest load, but my truck had four-wheel drive, too. Luckily, the chain spanned the wash to Pichi's truck, and we eased across without mishap.

Crawling along, we crossed the Río Asunción floodplain, a vast area of abandoned farms where rusted pumps still perched over dry holes, like we had seen four years ago in Quitovac, multiplied many times over. Once, the land had produced crops of cotton, vegetables, grain, table grapes, and alfalfa, but over time, pumping had depleted the underground aquifer—in effect, killing the Corúa. The abandoned farmland turned to hardpan, crusted with salt leached to the surface by flood irrigation. Stripped of vegetation, the barren landscape had the look of cataclysm. In 1693, Manje praised this area as excellent for raising horses and cattle and, together with irrigated farms on the river, could support three thousand Indians.

"I bet this was beautiful when the farms were operating," I mused out loud, but Lea's mind was on something else.

"Oh, aren't the families nice?" she remarked. "María José with her boyfriend and her brother, too. I remember the first time Oscar rode; it was Chepo's first time, too. MaJo—that's what José Luis calls her—MaJo got *so* mad. 'I'm a better rider than he is, so why can't I go?' she complained."

"When was that?"

"Let's see. They rode from Moctezuma across the mountains to Huepac—1998, I think. Well, the next year, she came too."

"Chepo is the oldest, right?"

"Yes, but María José is the one who rides all the time."

"Her dad told me she won the barrel-racing championship last year at Hermosillo," I said, remembering the e-mail I got after their big livestock show and rodeo, "on Daisy, the one she is riding today."

"She is *so* nice. She helped me put up Oscar's old tent last night."

We camped that night at an abandoned farmstead with a well that still pumped enough water for the horses. As it was Saturday night, the Salgados threw a big party, inviting friends and fellow Kino fans from Caborca, about twenty miles away. To accommodate the big crowd, Gaspar set up tables and chairs and began cooking while the rest of us cast about for a place to pitch the tents before dark. A cavernous building looked promising, until Dr. Heriberto Robles, the toxicologist, gave it the sniff test, saying it had been used to store insecticides, probably DDT and parathion.

Leading up to the building was a large, open area far enough away from the dining tables so the early-to-bed people would not be run over by the late-night merrymakers driving home. The main road to Caborca ran close by just on the other side of a concrete irrigation ditch, but there didn't seem to be another more out-of-the-way place.

At the party, Lea introduced me to Carlos Venegas, whose family owned the motel in Caborca where the Kino mission tours had stayed. Tourism had dropped to nothing as the notoriety over the border violence increased, and the Southwestern Mission Research Center had canceled the tour last year for the first time in thirty years. Venegas wanted Lea to reorganize tours away from the main trouble areas. The starting point would be Yuma, Arizona, he said, to pull crowds from the thousands of snowbirds flocking there each winter. The buses could cross the border at San Luis Río Colorado, follow Mexico's Highway 2 through Sonoyta, and stop overnight at Caborca. Seeing the Caborca Church and the petroglyphs at Proveedora Hills would take up two days, he said. Afterward, they could take the new toll road from Altar to Santa Ana and then go north to Magdalena to see Kino's tomb and the San Francisco church, avoiding the conflicted areas in the upper Altar River valley.

"That sounds like a good idea!" Lea said, enthusiastic as always. Mike Weber, who was sitting with us, agreed. Privately, I wondered if they would get any takers, considering the bad publicity. Last July, local gangs from Caborca and Altar, loyal to the Sinaloa cartel, had been ambushed by the Beltrán-Leyva gangsters in the mountains near Tubutama on the Altar River, killing twenty-one and wounding nine. Newspapers from Tucson, Phoenix, and Los Angeles had splashed the story over their headlines.

Two days later, driving back to Tucson, Lea said someone else would have to take up the task. "I did it for thirty years, and they will have to find somebody else now."

"With the State Department's travel warning, not many will come," I ventured.

CABORCA AND THE adjacent Altar River valley had been the sites of another bloody collision of cultures that sorely tested Kino's considerable diplomatic skills. By 1695, the energetic Jesuit had placed three new missionaries in the Pimería Alta, including Father Daniel Januske at Tubutama and Father Francisco Xavier Saeta at Caborca. He urged the neophytes to be kind and loving to the poor Indians and to spend themselves wholly on their behalf. Their welfare, he admonished, should be the missionary's one and all-absorbing happiness. Even so, not everything was sweetness and light. Kino's missionary goals conflicted with the designs of Spanish settlers on lands, livestock, and especially Indian labor. Also, frequent raids by Apache and Seri Indian bands had made the colonizers edgy and not inclined to differentiate between Christianized, friendly Indians and hostiles.

But Jesuit ignorance of long-standing cultural differences between native tribes finally ignited the fuse. Januske had brought Christianized Ópatas from the Río San Miguel to oversee the neophyte Pimas. The Ópatas long looked down on the Pimas as inferior and treated them as such, backed up by the Spanish military. Finally, Januske's Pimas got fed up with being whipped and scorned, and they killed three Ópata overseers in retaliation. This act of revenge broke the dam holding back long-repressed hostilities. The Pimas revolted against missionary rule. Januske escaped, but the rebels surged downstream on the Río Altar. They sacked the town of Altar and then entered

Caborca and killed Saeta, who had arrived on the job only a few months before. Most of the other Pimas fled, fearing Spanish reprisal, even though they had nothing to do with the rebellion.

Spanish reprisal was swift, but the army could find no organized opposition and managed only to kill a few women and burn some rancherías. Kino interceded, calling the Pima leaders to a meeting at El Tupo Village with General Jironza's army by persuading them that only those who took part in the massacre would be punished. The plan backfired when a Spanish officer beheaded the first tribesman identified as one of Saeta's killers. Panic ensued, and the Spanish army killed another fifty Indians, most of whom were innocent and had been promised immunity. That event was etched in Pima legend as "La Matanza en El Tupo."

Then a real war broke out. The enraged Pimas got organized and completely destroyed Caborca and Tubutama, as well as two missions on the Río Magdalena. As soon as their revenge was satisfied, the Indians dispersed and went home. Jironza marched through Pima country, killing men and women in a few places and destroying their crops. Soon, the Pima headmen became convinced that they could not win, and they sued for peace. Kino again intervened, offering immunity for those who had no part in the first uprising. This time he made good. The chiefs turned over the people who murdered the Ópata overseers and engineered the rebellion, and the Spaniards offered them the courtesy of baptism, confession, and the sacraments before they were hanged. The soldiers then returned to their presidios, the Pimas to their rancherias, and the indefatigable Kino started all over again.

After Kino's death in 1711, the mission system in the Pimería Alta languished. The twenty-year exemption of natives from tribute and forced labor had expired. Manje, who had become the *alcalde mayor* (governor) of all Sonora, sided with the settlers and moved toward opening Indian lands to Spanish settlers and the missions to lay clergy. Under the colonial labor system known as *repartimiento*, the Indians were forced to work on Spanish-owned mines, farms, and ranches. Many of the natives living on Kino's missions dispersed, returning to their remote rancherías. Within thirty years of the missionary's death, only 1,500 remained, about half that number around Caborca. With repartimiento, the culture of peonage that Mexico struggles with to this day became firmly established.

THE SALGADOS' PARTY looked like it might last until dawn when I left at ten. Walking back to the tent area, I nearly tripped over Father Sinohui, asleep on the ground, snoring softly. His mattress was made of saddle blankets laid over a ground tarp to keep out the dampness; his coverlets were two *frazadas*, or rough wool blankets, not nearly enough to keep out the cold. His denim jacket was rolled up in his leather chaps, with the straw hat perched on top of his boots. Much later, I came across Juan Mateo Manje's opinion of his traveling companion, written eleven years after Father Kino's death:

> He accomplished as much as two or three fervent workers. He was almost seventy years old when he died [he was 66]. His death resembled his life...one of great simplicity and poverty...His bed consisted as always of two sheepskins for a mattress, two rough quilts, and a pack saddle for a pillow.[5]

FEBRUARY 6

THE NEXT MORNING, I reclaimed my horse to ride to the petroglyphs with the others. Ten miles from Caborca, the volcanic San Juan and Proveedora Hills thrust up from the alluvial plain like dark slabs of bark cleaved by a giant axe, with a remnant of the Río Asunción running between them. On boulders above the riverbed, the animated emblems of an ancient human existence had been etched in stone with a sharpened bone or rock. Most of the figures were animals hunted for food: mule deer with enormous antlers; desert bighorn sheep, including one with a full curl; turtles; antelope; rabbits; lizards. Squiggly lines with a head seemed snake-like, but whether or not this was an O'odham water serpent, I could not say. In their midst stood a tall hunter in full head-dress, carrying a spear and enormous rings in his ears. I looked for horses but found none, so these etchings must have predated Kino and the Spanish. The arrangement of the figures had a ceremonial sense of order that must have originated in the simple-hearted ferocity of these desert nomads, long disappeared. Scholars debate whether these petroglyphs were drawn by the proto-O'odham, Hohokam, or another vanished people, yet such inquires seemed trivial to me at the moment. It was enough to know that the artists were all flesh and bones and nerves, with thoughts about their future well-being, just like us.

Caborca, a sizable city of sixty thousand, had two main roads entering from the west: Highway 2 from Sonoyta and Avenida Álvaro Obregón from Puerto Peñasco and the Sea of Cortés. We rode down the *avenida* through an industrial section of the city, crossing Avenida Luís Donaldo Colosio, and entered a residential area of small homes and corner stores. By now, we numbered over forty horses and riders, much to the delight of spectators lining the streets, who waved as we passed. Parked cars narrowed the two-lane street, and we rode in single file or two abreast, so that approaching vehicles could squeeze by. Cars coming from the rear took a detour or crawled along behind, curious to see what was up. By the time we reached Avenida 6 de Abril, the motorcade extended behind us for at least a mile.

Sonorans often name their streets after their heroes or significant dates related to one of Mexico's many battles and revolutions. Álvaro Obregón was a garbanzo farmer from southern Sonora who rose during the Mexican Revolution of 1910–20 to become Mexico's president. A brilliant military leader, he was fluent in Indian languages and strongly supported education, instituting land reforms that included farmer training for peons. Obregón was popular in the United States, too, selling his entire garbanzo crop to Woodrow Wilson to help feed the United States Army in World War I. Like many of Mexico's politicians, he was assassinated, shot by a religious fanatic in 1928, before fulfilling his second term.

Luis Donaldo Colosio, a native son of Magdalena de Kino, ran for the presidency in 1994. Extremely popular in Sonora, he had been handpicked by the Institutional Revolutionary Party (PRI) to succeed President Carlos Salinas de Gatori. During a campaign appearance in Tijuana, Colosio was shot in the head by an assailant who claimed that he acted alone, although rumors persisted he acted under orders of a Tijuana drug lord or a political rival.

We turned south on 6 de Abril, which took us alongside the expansive plaza fronting La Purísima Concepción de Nuestra Señora de Caborca church, founded by Father Kino in 1692. Turning to the west on Avenida General Ignacio Pesqueira, we followed it a little way to a stockyard, where we unsaddled the horses and hurried around to the back entrance of the cathedral to attend Mass.

In the 1850s, the general was embroiled in a struggle to seize power from Sonora's incumbent and corrupt governor, Manuel Gándara. Henry A. Crabb, a California land pirate (*filibustero*) was related to a prominent Sonoran family by marriage. Crabb thought he had struck a deal with Pesqueira to receive a large land grant in exchange for troops and military support. Pesqueira prevailed without his help and warned Crabb to stay home, calling on the people of Sonora to beware of an American invasion.

Crabb and one hundred volunteers came anyway, marching over the El Camino de Diablo to Sonoyta. On the outskirts of Caborca, Capitán Lorenzo Rodríguez and Mexican troops intercepted Crabb and his followers. Rodríguez advanced to speak, but the Americans opened fire and killed the commander and several others. The survivors retreated to the La Purísima church. Instead of pressing their advantage, Crabb's brigade commandeered several adobe houses on the opposite side of the plaza. A week-long battle ensued, with Mexican and Indian reinforcements laying siege. Crabb had not expected such stiff resistance and foolishly had left most of his ammunition and horses on Caborca's outskirts. After the Papago fired the straw roof with flaming arrows, Crabb and the fifty-eight survivors surrendered on April 6. The Mexicans treated the Americans as terrorists, having taken many casualties during the fight after warning Crabb to stay away. The next day, the filibusters were lined up against the wall and executed by firing squad, all save a sixteen-year-old youth who was set free to tell the story. The Mexicans preserved Crabb's head in a jar of mescal as a souvenir of war and a deterrent to other like-minded *filibusteros*.[6]

I entered the Caborca church through the west transept and sat down on a front pew beside Lea and Mike Weber. The Salgados and the other cabalgantes had already taken seats on the opposite side. The Sunday-afternoon light of midwinter streamed through the main entrance to the nave, where some of Caborca's faithful citizens sat in quiet meditation. The tall, whitewashed walls and arched pinnacles drew my eyes upward toward the plain statuary and paintings of saints, the Virgin Mary prominent among them. Outside, the large plaza of polished clay tile positively gleamed while the scalloped arches imparted a sense of movement toward the steps leading up to the entryway.

Father Sinohui stood at the altar, bereft of cowboy clothes, now white-robed and bareheaded, with a large bronze crucifix hanging from his neck. He went through the ritual chants of Catholic Mass and then offered a brief homily recapitulating Father Kino's life work, including the founding of Caborca's church. For the others in attendance, he explained the cabalgatas as a veneration of Father Kino by retracing his journeys, showing respect for his accomplishments, and continuing their devotion to the cause of his sainthood.

Father Sinohui then offered communion. Watching my friends come to the altar, one by one, to receive the sacraments, I realized that these journeys were not just horseback adventures but deeply religious acts, uniting them in a personal way with their exemplary Jesuit in those exact places where he had wrought so many extraordinary achievements. To them, Father Kino's legacy was not an abstraction or an academic curiosity but embedded in their everyday lives.

Despite its gloomy emphasis on sin—original and other—I felt new admiration for Father Kino's venerable church, with its rigid rituals and supposedly infallible pope as backstops. Though not perfect, Catholicism has anchored its faithful in a constantly changing world. Also, for the indigenous Mexican, the church has been warmly inclusive. Because Catholicism was, in effect, Mexico's state religion, natives and mestizos were incorporated into the fabric of Mexican society, albeit at the bottom of the economic and social pyramids.

By contrast, Puritan Anglo America followed a cold policy of exclusion for the Native Americans who survived the settling of the West. Confined to reservations and deprived of their birthright, they remained outside of American society—and remain so even today. To enforce their internment in the early years, the United States Army

Padre on Horseback

resorted to seizing and slaughtering their horses. But today, they are getting a measure of justice (some call it revenge) with court decisions that uphold their water and land rights and gaudy gambling casinos where they relieve their Anglo neighbors of their social security checks.

In a larger sense, the human impulse for pilgrimage traces back beyond written history to one bright morning when humankind awoke and began to reflect on its impotence in the face of nature. Stripped to its roots, religion probably began as a response to such metaphysical anxieties. That awakening to self was the beginning of our search for divine beings that might control nature's primal powers, bringing relief from drought and flood, hunger and disease, and the defeat of enemies. Thus, the O'odham made journeys to sacred places, like the blessed springs of Quitovac and the caves of the Pinacate, performing ceremonies to bring rain and earning the favor of deities that might bring them a bighorn sheep to fill their bellies. The Spanish and most of the Jesuits dismissed these customs as stupid and heathenish, while the affable, optimistic Father Kino directed his enormous energy and intelligence toward making their lives more secure.

After the service, Enrique, Dr. Mike Weber, and Father Sinohui recessed to a large podium that had been set up on the plaza in front of the church. A crowd had assembled to see a video that Enrique had produced, encapsulating the Los Caminos de Kino rides over the past twenty-four years. Then Dr. Weber presented the significance of the journeys from the American point of view, emphasizing the fact that until one travels the Pimería Alta as Kino did the historian can only appreciate Kino's achievements from the standpoint of a librarian. After my four cabalgatas, I wholeheartedly concurred and only wished that I had started the rides years ago, when Oscar first invited me to come along.

Part 5

Coda

Coronado National Monument Fire

Today's Changing Border

JUNE 2011. FEW climes lack a lean season. On the borderlands, ours falls during the arid pre-monsoon months of May and June. By noon, the temperature is already ninety-eight degrees. Even our resident mockingbird is subdued, perched open-beaked and panting in the shade. These are the relentless, nosebleed days, the kind that dry out the sinuses and curl the hair on the back of your neck. Our last rain fell on December 22, a sumptuous, one full inch, followed by light snow dusting the bald knob of Mount Wrightson. The landscape has long since lost its graceful touch. The grasses now are like straw and don't have much strength. In April, we moved half of the cattle off the ranch to the farm.

That last rain concluded the wettest year in my two decades in Sonoita; twenty-one inches fell at our house, a little more in the monsoon than during the winter. The Canelo Hills dressed up for spring in bright yellow and green from the annual golden-eye and lush grama. When the cabalgata rode the San Pedro River in April 2010, grass brushed our horses' bellies, and the nearby Huachuca Mountains were still streaked with snow.

But so far this year, we've had no moisture: zero, zilch, *nada*. Adding to the fuel load, January's sub-zero weather killed many trees. The combination of heavy leftover grass and drought caused a perfect storm for wildfires, to the delight of the local arsonists, the *narcotraficantes*.

Two days ago, I noticed a puff of smoke rising from the south end of the Huachuca Mountains. This morning, it had grown into a mushroom cloud, billowing over Montezuma Peak, as if the army at Fort Huachuca tested a nuclear bomb. By midday the winds were strong enough to blow Christ off the cross, driving the plume eastward into

New Mexico. A month ago, that same offshore wind from the California coast pushed smoke our way from the massive fires west of Nogales—so thick I wore a wet bandanna over my face. The air smelled barbequed.

No one has officially said who started these fires, but the narcos are the prime suspects because they've done it before as a diversionary tactic. The Park Service and Border Patrol said it started just across the line in Mexico, at the edge of the Coronado National Memorial near Smuggler's Ridge. The Murphy fires started north of the border along known drug trails that stream up Nogales toward Tucson. Both were human-caused, because the sky had been cloudless for months. Last week, a few miles north of Sonoita, some nitwit started a smaller fire by welding on a windmill. Firemen killed it after it burned a thousand acres.

Later that morning, I drove south on Highway 92, headed for Palominas, dragging a stock trailer. Friends had livestock that had to be moved out of the fire's path. Before reaching the turnoff to the memorial, the road was blocked by fire trucks and police cars. The wind-driven flames had topped over Montezuma Peak and raced down Ash Canyon eastward into a subdivision of lovely homes overlooking the San Pedro River valley. Through binoculars, I saw the wind-whipped flames bursting through the windows of one house. Next door, the chapel of Our Lady of the Sierras was already a smoldering ruin. Firefighters tried to stop the flames by cutting a firebreak up the steep hill behind it. Giving up, they now trudged in single file over the next ridge, masked and roped together for safety. Mother Nature has many ways to humiliate its most adventurous creature—drought, flood, and fire, foremost among them. A little flood would have been nice right then.

On the way home, I parked on Three Canyons Road, looking west into the maelstrom. The fire was marching down a different ridge, threatening the strip malls that line Highway 92. Sky-crane helicopters circled the flames like a squadron of gigantic miller moths, each one with a refill tube dangling from its abdomen. Swooping down into the billowing smoke, they released their two-thousand-gallon loads in a single massive spray on the fire's leading edge and then circled back to the parking lot to refill.

While I watched the sky-cranes hover over the refueling tanks, a motorcade of thirty Border Patrol trucks rushed by to help with the on-ground evacuations, each truck carrying four patrolmen. If the narcos bastards did set this fire as a diversion, they succeeded beyond their wildest imagination, destroying sixty homes and businesses in the process and costing millions of dollars to fight. I called Rich and Diane, advising them to be on the lookout for burreros coming up on our side through the San Rafael

Valley toward Patagonia and Red Rock Canyon. On the San Pedro River, *El Embudo* in the border fence would be crowded tonight with drug mules making a dash for Interstate 10. The gatekeepers were otherwise occupied.

El Embudjo

The *Arizona Daily Star* ran a full-page story recently about how the illegal border traffic has slowed down so much that Border Patrol officers were getting bored. With few jobs available in the United States because of the recession, more border protection, and tons of publicity over Arizona's SB 1070 anti-immigration law, immigrants no longer come in waves as they once did, and some of those already here were going to other states or back home to Mexico.

Arizona's politicians claim their anti-immigrant policies are working. Perhaps so, but the narcos don't read gringo newspapers. A mile south of our house along a Forest Service road, the brush thickets were littered with yellow rope and black plastic sheets, used to bundle the marijuana. I showed the local officers the evidence and asked why they didn't stake out night patrols on the drop spots. "Too dark and too brushy," they replied. But they do drive by and sometimes park there during the day.

I go to the community meetings and tell them what I see, but the Border Patrol seems glued to the upholstered seats of their four-wheel-drive trucks, at least in our area. Their checkpoint on Highway 83 going toward Interstate 10 shuts down for inclement weather, like schools on snow breaks, while the narco scouts keep watch. In the last twenty years, I have seen only one Border Patrol patrolling on foot. The borderlands would be safer for everyone if Homeland Security had developed a competent horse cavalry instead of pissing away a billion dollars on a virtual fence that did not work. A modern-day Compañía Volante could cut down on narcotics trafficking and save lives too.

The backcountry border-crossers are a different breed these days. It used to be that most of them were honest country people, returning to a job in El Norte, or new immigrants looking for work. Nowadays, they are often burreros from Mexico's cities and towns. Some, perhaps many, are still honest people, driven by poverty and the cartels into carrying drugs. An elderly gentleman with a green card from Nogales, Sonora, who does yard work around our town claims half of the young men in his barrio are so employed.

"*No hay otro trabajo,*" he says with a shrug.

So we've had to become more cautious. Now, when I ride and see someone lying under a tree, instead of going to see what's up, I stay back. Last week, in Red Bear Pasture, I watched a Mexican FedEx delivery of cannabis from the Sinaloa cartel, destined for America's Heartland. Through binoculars I counted ten men trudging up a ridge, their foreheads cut by tumplines that supported the black rectangular bales on their backs. The lead burrero carried a long gun.

Still, it is impossible to anticipate every encounter. Four days after the Coronado Memorial fire, I rode out to check pipelines in Dark Canyon Pasture. The horse saw the men first, shying away from a juniper thicket. Ben heeled up behind me. Sis wagged her tail and walked toward their camp, following her nose to the half-empty pan of chorizo and beans. Too late to turn away, I called out, "*Buenas días, señores,*" to the two men rising up on their elbows. I told them I was looking for cows, and they pointed up the hill, where I'd already seen a bunch.

"*Andan solos?*" I asked, inquiring if they were alone.

"*Si, solo. Vamos por Tucson,*" they replied.

I rode around the thicket to get a better look. At first, they said they were from Nogales, but when I asked where they crossed the border, they replied Santa Cruz, a three-day walk directly south.

"*De donde son en México?*" I asked where they were from.

"*Tijuana*," the one in the red cap answered.

"That's a long way from here," I mused, asking why they didn't cross in California.

"*Es muy difícil ahora*," he answered, complaining how hard it was to cross into Southern California now. (Operation Gatekeeper fencing and enforcement started in 1994, pushing illegal border traffic into the wildernesses.)

"*Son burreros?*" I asked and then instantly realized that was a stupid question, asking if they were packing drugs.

"*No, no, señor,*" they replied quickly.

I didn't see any marijuana bales, but they had full shoulder packs leaning against the tree, along with a gallon of sweet green tea, a milk jug full of water, and a half-full bottle of mescal.

"Ándele pues," I said, roweling the horse up the hill.

People meet in the tangled brush on a sharp hillside twenty-five miles from the border: one, a rider on horseback with a pair of cow dogs; the other two, Mexicans bedded down in a thicket with full packs. They greet each other. The conversation is casual, not threatening. The rider asks questions.

Beyond that, what else could be known? That the rider is not Border Patrol—he is obviously a gringo looking for cows; that he speaks Spanish. And that he is exposed like a worm under a kicked log as he rides off—that his cell phone does not work in Dark Canyon.

Beyond these things, neither could tell for sure if the other was armed. Neither could be certain of the other's destination or intent. But the friendly salutations were wise. Mexicans are a congenial folk, generally speaking.

What could be guessed? That the Mexicans are immigrants, as told? Or perhaps burreros on their way to make a drop? Or that they are "go backs," taking a nap before heading back to Santa Cruz under a full moon? Or that the overly curious gringo might bring back the Border Patrol?

LATELY, I'VE THOUGHT about carrying a pistol. My neighbor, whose ranch has drug trails running through it, carries a hog-leg six-shooter strapped low on her hip when she is outside working. She says the gun enlightens the burreros of the fact that she is not an easy mark, in case they get careless ideas.

A friend whose ranch has five miles of border fence has carried a .38-caliber Smith & Wesson ever since the border heated up a couple of decades ago. The gun has only a two-inch barrel and sits neatly on his right hip, out of his way on horseback but easy to reach. Now, the border in his area is fenced with vehicle barriers made of railroad track, top rails twenty feet long that are supported by jack-legs at either end. Behind the new fence is a sagging barbed-wire cattle fence, erected in the mid-twentieth century. A graded road for the border patrol parallels the new fence.

The new fence has stopped most cross-border vehicle traffic, although occasionally the narcos will push the fence aside with a front-end loader or use a flatbed tow truck to drop a drug-loaded pickup over it. In the old days, the barbed-wire fence was cut so often and in so many places that cattle guards were needed to keep the cows from becoming illegal aliens. Also, Texas-style wire gates allowed ranchers from either side to get back stray cattle. Neighbors from both sides used to help each other on roundups. The new fence has stopped most of that cross-border neighborliness. Rarely, when cattle do get through (the top rail is three feet high), getting them back is more difficult and dangerous. The Border Patrol trucks stir up a lot of dust and they don't help maintain the roads they use.

Even so, my friend much prefers the present situation to the past. Before the vehicle barrier, drug and people smugglers made their runs in broad daylight almost every day, speeding over ranch roads, sometimes with the Border Patrol in hot pursuit. Now, the burreros mostly move at night and stick to the mountain trails. This rancher has lived on the border in the same place for seventy years, and he plans on staying put, as his father and grandfather did before him.

But opinions vary. Another longtime rancher next to the border wall in the San Pedro River basin sees things differently. He says the wall and Border Patrol have done more damage to his land and livestock than the illegal immigrants and burreros ever did. Whenever possible, he keeps the Border Patrol off his land, although the law allows them to go anywhere they want within twenty-five miles of the border.

My take on the gun question is that a pistol is like any other precision tool that must be used regularly to stay proficient, and I don't take the time to do so. Also, I have no experience in judging the level of the threat that I might be faced with, as would a policeman or soldier. At a certain critical juncture, it may be impossible to tell, like when the panicky immigrant jumped at me from behind a juniper thicket. Like most borderlanders, my first impulse is to help. In an interview given several years before his death, Rob Krentz remarked, after his house had been robbed, "If they ask for water, well, I'll still give them water. I mean, that's just my nature."

Late last fall in Sonoita, the weather got cold and the new pot crop had been picked and packaged for delivery to America's heartland. One morning, Diane looked up from her desk in time to see seven men dressed in black, running down our fence line, a scant one hundred feet away. She ran to lock the doors and dialed up the Border Patrol, who surrounded the house in white and green pickups fifteen minutes later. But the burreros had already faded like smoke into the Canelo Hills. That afternoon, the officers found several hundred pounds of marijuana stashed near a windmill located a mile north of our headquarters. We have the advantage of a Border Patrol station on the Sonoita crossroads located just six miles away. For others who live in more isolated areas, the response time may be hours or days. Now, I keep a loaded gun in the house, but Diane refuses to touch it.

"I don't do guns," she says.

Yet I know that eventually, I will bump into people who would shoot first if I threaten them. That danger is minimized by cartel standard operating procedures. The business organization that employs burreros values secrecy, maneuvering under the radar with as little publicity as possible. This last argument could be moot if one of them is spaced-out on meth or hates gringos for whatever reason. Rob Krentz was armed, and I suspect a gun wouldn't do me any good either.

Borderland ranching has always had its dangers, mostly because of the terrain, weather, and working with livestock. The vaqueros have a saying: things that don't happen for years happen in a second. A covey of stick-tight quail bursts out of the grass, and that old reliable gelding dumps you on the rocks; or you get careless and step off the horse with a spur hung in the lariat rope; or you get clothes-lined out of the saddle by a tree limb. Belligerent bovines are another caution. I have a brindle-colored cow with a strong sense of personal space. I can see danger in her almond-colored eyes when I ride too close to her scrawny calf. If I penetrate their circle, the old lady drops her head and charges. Every year, I say I'm going to sell her, but every year she weans a decent calf.

Weather is still a rancher's biggest risk: drought, thirst, heat, and cold—especially drought, when the land burns up, the grasses wither, and the livestock becomes a tapestry of bones. Even so, a new menace looms just across the border in the form of Mexico's criminal cartels, a threat that feeds on America's addictions and cannot be stopped with a wall or border army.

Jack-Leg Border Fence

The Rising Drug Threat

DURING THE LAST ride, the cabalgantes said they also were adjusting to the rising narco violence in Sonora. Yet accommodation to Mexico's level of lawlessness could ultimately be self-destructive. Once ingrained in the economy and culture, it becomes a cancer and threatens to create a republic without laws except who has the most guns, commits the most horrible atrocities, and has the most money.

This calamity has a proximate cause: the addictions of twenty-five million Americans who buy $25–40 billion of illegal narcotics each year, most of it coming in through the southwestern border. Writer Charles Bowden has cleverly labeled this as a case of Gabriel Garcia Márquez's magical realism bumping up against Adam Smith's iron laws of supply and demand. Every time someone in the United States snorts a line of coke, or courts the muse by smoking a joint, or a group of teens score meth on a dare—each one of these individual acts fuels the cartel machine and resonates back along the supply chain to the borderlands. From the Mexican perspective, America's insatiable demand carries a greater responsibility for the drug wars than Mexico's admittedly imperfect law enforcement and criminal justice systems. And they have a great deal of right on their side.

The cabalgantes were acutely aware of how one criminal gang, the Zetas, have shifted operations from the border to Monterrey, a major industrial city in northeastern Mexico, and they worry that the same might happen in Sonora. The Zetas were formed by renegade Mexican Army Special Forces in the late 1990s. Over time, they recruited new members from corrupted Mexican law enforcement, growing into the most violent and ruthless cartel in Mexico, according to President Felipe Calderón and the US Department of Justice. Lately, they have branched out into extortion and kidnapping. For those who can't pay, like the hapless immigrants on their way to *El Norte*, the Zetas force them to carry drugs across the border, murdering those who refuse. In April 2011, Mexican police uncovered seventy-two bodies in a mass grave near the Texas border, most of them Central Americans.

A recent poll by the Pew Research Center found that a large majority (83 percent) of Mexicans supported Calderon's use of the military against the cartels.[1] Yet an undercurrent of opposition surfaced last year in the nationwide marches of the Movement for Peace with Justice and Dignity. Led by poet Javier Sicilia after his son was killed by crossfire between cartel gunmen, the movement made the case that criminals are also victims and called for peaceful reconciliation. Mexico is overwhelmingly Catholic, and the moral tenets of the church make allowances for the seriousness of a crime if the causes and conditions of the criminal are known and understood. Most cartel killers come from a background of poverty and social depravation, created in part by Mexico's culture of peonage and corruption. Even so, the flaws in government and Mexican society do not absolve them of guilt. Their barbaric acts against innocent people have inexcusably crossed an irreversible moral boundary. The nation has the right and moral obligation to defend itself and its citizens against the criminal assault of the cartels, according to Felipe Calderon's administration, and most Mexicans agree.

Meanwhile, the United States shoots itself in the foot by supplying high-powered weapons to the cartels. Ricardo Ramonet's prediction that the narcos would soon be killing Americans with their own guns came to pass last December. Border Patrol agent Brian Terry was killed in a shootout with a drug gang near Nogales, Arizona. Two AK-47 assault rifles were found at the scene. They had been purchased from a gun dealer in Glendale, Arizona, and smuggled across the border in Columbus, New Mexico, by a supplier to the Sinaloa cartel. On February 15, 2011, two Immigration and Customs Enforcement officers were shot in Mexico with weapons purchased from a gun dealer in Texas. In both cases, a botched sting operation called "Fast and Furious" gave these guns (and thousands more) a free ride into the hands of cartel killers in the hope of identifying weapons-trafficking operations in the United States. In Mexico, of the nearly thirty thousand weapons recovered at crime scenes, almost 70 percent were traced back to America, according to a congressional investigation.[2]

Our Mexican allies were outraged. President Calderón accused America's weapons industry of complicity in the deaths of thousands of Mexicans and called for reinstating the ban on sales of assault weapons that expired in 2004. Others saw it as a double standard and an example of America's cultural attitude of contempt for Mexican lives.

One has to ask if the United States would have done this in Afghanistan or Pakistan, knowing those guns would be used by the Taliban to kill NATO soldiers. Why ordinary citizens should have a need for and be allowed to easily purchase military assault weapons baffles Mexicans and many Americans as well.

In 2009, Vicente Fox Quesada, Mexico's president from 2000 to 2006, made headlines recently by calling for legalization of marijuana production in Mexico. Later, he enlarged that to all narcotics, proposing that production be turned over to law-biding businesses that pay taxes and provide jobs for Mexicans. America's contribution to Mexico's battle with the cartels has been little more than a *propina* (tip), he claimed, with forty thousand Mexicans killed and the army mobilized and the streets.

In the United States, legalizing marijuana production and use makes sense for other reasons as well. The principal deterrent to pot (and other illegal narcotics) has been incarceration, even for minor offenses. As our prisons have filled, America has become the world's leading jailer, with 3 percent of its population detained in one way or another.[3] Canada and European countries have incarceration rates one-seventh to one-eighth of ours. Only Russia and South Africa came close to the US rate. If legalized, marijuana could be taxed, regulated, and controlled, like alcohol and cigarettes.

On our last ride, one of the cabalgantes commented that laws should reflect the realities of society. In the United States, marijuana use is widespread, and the drug is ridiculously easy to get, despite being against federal laws. Legalizing marijuana would relieve our penal system of a large number of its jailbirds. The criminal cartels would be starved of an important source of cash. The rural borderlands would be less dangerous, less trampled, and less property damaged. Some of the border enforcement troops could be retrained and reassigned to areas where the most dangerous drugs are smuggled in and focus their attention on the really bad guys in America as well as Mexico.

Immigration and Neighborliness

TODAY, THE ARIZONA-SONORA border lies between fear, hypocrisy, and hope. The reality is that two borders exist: one physical and the other cultural. The United States has constructed a new fence on all but about eighty miles of Arizona's physical frontier. Unsatisfied and still afraid, Arizona's politicians have plans to finish the job using public donations and prison labor. People hope the wall will protect them from Mexican and Central American immigrants and the criminal drug cartels. But the fence separates families and isolates cultures, and therein rests the hypocrisy.

Southern Arizona was added to the Union in 1854 by the Gadsden Purchase, a treaty that extended US citizenship and property rights to thousands of Mexicans living in the thirty thousand square miles and guaranteeing their constitutional rights. Yet today, one and one-half centuries later, many Arizonans still fear the cultural border—the brown wave sweeping north that threatens Anglo cultural and political dominance with a healthy change to multicultural integration. Yet wanting Arizona's demographics to remain static is "a backward-looking, codger's way to live...and ultimately a lost cause."[4]

Every nation should police who comes and goes across its borders. There are a few people seeking to do the United States serious harm—but not Mexico and the Mexican people. They are allies, not enemies, and Americans ignore that fact at our peril, especially in the current high-stakes conflict. The fight against the drug cartels requires the mentality and language of "we" instead of "them and us," as writer Rubén Martínez has urged. Mexico's greatest strengths are its tight-knit families, a deep belief in the tenets of the Catholic Church, and the courage and willingness to fight. These are assets to be treasured and used against the cartel terrorists, not spurned and looked down upon.

Two weeks after the 2010 San Pedro River ride ended, Governor Jan Brewer signed Senate Bill 1070, Arizona's anti-immigration law, setting off protest demonstrations at the state capitol. Legal scholars claimed that had the complete bill gone into effect, the constitutional protections of due process, equal protection under the law, and prohibition against unreasonable search and seizure would have been suspended for a certain demographic class. In other words, it would have undermined the constitutional and civil rights for Hispanic and Native American citizens. Also, state laws would have preempted federal immigration laws.

Although the governor signed a companion bill designed to remove race as a consideration, in actual practice, racial profiling and bias would be guaranteed. The law specifically was aimed at identifying Hispanic immigrants without papers who happen to have black eyes, black hair, and dark skin and who speak Spanish, as do a quarter of the state's legal citizens. Also, it would have led to profiling Native Americans, the original citizens of the state. Some Hispanic police officers, recognizing that they would be in double jeopardy, also filed lawsuits against SB 1070.

How had this mind-set developed in my native state that for most of the twentieth century had been forward-looking, confident of its future, and caring of most (though not all) of its people?

During the last third of the century, another exodus took place. Phoenix, Tucson, and Yuma fetishized their sunshine, and Arizona became a Sunbelt state. Hundreds of thousands of retirees and others fleeing the freezing Rust Belts of the East and Midwest moved each year into new subdivisions and retirement communities to live out a new version of the American dream. Before long, this swelling demographic became fifty-, sixty-, seventy-, and eighty-year-olds.

But the dream suffered a devastating blow from the attack on the World Trade Center, shattering America's illusion of invulnerability, creating in its stead a deep-seated mood of insecurity and fear of anyone foreign.

A half dozen years later, as the recession took hold, the second pillar of the dream—the assumption of continued unlimited economic growth—crumbled amid the schemes of corporate shysters, abetted by government incompetence. Retirement accounts plummeted along with interest rates paid on savings. The value of that new house they moved into a few years ago dropped to below the purchase price or the amount owed on the mortgage. For people on fixed incomes or whose jobs were in jeopardy, signs of insecurity appeared everywhere. In the midst of economic hard times, a strong wave of nativism surged over the United States and especially in Arizona.

Modern Arizona's version of the dream had been built on a third shaky pillar—a sense of place weakened by the lack of local community history and family context. In the minds of many new residents, Arizona began on the day they arrived. These new Arizonans had traded their families and neighborhoods for a dwelling in a sun-stricken, homogenized mega-suburb, where every house looked like every other house, where the street corners were crowded with fast food joints and strip malls. Or they moved into sleek retirement communities where everyone was over fifty-five years old, well-to-do, and played golf; where basketball courts in driveways, backyard tree houses, and the laughter of children were not allowed. The retirees had left their children and grand-children back East and so voted against funding education here. Today, Arizona ranks at the very bottom in crucial childhood education and near the top in the percentage living in poverty. Meanwhile, these new Arizonans elected politicians and sheriffs who played on their fears by vowing to protect them from the state's inevitably changing demographics.

Few Hispanics lived in the places the new Arizonans had left behind. So when Spanish-speaking people flooded into Arizona's cities for jobs, building and maintaining the new homes and retirement services, the newcomers began to fear that Mexicans were out to steal the remnants of the dream. Unschooled in Southwestern history and culture, they lumped all Hispanics into a single category of suspects. They all spoke the same foreign language, they were younger and dark-skinned, they had an unfamiliar culture, and they lived in separate communities. They were all different in the same ways.

The new border wall and anti-immigrant laws were intended to relieve anxieties by keeping a certain class of people out. The next logical step in the sequence of repudiation would be to start asking who belongs within. Ominously, new proposals began to circulate for the repeal of the Fourteenth Amendment of the US Constitution that grants citizenship to anyone born in America, regardless of parentage. Arizona was on a path toward becoming the 1950s Mississippi of the new millennium.

But other cultures have come to America as immigrants, multiple millions passing through Ellis Island, and the nation is better and stronger because of them. The rugged, rowdy Irish, a clannish people, fled their insular island—my ancestors among them—leaving behind its grimy poverty and potato shortages and settling in urban East Coast cities. They blended in rather quickly, not by choice but because they were separated from their homeland, schools, and culture by three thousand miles of the Atlantic Ocean.

But Mexico is unlike any other mother country of immigrants, because it shares a common border of two thousand miles with the United States. Before the Gadsden Purchase, much of the Southwest was Mexico. And for many years after, the border was little more than a "line in the sand," as historian Rachel St. John observed. Mexican, Anglo, and O'odham moved easily back and forth, renewing family ties and enriching the cultural exchange. Historically, the borderlands provided a venue where people from both sides met, did business, and often became friends; a mutual appreciation of neighborliness overcame most cultural differences.

Nowadays, some politicians and sheriffs frame undocumented immigration as an intrusion on Anglo Arizona's supremacy and a danger to public safety that requires racial discrimination to enforce, a 389-mile-long wall and a bigger border army in order to manage the threat. And the latest national immigration reform bill calls for nineteen thousand more Border Patrol soldiers, round-the-clock border surveillance, and seven hundred miles more fence, all at a total additional cost of $46 billion.[5]

Even if it were possible to seal the border, could we afford the consequences? Would we want to? Mexico is our third largest trading partner and the original homeland to forty-five million of its legal citizens. For Arizona, 30 percent of its citizens are Hispanic, and Sonora is its largest trading partner.

George Miller, Tucson's two-term mayor and longtime borderland resident, came up with a better plan almost a decade ago: Put an Ellis Island at Nogales (and other big border cities), where Mexicans and others looking for work could be matched with unfilled jobs.[6] Qualifications would include a clean police record and family ties back home to help ensure they would return. Employers would have to pay a fair wage and safe working conditions. The Border Patrol could become the clearing house for prospective workers and employers, inspectors on the job site, and provide transportation back to Mexico when the job was done.

Workers would pay a fee for safe passage and job placement, something like the $2,000 to $5,000 they now pay to the cartel coyotes, with no guarantee of a job after the crossing. Undocumented migrant workers would be decriminalized; they would not be exposed to the dangers and degradations of illegal border crossing; and American farmers, ranchers, and many other industries would have a legal cadre of workers they badly need.

There will be some abuses, of course. A few workers will fly the coop to stay in the United States. Some employers might try gaming the system by paying substandard wages. Even so, the program could pay for itself from fees and reduced costs of border enforcement. The Pew Hispanic Center estimated that five hundred thousand immigrants crossed over in 2005; in 2009, during the recession, the number was still over three hundred thousand. But American businesses and industries are as much addicted to cheap labor as drug addicts are to heroin and cocaine, so there will always be demand for good workers from the poor communities south of the border.

Such a system would also eliminate much human suffering. From 1994 when Operation Gatekeeper started, body counts on both sides of the border for all nationalities have totaled over six thousand.

Reality and Myth

THE POPULARIZED PICTURE of Arizona's borderlands is a bloody one, in which drug violence in Sonora has turned the region into a war zone. Governor Jan Brewer has warned of beheadings and decapitated bodies lying out in the desert. Talk show pundits call for citizens to arm themselves for the coming invasion of Mexican mafia slithering across the sand armed with AK-47s and grenades, bent on murder and mayhem. Soldier-of-fortune writers drive around the borderland for a few days and return home to write "Hell on the Border" stories for adventure magazines.

The truth is that most Arizona borderland towns and rural areas have lower rates of violent crime than do the cities and suburbs of Tucson or Phoenix, according to FBI statistics and local law enforcement agencies. The last thing the cartels want is the notoriety that accrues from assaulting United States citizens, in either Arizona or Sonora. But these comforting statistics mask other grave realities.

First, the massive buildup of border protection by the Department of Homeland Security has concentrated on shielding the population centers and ports of entry. The announced strategy has been to push drug smugglers and immigrants into the hinterlands of Santa Cruz, Pima, Cochise, and Yuma counties, making the crossing more difficult and dangerous. This has made life more dangerous for people like ranchers who live in these isolated areas. The dominant Sinaloa cartel has responded by becoming more spread out, more technologically sophisticated, and more diversified. They now control movement of illegal immigrants across the border, as well as drugs. The multibillion-dollar prize in illegal drug sales in the United States has not shrunk, and the borderlands are only a conduit to the big distribution and market cities of Tucson, Phoenix, Denver, and others.

Second, crime statistics don't record the murders, rapes, assaults, and extortions that occur on the overland trails and canyons of the hinterlands, mostly to immigrants and burreros. Every immigrant has a phone number of folks back home or in the United States, and the cartel thugs will hold them in safe houses in Tucson or Phoenix until a ransom is paid. Phoenix, according to the FBI, has become the kidnap capital of the United States. Many of these assaults go unreported because the victims are undocumented and fear arrest and deportation. Also, a running battle is going on between the cartels and local rip-off gangs, who steal their cargo as they make their way up the trails toward the interstate highways. Those trails became more active when the highway checkpoints on I-19 and Highway 90 were made permanent. An unofficial indicator of the amount of illegal traffic flowing up from the border cities was the huge spike in trash, property damage, and lost immigrants and burreros on the adjacent rancher's property when the checkpoints were open, versus when they were closed.

Third, the "War on Drugs" declared by Richard Nixon forty years ago has already been lost, according to experts who don't have a vested interest in continuing the conflict.[7] Use of illegal narcotics has increased over time, as have drug-related crimes in the United States generally. Nixon's war used the same failed strategy as prohibition of booze did in the 1930s. Instead of focusing on prevention of narcotics use through education or treating addiction like the health problem it is, we have made it a moral issue and criminalized the stresses and frailties of life. Drug-use prevention programs and legalization of marijuana would presumably mean lower demand for illegal narcotics, less trafficking across the border, and less crime. These approaches have worked in European countries.

POPULAR HISTORY OFTEN evolves to the symmetry of myth to explain away the dark side of the dominant culture—in effect, making a pilgrimage back to the way things never were. The greed and brutality of the drug cartels are mirror images of the tactics and motives of those who conquered the lands and native people of New Spain. Hernán Cortés defeated the warrior Aztecs with a combination of cavalry, superior weapons and tactics, and alliance with enemy tribes, as well as by holding their ruler, Moctezuma, hostage with what amounted to a choice between *plata o plomo* (take a bribe or a bullet).

Spain's conquest led to a potent commingling of Spanish and native bloodlines that eventually created the Mexican race. Even so, Mexico's frontier societies retained a tiny aristocracy, whose position and wealth derived from family lineage, ecclesiastic status, or ownership of land and livestock. The economic elite include today's business tycoons, and they still rule Mexico, despite the illusion of democracy with equal opportunity for all. Their unwillingness to equitably share the country's enormous wealth has led to Mexico's many revolts and revolutions and fueled the exodus of its poor people to America. Mexico's new rulers would do well to take a fresh look at Father Kino's example of compassion and generosity toward his fellow human beings. The exceptional people in history have been those who rose above the conventional wisdom of their time and place. Father Kino was one of those rare individuals.

Another myth is that the flow of drugs across the border can be stopped by more walls and more Border Patrol. The best that can be done is to slow it down. The bad guys will climb over, tunnel under, fly an ultralight, or take a boat up the seacoasts. It becomes a sometimes deadly game of cat-and-mouse. In the last four years, sixty tunnels under the border have been discovered below Ambos Nogales alone.[8] As border enforcement has tightened, the *coyotes* have also taken to the seas in *pangas*, the traditional Mexican fishing boats. They carry twenty-five *pollos* every trip without wetting their feathers. At $5,000 each, one trip generates a hundred grand.[9] In the United States, the clarion call for "securing the border" is fantasy food for the politician's ego because "the border" is not some straight line on a map or computer screen. Instead, it is a spiny landscape of mountains, deserts, and rivers—some of the most rugged country on earth. And the bad guys and their accomplices are at home there and know the terrain better than US or Mexican lawmen do.

The reality is that most of the high-value stuff comes in through the busy ports of entry, concealed in myriad ways. The recent opening of American highways (as required by the NAFTA treaty) to Mexican truckers have the cartels grinning from ear to ear. The Nogales port of entry was designed to cross four hundred trucks per day, but now handles 1,500 during produce-shipping season. In Laredo, Texas, five thousand Mexican trucks head north every day, with everything from maquiladora-made widgets to vegetables and electronics imports from afar.

A small percentage will also carry narcotics. The inspection process is imperfect. Flush with American drug dollars, the cartels bribe customs inspectors to flag those trucks through. Examples: in Brownsville, Texas, Luis Enrique Ramírez was found guilty of taking $500,000 in bribes for passing vehicles carrying cocaine and illegal immigrants;[10] recently, fifty-nine pounds of crystal meth was found in a truckload of cucumbers;[11] in a more sinister development that sounds like a Cold War spy novel, the *New York Times* reported that drug cartels are sending clean undercover operatives in to apply for jobs as customs inspectors. One, Luis F. Alarid, was convicted of flagging drug-carrying trucks through his lane, pocketing $200,000 in payoffs.[12] In May 2012, $1.9 million in pot was pulled from loads of peppers and limes at the Nogales Port of Entry.[13] Since 2004, 127 US Customs employees have been indicted or arrested for acts of corruption.[14]

The Borderlands I Know

THE STACKED AND shelving clouds parted over Mount Wrightson as I walked to the barn. Below, the Sonoita Creek drainage was filled with tattered mists left over from last night's rain, a scene dim and vague and shifting. The dawn air was crisp with the promise of fall. The monsoon had started promptly on cue—San Juan's Day, June 24—and it was still raining now at September's end. In the foreground plain, the tawny grasses were bent with heavy dew. Around the barn, the oaks dripped with moisture. A family of Mexican jays squawked, protesting my intrusion into their leafy space. I wished I had known their language. They may not be what we humans call intelligent, but they knew all they needed to know. Oscar said jays organized their flocks from close family members, a morsel of natural history that I find uplifting.

Mount Wrightson glistened as the rising sun chased the night shadows back into the canyons. In our westerly, wide-open view, not a single man-made structure marred the setting: not house or road, concrete or asphalt, pole line or fence. As always, this landscape renewed my sense of enlargement: the feeling that life on the borderlands does not have to be cramped and fearful.

It may come as a surprise to politicians and the Department of Homeland Security that there are many places and people on the borderlands who do not want or need another nineteen thousand Border Patrol, seven hundred more miles of fences, and around-the-clock snooping into our lives. Let the Department of Homeland Security retrain and reassign the available personnel and assets to make them more effective, but please don't militarize our homeland any further.

Yesterday, I traded e-mails with the cabalgantes about making the next leg of the lower San Pedro River this year. "Okay," I replied. "I'll look for horses and start scouting the trail." From Cascabel to the confluence of the Gila River, it looked like about ninety miles—three days at Father Kino's pace. A lot of the route would be on highway right-of-ways and canal banks, with time passing at about the rate it does in a dental chair. The country on the lower San Pedro River was more settled and ordinary than in Sonora—except for the Galiuro Mountains and Aravaipa Creek, where on second night we would camp at the site of the infamous Camp Grant massacre.

At dawn on April 30, 1871, 140 Apaches, almost all women and children, were murdered in their beds by a vigilante militia called the Committee of Public Safety, formed and led by Tucson's leading citizens: ranchers Juan and Jesús María Elías, prominent businessman William S. Oury, and O'odham leader Francisco Galerita. The killers also kidnapped twenty-seven Apache children, later sold as slaves into Sonora.[15]

How this improbable combination of opposing cultures—Anglo, Mexican, and O'odham—had joined up against a band of peaceful Aravaipa Apache seems impossible today, until one considers the four hundred years of violent borderland history that engendered the deadly urge for blood revenge among all frontier societies, indigenous and foreign. These dark and dangerous emotions persist today, as a few O'odham still remember details of this event in their oral histories and for decades retained Apache scalps taken from the Aravaipa massacre.[16]

Years ago before I knew the full story of the massacre, I had ridden Aravaipa Canyon and hunted deer and lion all over the surrounding Galiuro Mountains. Looking at the map now, I tried to imagine how it would feel to lie in my bedroll, looking up at the burning stars, as the killers crept toward our dead campfire. But the images would not come—not here, sitting at the table with the afternoon light streaming through the window and hummingbirds assaulting the flowers outside. This Apache clan had camped on the reservation at Camp Grant under the known protection of the US Army, but the cavalry was unwittingly on duty elsewhere that deadly morning. The multicultural assassins struck the defenseless village when the Apache men were away hunting in the nearby mountains. President Ulysses S. Grant, a battle-hardened veteran of the Civil War, called the massacre "purely murder." Brought to trial, a jury of Tucsonans quickly acquitted the assailants of wrongdoing.

Those who do not learn from history, philosopher George Santayana once remarked, are condemned to repeat it. The Tucsonans of 1871 claimed they had no choice but to act, because the US government failed in its duty to protect them, the very same complaint heard today from Arizonans who fear the borderlands—only now the perceived threats come from Spanish-speaking immigrants. But the immigrant feared today is a stereotype, a lumping together of all Hispanics as a single homogenous group, just as 140 years ago, all Apaches were considered a unified tribe of murderous savages.

At the end of the ride, the national monument held a trove of Hohokam and O'odham artifacts and lore. Maybe the Park Service would let us camp there the last night. So once again, I'm on the brink of embarking on Father Kino's trails with the hope of new visions, some further understanding, and the compañerismo urging me along.

Acknowledgments

My deep appreciation goes to Jesus Enrique and José Luis Salgado, for inviting me to come along and for organizing the many details of our pleasant and enlightening journeys, as well as for allowing brief quotes from their travel journal; to the veterinarians Pichi and Pichito Salgado, for taking good care of the horses and for many good stories; to Ricardo Ramonet and Arturo López, who mounted me on their horses; and to all of the *cabalgante* riders, whose friendship and fellowship taught me so much about the borderlands and Sonoran-Mexican culture. This book is as much theirs as it is mine. Knowing them and their families gives me hope that Mexico and the United States have the capacity and compassion to confront the migrant/immigrant and drug trafficking problems together.

I extend my thanks to my neighbor Gary Paul Nabhan, who read an early draft of the book and thought it had merit. The helpful comments by this renowned borderlands scholar encouraged me to keep researching and revising. Any errors of scholarship, however, are mine, as are all of the opinions expressed. I am a slow writer and getting to the final draft took many months.

Much gratitude and love goes to my family, especially Diane for her patience with my sometimes reclusive behavior during the writing of this book; also to Richard West, who took over the ranch responsibilities, giving me both the space and time I needed; to Leslie and Tyler who came along on a later ride; and to a whole bunch of horses over the years, both ornery and willing. Ranching requires affection for these large, semi-domesticated herbivores, as well as a healthy, uncluttered landscape. Without them, the cowboy life is just another dirty job.

Endnotes

Prologue

1. See Silvia Longmire, *Cartel: The Coming Invasion of Mexico's Drug Wars* (Palgrave Macmillan, 2011).

Part 1: The Western Desert, 2008

1. Jesús Enrique Salgado and José Luis Salgado, *Por Los Caminos de Kino.* Hermosillo, Sonora, Mexico (Kino Cabalgata, 2010), 79.
2. Herbert Eugene Bolton, *Rim of Christendom* (New York: MacMillan, 1936), 281.
3. Bolton, *Rim of Christendom*, 58–60.
4. Diana Hadley, "Kino's Cows," *Archaeology Southwest* 23, no. 2 (2009): 20–21.
5. Gary Paul Nabhan, *The Desert Smells Like Rain* (Tucson: University of Arizona Press, 1987), 89.
6. Tyche Hendricks, *The Wind Doesn't Need a Passport* (Berkeley, CA: University of California Press, 2011), 98.
7. Ted Robbins, *National Public Radio News*, "Border Tribe in Midst of Smuggling Crisis," May 19, 2009.
8. Henry Ramon, Tohono O'odham Chairperson, *Indigenous People and the Modern State* (2005), 24.
9. Ed Vulliamy, *Amexica: War along the Borderline* (New York: Farrar, Straus, and Giroux, 2010), 93.
10. Bernard L. Fontana, *Of Earth and Little Rain* (Tucson: University of Arizona Press, 1989), 32.
11. D. J. Howell, "Plant-Loving Bats, Bat-Loving Plants," *Natural History* 85 (1976): 52–59.
12. Quoted in Louis Urrea, *Devil's Highway* (New York: Little, Brown & Co., 2004), 5–6.

Part 2: The Sierra Madre Occidental, 2009

1. Kino's discovery of the Pacific Ocean shells in the hands of Pimería Alta natives led him to suspect that there must be a land connection with Baja California.
2. Eric P. Perramond, *Political Ecologies of Cattle Ranching in Northern Mexico* (Tucson: University of Arizona Press, 2010), 120–22.
3. Perramond, *op. cit.*

Part 3: Discovering the Sobaipuris, 2010

1. Dept. of Human Services, Office of Immigration Statistics.
2. Ernest J. Burrus, *Kino and Manje* (St. Louis, MO: Jesuit Historical Institute, 1971), 197–222.
3. Burrus, *Manje's Journal of the Fourth Expedition* in *Kino and Manje*, 1971, 200.
4. *Op. cit.*
5. Bolton, *Rim of Christendom*, 382.
6. Eusebio F. Kino, *Kino's Historical Memoir of Pimeria Alta*, trans. H. E. Bolton (Cleveland, OH: Arthur H. Clark Co., 1919), 44.
7. Burrus, *Kino and Manje: Explorers of Sonora and Arizona*, 91.
8. Ignaz Pfefferkorn, *Sonora: Description of the Province*, trans. Theodore E. Treutlein (Tucson: University of Arizona Press, 1989), 221–2.

Part 4: Cerro El Nazareno, 2011

1. Bolton, *Rim of Christendom*, 280.
2. Bolton, *Rim of Christendom*, 276.
3. Burrus, *Kino and Manje: Explorers of Sonora and Arizona*, 91.
4. *Manje's Journal of the Seventh Expedition*, in Burris, *Kino and Manje*, 264–273.
5. Burrus, *Kino and Manje: Explorers of Sonora and Arizona*, 13.
6. Diana Lindsay, ed., "Henry A. Crabb, Filibuster, and the San Diego Herald." *J. San Diego History* 19, no. 1 (1973), http://www.sandiegohistory.org/journal/73/winter/crabbe.htm (accessed October 10, 2012).

Part 5: Coda

1. "Mexicans Back Military Campaign against Cartels," Pew Research Global Attitudes Project, June 20, 2012.
2. "Operation Fast and Furious," Report by the Committee on Oversight and Government Reform, United States Congress, October 2012.
3. Adam Gopnik, "The Caging of America," *The New Yorker*, January 30, 2012, 72–77.

4. Ted Conover, *Coyotes: A Journey across Borders with America's Illegal Immigrants* (New York: Vintage, 2006), *xix*.

5. "A Guide to S. 744: Understanding the 2013 Senate Immigration Bill," The Immigration Policy Center, July 10, 2013.

6. Guest Opinion, *Arizona Daily Star*, October 26, 2006, A13.

7. "War on Drugs," Global Commission on Drug Policy, June 2011.

8. Maggie Pingoly, "Nogales Is the Site of Majority of Border Tunnels," *Nogales International*, June 21, 2011, 2A.

9. Associated Press, "Frustrated on Land, Illegal Crossers Take to the Sea," *Arizona Daily Star*, August 27, 2010, A14.

10. Richard Connelly, "Luis Enrique Ramirez: Border Guard Admits Letting Coke and Aliens," *Houston Press*, March 3, 2011. http://houstonpress.com/03/03/11 (accessed April 21, 2011).

11. US Customs and Border Protection Newsroom, January 2012.

12. Randal C. Archibold, "Hired by Customs, but Working for Mexican Cartels," *New York Times*, December 8, 2009. http://www.nytimes.com/12/08/09 (accessed January 10, 2010).

13. Nogales International, Friday, May 11, 2012, 3A.

14. Brady McCombs, "Border Corruption Cases Grow," *Arizona Daily Star*, August 16, 2011. http://www.azstarnet.com/o8/16/2011 (accessed November 10, 2011).

15. Karl Jacoby, *Shadows at Dawn: A Borderlands Massacre and the Violence of History* (New York: Penguin Press, 2008).

16. Gary Paul Nabhan. Personal communication [2011].

Selected Bibliography with Commentary

Asterisks (**) denote engaging, easy-to-read narratives about the borderlands, its history, and present-day state of affairs for the nonacademic reader.

Annerino, John. *Dead in Their Tracks*. New York: Four Walls Eight Windows, 1999. Annerino walks with immigrants over the Devil's Highway and photographs their corpses.

** Bolton, Herbert Eugene. *Rim of Christendom*. New York: MacMillan Co., 1936. A detailed but embellished biography of Kino's missionary efforts in the Pimería Alta.

** Brenneman, D. S., and Diana Hadley. "Preserving Missions in the Pimería Alta." *Archaeology Southwest* 23, no. 2 (2009): 1–24.

** Broyles, Bill, et al. *Last Water on the Devil's Highway*. Tucson: University of Arizona Press, 2012. Detailed treatment of the Pinacate-Altar region, from pre-history up to the present, by people who know the landscape firsthand. Excellent maps and photographs.

Burrus, Ernst J. *Kino and Manje: Explorers of Sonora and Arizona*. Vol. 10 of *Sources and Studies for the History of the Americas*. St. Louis, MO: Jesuit Historical Institute, 1971. Includes Manje's *Luz de Tierra Incognita* journal/memoir.

Cabeza de Vaca. *Adventures into the Unknown Interior of America.* Translated and edited by Cyclone Covey. Albuquerque, NM: University of New Mexico Press, 1983.

** Conover, Ted. *Coyotes: A Journey across Borders with America's Illegal Immigrants.* New York: Vintage Books, 1987. One of the first and most perceptive accounts of traveling the Mexican migrant trails.

Cremony, John C. *Life among the Apaches.* Lincoln, NE: University of Nebraska Press, 1983. Reprint of the first edition published in 1868. Firsthand experience with the Apache that corroborates their raiding and warfare behaviors given in Grenville Goodwin's anthropological studies done in the 1930s. Cremony's experience illustrated the critical importance of good horses in surviving on the southwestern frontier of the 1800s.

Davis, Goode P. *Man and Wildlife in Arizona: The American Exploration Period, 1824–1865.* Phoenix, AZ: Arizona Game and Fish Department, 1982. Documents the presence of beaver on the Gila and San Pedro Rivers drainages.

De Steiger, J. Edward. *Wild Horses of the West: History and Politics of America's Mustangs.* Tucson, AZ: University of Arizona Press, 2011.

Diaz del Castillo, Bernal. *The Bernal Castillo Chronicles: The True Story of the Conquest of Mexico.* Translated by Albert Udell. Garden City, NY: Doubleday and Co., 1956. Firsthand, detailed account by a conquistador/participant.

** Fontana, Bernard L. *Of Earth and Little Rain.* Tucson, AZ: University of Arizona Press, 1989. Delightful, well-written small book that encapsulates the culture of the O'odham by an anthropologist who lived next to them for three decades.

Goodwin, Grenville. *Western Apache Raiding and Warfare.* Edited by Keith H. Basso. Tucson, AZ: University of Arizona Press, 1971. Authoritative account based on oral histories taken in the 1930s; especially valuable when read with Cremony (see above).

Grandin, Temple, and Catherine Johnson. *Animals Make Us Human.* New York: Houghton Mifflin Harcourt, 2009. Ethnology in service to domestic animals, especially horses and cattle.

** Griffith, James S. *A Shared Space: Folklife in the Arizona-Sonora Borderlands.* Logan, UT: Utah State University Press, 1995. Contains the El Moro de Cumpas legend, a description of the October festival in Magdalena de Kino, and other borderland folklore.

** ——. *Victims, Bandits, and Healers: Folk Saints of the Borderlands*. Tucson, AZ: Rio Nuevo Publishers, 2003. The stories of Teresa Urrea and Jesús Malverde.

** Hendricks, Tyche. *The Wind Doesn't Need a Passport*. Berkeley, CA: University of California Press, 2011. An in-depth, journalistic investigation of the lives of borderland people on both sides of the line.

Jacoby, Karl. *Shadows at Dawn: A Borderlands Massacre and the Violence of History*. New York: Penguin Press, 2008. The Camp Grant massacre presented from the viewpoints of its victims and assassins, before, during, and after the event.

Kessell, John L. *Friars, Soldiers, and Reformers: Hispanic Arizona's Mission Frontier, 1767–1856*. Tucson, AZ: University of Arizona Press, 1976. Scholarly and readable account of the Franciscan missionaries after the Jesuits were expelled.

——. *Spain in the Southwest*. Norman, OK: University of Oklahoma Press, 2002. I am grateful to Professor Kessell for his admonition that stereotypes are not useful in understanding Spain's conquests of indigenous Americans. Unfortunately, racial stereotypes still drive the attitudes of many people on borderland issues.

** Kino, Eusebio F. *Kino's Historical Memoir of Pimería Alta*. Translated by Herbert Eugene Bolton. Cleveland, OH: The Arthur H. Clark Co., 1919. Kino's own account of his journeys and accomplishments, highlighting his deep religious convictions, instincts as an explorer, and empathy and rapport with the native people.

Longmire, Sylvia. *Cartel: The Coming Invasion of Mexico's Drug Wars*. New York: Palgrave MacMillan, 2011. Longmire, a security analyst, traces the rise and spread of Mexico's criminal drug organizations, using security documents and journalistic accounts.

Lumholtz, Carl. *New Trails in Mexico*. Tucson, AZ: University of Arizona Press, 1990. Lumholtz's trails were not new, but he did make detailed observations on the people and natural history of the Pimería Alta, especially the western deserts and Hia C-ed O'odham.

Martínez, Rubén. *Crossing Over: A Mexican Family on the Migrant Trail*. New York: Picador, 2001. I am grateful to the author for his essay emphasizing the need for the language of "we" between the United States and Mexico when confronting the drug cartels.

Myer, Michael C., and William H. Beezley, editors. *The Oxford History of Mexico*. New York: Oxford University Press, 2000.

**Nabhan, Gary Paul. *Gathering the Desert*. Tucson, AZ: University of Arizona Press, 1987. Ethnobotany and history of the Sonoran Desert. Detailed chapter on bootleg mescal.

** ——. *The Desert Smells like Rain*. Tucson, AZ: University of Arizona Press, 1982. A small collection of personal encounters with the O'odham and their desert homeland by a noted ethnobotanist and scholar.

** ——. *Cultures of Habitat: On Nature, Culture, and Story*. Washington, DC: Counterpoint, 1997. Nabhan's research exposes the environmental movement's damaging fiction that wildness exists only in the absence of human impact.

** Officer, James E., Mardith Schuetz-Miller, and Bernard L. Fontana, eds. *Pimería Alta: Missions and More*. Tucson, AZ: The Southwestern Mission Research Center, 1996. This delightful book was written by recognized authorities and given to all who traveled the Kino Mission Tours initiated by Lea Ward. An easy-to-read, informative classic.

——. *Hispanic Arizona, 1536–1856*. Tucson, AZ: University of Arizona Press, 1987. The Arizona Territory under Spanish and Mexican rule. This thoroughly researched history includes the influential Elías Gonzáles clan and their struggles against Apache depredation, making the Camp Grant massacre plausible though deplorable.

** ——. "Kino and Agriculture in the Pimería Alta." *The Journal of Arizona History* 34, no. 3 (1993): 287–306. Well-researched account of Kino's role in establishing European agriculture.

Paz, Octavio. *The Labyrinth of Solitude and Other Writings*. New York: The Grove Press, 1985. Probes the historical formation of the Mexican character and culture and includes the perceptive essay "Mexico and the United States."

Perramond, Eric P. *Political Ecologies of Cattle Ranching in Northern Mexico*. Tucson, AZ:

University of Arizona Press, 2010. Founded on field research and rancher interviews of seventeen private properties on and near the Río Sonora.

Pfefferkorn, Ignaz. *Sonora: A Description of the Province.* Translated by Theodore E. Treutlein. Tucson, AZ: University of Arizona Press, 1989. Of all the Jesuits, Pfefferkorn, with Germanic thoroughness, recorded detailed descriptions of Sonora's indigenous people, climate, and natural history, although he disliked most of it, except for the Spanish horses.

Phillips, Steven J., and Patricia Wentworth Comus, editors. *A Natural History of the Sonoran Desert.* Tucson, AZ: Arizona Sonora Desert Museum Press, 2000. A valuable reference for the layperson.

** Polzer, Charles W. *Kino, A Legacy.* Tucson, AZ: Jesuit Fathers of Southern Arizona, 1998. A valuable though partisan portrait of Kino's life and missionary work, written by a fellow Jesuit. Covers the discovery of Kino's tomb in Magdalena de Kino in 1966.

Salgado, Jesús Enrique, and José Luis Salgado. *Por Los Caminos de Kino.* Hermosillo, Sonora, Mexico: Kino Cabalgata, 2010. Copyrighted journal of the Kino Cabalgata from 1987 through 2010. Written in Spanish with a limited distribution, this amazing book covers twenty-three Cabalgatas.

Seymour, Deni J. "The Dynamics of Sobaipuris Settlement in the Eastern Pimeria Alta." *Journal of the Southwest* 31, no. 2 (1989): 205–222. Describes the scattered nature of O'odham Sobaipuris settlements on the San Pedro River.

** Sheridan, Thomas E. *Arizona: A History.* Tucson, AZ: University of Arizona Press, 1992. Well-written, easy-to-read, authoritative history of the state, starting at the colonial era. A revised edition for 2011 is now available. Perhaps the best single reference to Arizona's past and present.

Spicer, Edward H. *Cycles of Conquest: The Impact of Spain, Mexico, and the United States on the Indians of the Southwest, 1533–1960.* Tucson, AZ: University of Arizona Press, 1976. Magisterial synthesis of the history and impact of Western civilization on southwestern native cultures and of how they responded to these collisions. A balanced interpretation of Jesuit (including Father Kino's) influence on these tribes.

** Tellman, Barbara, and Diana Hadley. *Crossing Boundaries: An Environmental History of the Upper San Pedro River Watershed, Arizona and Sonora.* Tucson, AZ: Arizona State Museum, 2006. Up-to-date, well-illustrated and readable but does not cover the impact of illegal immigrants on the river.

** *War On Drugs.* Report of the Global Commission on Drug Policy, June 2011.

Urrea, Luis Alberto. *The Devil's Highway.* New York: Little, Brown and Co., 2004. Paced like a novel, this is a factual account of the diabolical and deadly effects of border policy when fourteen Mexican immigrants died in a single crossing from Sonoyta to Interstate 8.

———. *Hummingbird's Daughter.* New York: Little, Brown, and Co., 2005. A historical novel based on the life of Teresa Urrea, Santa de Cabora.

Vulliamy, Ed. *Amexica: War along the Borderline.* New York: Farrar, Straus and Giroux, 2010. A reporter's eyewitness account of present-day violence due to drugs, poverty, and immigration policy in border cities ranging from McAllen, Texas, to Tijuana.

** Yetman, David. *Organ Pipe Cactus.* Tucson, AZ: University of Arizona Press, 2006. All anyone ever wanted to know about *pitaya* cactus.

Zepeda, Ofelia. *Ocean Power: Poems from the Desert.* Tucson, AZ: University of Arizona Press, 1995. O'odham poet and linguist Zepeda writes eloquently of the critical importance of landscape, seascape, weather, and seasons in O'odham culture.

———. *Where Clouds Are Formed.* Tucson, Arizona. University of Arizona Press, 2008.

Photography Credits

"At the Caborca Corrals" by José Luis Salgado. Oscar and Lea Ward front-center; Enrique Salgado far right; Author second from left. Used with permission.

"The Border Wall" by Jim Holmlund, copyright Western Digital Mapping. All Rights Reserved. Used with permission.

"The Monument Fire," *Arizona Daily Star*, June 13, 2011. Photograph by Dean Knuth. Used with permission.

"About the Author," by Kristina Holt, copyrighted. Used with permission.

All other photographs are by Diane and Richard Collins.

Cover photo by Diane Collins: The author looking south from the San Rafael valley into the Chivitos Mountains of Sonora

About the Author

RICHARD COLLINS WAS raised on a ranch near Phoenix, Arizona, where he lived until leaving for college. He was educated at Arizona State University (BS) and the University of Arizona (MS and PhD), where he also competed on the rodeo teams, winning regional titles. During the decades of the 1970s and '80s, he worked in the rural villages and farms of Central America and Mexico for the Centers for Disease Control, where he witnessed the environments of poverty, disease, and violence that are the root causes of much of today's turmoil on the borderlands. Since 1983, he has owned and operated farms and ranches in southern Arizona, including the thirteen-thousand-acre C6 Ranch, located twenty-five miles north of the Mexican border, where he has lived for the last twenty years. Writing credits include work in *National Geographic Traveler*, *Science and Spirit*, and *SN Review* magazines, along with a local history series for the *Sonoita Bulletin* and essays selected twice for the Environmental Writing Institute at the University of Montana.